MINGLEMENTS

PROSE ON POETRY AND LIFE

Renée Ashley

—

Del Sol Press

Del Sol Press
Washington, DC

minglement: n. 1. The act of mingling, or the state of being mixed.

Webster's Dictionary, 1913

Also by Renée Ashley

Poetry

The View from the Body
Because I Am the Shore I Want To Be the Sea
Basic Heart
The Verbs of Desiring, a chapbook
The Revisionist's Dream
The Various Reasons of Light
The Museum of Lost Wings, a chapbook
Salt

Novel

Someplace Like This

TABLE OF CONTENTS

ACKNOWLEDGMENTS

AWP Chronicle: Writing on the Brink: Peripheral Vision and the Personal Poem

The Book of Worst Meals: 25 Authors Write about Terrible Culinary Experiences: Her Very Worst Meal and How It Was Much Like the Three Fat Men—One of Whom Was Wearing a Beret—She Saw Today

Fulcrum: an annual of poetry and aesthetics, Ut Pictura Poesis: The Painting in the Poem, or, Simple Perspective for Poets: A Mini Essay

Gently Read Literature: True Lines Not Mere Sentences: Renée Ashley on Dennis Hinrichsen's *Kurosawa's Dog*

The Inner Music: Interview with Poet Renée Ashley by Michael T. Young

IthacaLit: A Possibility of Memoir; Interview by Michele Lesko

The Literary Review: Editor's Choice: *The Art of Subtext: Beyond Plot* by Charles Baxter and *The Art of Attention: A Poet's Eye* by Donald Revell; Editor's Choice: *Elegy* by Mary Jo Bang; Editor's Choice: Fanny Howe's *Selected Poems*; Editor's Choice: Tess Gallagher's *Dear Ghosts,*; Minglement: Mixed Fruits, My Mother, and the New American Poem, Essay/Review of *American Hybrid: A Norton Anthology of New Poetry*; Line or No Line: An Essay/Review of Longenbach's *The Art of the Poetic Line* and *The Rose Metal Press Field Guide to Prose Poetry: Contemporary Poets in Discussion and Practice,* editors Gary L. McDowell and F. Daniel Rzicznek; Essay/Review of Mary Jo Bang, *The Bride of E* and Louise Glück, *A Village Life*; Essay/Review: Damn Sad Stories, *One More Theory About Happiness: a memoir* by Paul Guest, and *Happy: a memoir* by Alex Lemon; Editor's Choice: Albert Goldbarth, *The Kitchen Sink: New and Selected Poems 1972-2007*; *We Mad Climb Shaky Ladders*, Pamela Spiro Wagner; *White Papers*, Martha Collins; *Wings Without Birds*, Brian Henry; *Without Wings*, Laurie Lamon

Thanks are due to so many people . . . to the editors of the journals who published these essays; to the interviewers: J.P. Dancing Bear, Michele Lesko, Kim Nagy, Matthew Thorburn, Michael T. Young, Jacklene Oakes and Anastasia Cyzewski; to Walter Cummins for friendship, inclusions, hours and hours and hours of his time, and his perpetual good nature; to Minna Proctor for allowing and encouraging the pieces included in *TLR*; to the McDowell Colony and to the Virginia Center for the Creative Arts— without their hospitality I would never have completed the work; to Noni Diamantoupolos for the use of the Hide Away; to the women, long ago, at Ringwood Public Library who probably wanted to kill me during the building of the Edward Taylor essay; to my proofreaders, poor, patient souls: Nedra Behringer, Melanie Kershaw, Heather Lang, Tim Lindner, and Louise Stahl; to Stephen Dunn and Catherine Doty for permission to include their poems; to Mark Hillringhouse for the flattering author photo; to Jack Pirkey for his forbearance; to Mike Neff for his enthusiasm; to Mira Sadorge for her fabulous cover art, and to David Pischke for his striking cover design; and to Ma, without whom I'd've had much less fun and not-fun and much less to say about both.

NOTE

Louise Stahl is fiercely insistent on the *toward/towards* issue. She says *towards* makes her teeth hurt. *Toward* being the U.S. usage; *towards* being the British. And she is right to be vigilant; it's her job. However, for whatever reason, I say and write *towards* and, after much thought and many takings-out and puttings-back, along with myriad plosive attempts to read aloud with *toward*, I've chosen to assert my right to be wrong with *towards* because the *s* slithers so easily into the word that follows, because I don't have to think about it, and because it just generally makes life easier. It, that *s*, may just be the one thing in this life I'm consistent about. Sorry about the tooth thing, Louise. *Mea culpa.*

And, speaking of consistency, I have chosen to republish essays, here, in the forms in which they were originally published: some with footnotes, some with a works cited or works consulted pages. See what I mean about consistency?

When we try to pick out anything by itself, we find it hitched to everything else in the Universe.

John Muir

EXORDIUM

What else can there be but everything? And though we cannot consider all things at once, are we really able to bean-pick, to consider one single thing, one uncolored and utterly independent notion from that interconnected, cross-wired immensity?

The arts, philosophy—The Humanities, let's say—along with our understandings and misunderstandings of the sciences, natural and otherwise, and our every experience, action, and reaction—what we think we know, our opinions, and our states of mind—none are sealed off from the others, none run in discrete channels. We are the confluence of what streams through us. We read a novel that makes us think of our Uncle Barney, though there's no Barney-like character in the story, but the book evokes the feeling of what it felt like to be with him; we are startled by an abstract sculpture that recalls for us the landscape of the place our father lived after he left us and, then, are unable to really see that sculpture, or perhaps even another work by the same sculptor wholly unlike the first, even though the sculpture itself has nothing of leaving about it; or we attend a live performance of Levy's opera, *Mourning Becomes Electra*, and are jetted with bone-chilling rapidity back to the Iowa farm we visited long ago where we heard the all-too-human-like screams of a brown rabbit being tortured beneath a knee-high hedge—skinned alive—by a smallish barn cat.

Our connections and associations help make the world easier both to comprehend and articulate. We compare, consciously or not; we draw or observe parallels. *This is like that*, we say. *This makes me think of that other thing*—similar to the mapping that makes metaphor work; perhaps, sometimes, exactly the same kind. We recreate from our contexts—not simply the current ambient circumstance or the location in which our bodies, at any given moment, might take up space, but the catalog of contexts we have absorbed throughout our lives—via those accumulations, those personal and universal recognitions, sense-and-memory associations with their fractional samenesses—and whether those connections rise up into our consciousness at a given time—say, while you're writing a review or an essay on craft—that, no doubt, is another set of active connections, a subset of the whole and, experientially, not the least bit irrevelant.

In *Minglements,* some pieces are more mingled than others, and both the mingled and less-mingled are interspersed here in this volume, a small sampling of my own connections which, I hope you'll find to be, in one context or another, wholly or partially, straightforwardly or tangentially, related to your own.

MINGLEMENT: MIXED FRUITS,
MY MOTHER, AND THE NEW
AMERICAN POEM: AN ESSAY/REVIEW OF
AMERICAN HYBRID:
A NORTON ANTHOLOGY OF NEW POETRY
COLE SWENSEN AND DAVID ST. JOHN, EDS.

Did you know that a rutabaga is a hybrid, a cross between a turnip and cabbage? Did you know this crossbreeding is not the product of modern gene-splicing, but took place naturally sometime during the Middle Ages? The American Institute of Cancer Research (AICR) *eNews* of August 2007 says the rutabaga "contains qualities of both its parents, firmer than a turnip with a stronger flavor," and states, as well, that "[p]retty much all produce sold today are hybrids, but typical hybrids are crosses within the same type of fruit or vegetable." I didn't know that, though I probably should have. But have you been to an up-scale market lately? Have you seen the more obvious and fittingly-named manifestations? Pluots (plum + apricot, about 75% plum)? Apriums (apricot + plum, about 75% apricot)? Have you come across nectaplums or peacharines? Nectacotums? Peacotums? How about broccoflower or broccolini? They're out there.

It seems that, in just about any venue, a great many of the most interesting and viable things happen when their elements are mixed. For instance, all my dogs have been found-or-pound mongrels—and I've never had a bad or sickly dog. In fact, I'm a mixed breed myself: Jewish, Irish, Scandanavian, with dribs and dabs of other things, then, somewhere along the line, Kansas, California, who knows where else, and I'm a relatively healthy specimen, considering—and though I look more like my mother than my father, I have his disposition and eyes. A Mai Tai is a mixed drink, you know. And the glorious Margarita. Much of the food we eat is made by combining ingredients: a seafood paella doesn't come into the world fully formed. Even my best attempt at swimming falls somewhere between a breast stroke, a dog paddle, and a slow sinking. We take a little of this and a little of that, run them together, and we are our own result.

Without even thinking about it we have become ready users of the vocabulary associated with hybridization: *assimilation, incorporation, synthesis, fusion, amalgamation.* And *minglement,* to use a word we've lost but should find again. Whatever you want to call it, it's here. It's been here. And the astute editors of *American Hybrid: A Norton Anthology of New Poetry* have given us a volume to give us our footing while the word is spread and codified. It's a fine step in acknowledging the protean state of contemporary poetry, in moving to the foreground what Keith Waldrop could easily have been speaking of at the end of his poem, "First Draw the Sea," when he said, equal signs included:

=

. . . this corner turned.

=

Unattended ground.

We are categorists both at heart and out of necessity. Categories keep the world that comes at us in such rush and abundance—and from so many varied sources—manageable. And while I am neither a connoisseur of, nor a lobbyist for, categories (for the most part, I'm sure, determinations such as categories at best oversimplify and at worst mislead or even falsify), I also understand they're a necessary and expedient shorthand. But in the case of *hybrid,* as in *American Hybrid: A Norton Anthology of New Poetry,* it is, though admittedly vast and open-ended, spot-on. The dichotomous traditional and experimental categories no longer cover the range of possibilities (if they ever did). *Hybrid* is a category that is utterly apt and filled with possible and promising permutations; it's also a signal that a poetry reader's arena of expectation must be wide-open and poised for change. This is a good thing in both poetry and life. It strengthens both the figurative and literal gene pools.

Cole Swensen points out in her introduction:

> While the new is an important common denominator of much hybrid work, it is a combinatory new, one that recognizes that 'there is nothing new under the sun' and embraces the postmodern understanding of the importance of connection: that given elements are often less crucial than the relationships between them.

Ann Lauterbach's poem "After Mahler" is an excellent example of that "combinatory new." Within its confines it acts out its own evolutionary combinations, its combinations within its combinations. The first stanza consists of six end-stopped lines of syntactically correct sentences.

> A thousand minutes came out of the tottering state.
> The bed of thyme moved within its bearings like a dream.
> He answered, *tomorrow.*
> Someone else was screaming on the radio; people laughed.
> The cat has been dead for some time now.
> The wedding party's bright joy looked strange from the
> streaking jet.

But something has knocked that "correct" status awry: We find things just slightly strange. In the first line, "minutes" come out of the "state"—what? OK, we might think, we can work with that: It's a metaphor . . . But then the second line is slightly less intelligible: An herb bed is moving "within its bearings." The third line begins with a pronoun that has no antecedent. The fourth is plausible—but what does it have to do with the lines that come before? Who is that "screaming on the radio"? Someone *else*? Other than whom? The speaker? The "He" of the previous line? The fifth line, the one about the dead cat, comes out of nowhere as well—what cat? It's *the* cat, not *a* cat, but we haven't, before, heard anything about a cat. And the sixth line's perspective is that of someone "streaking" away on a jet. The speaker? The *He*? The cat? The people on the radio? No clue. Within a normative syntax there are content entries of lines with separate focuses without transitions. The usually smooth road is a tad rocky and the reader is knocked off-balance more than once.

The following stanza is quite different.

> Meanwhile persons are moving around outside. They have decided to
> foreclose on
> options pertaining to the new world. Instead, to allow themselves to
> live in a world
> neither new nor old, but which abides as in a balloon floating
> untethered above the trophies and noise so that
> truncated, wren-shrunk

A big shift in format: Not only do we now have enjambed lines, and truncated lines far removed from the left margin (which begins the introduction to the poem of more air, more white space), and, with the third line, we lose our normative sentence structure and the sense begins to wander, the misalignment of images is heightened and Lauterbach moves further into the world of abstractions. Already we are leaving rutabagas in the dust.

The third stanza begins with lines in a three-step remove from the left margin, but by the fourth and fifth lines extra white space is injected between sets of words, and the sixth line is merely a single word—and, visually, the poem seems to continue to come apart until the fifth stanza where, once again, the left margin holds firm and mixes whole sentences with fragments and continues its disjunctive message.

Combinatory. Excellent word. It explains so much.

Our human drive towards comingling—for whatever reason: nature, nurture, convenience, or the will of some capricious god—is a strong one. And I imagine that by now we're hard put to find purity in either line or lineage. For many of us, the hybrid personality, embracing some behaviors perhaps even more disjunctive than the variances of Lauterbach's poem, are part of the human package.

One example: At a time when it was uncommon, my mother had her first and only child at thirty-nine. Ma dressed "like a lady" and acted the lady until it suited her to do otherwise, until, as in the development of a poem, the traditional expression available to her let her down and her own nature, nature and perceived necessity, levered her into a mode of discourse that forced the observer to adjust his idea of how a woman—dressed "like a lady"—was free to act. Ma tells me strangers stopped her almost daily to comment on her adorable "granddaughter." It hurt her feelings and damaged her vanity; it pissed her off. But she set them straight, she assured me, in no uncertain terms. It was simple: She stood very straight, turned her smiling face towards their own, and said in a tone that could have stripped the enamel right off their teeth, "She's my daughter, *asshole.*" She'd be tugging on her gloves as she said it.

There always were—and still are, I might add, and she's ninety-eight now—disparities between Ma's appearance and her actions that manifested even without unintentional baiting from total strangers. I didn't understand this until later. I was a child then—what did I know? My mother was the whole world. I knew nothing about adults other than her, my gentle and absent father, and my teachers who were, without exception, singular paragons of virtue. Really. They were. So as far as I knew there were three camps of adults: teachers, kind and absent fathers, and Ma. I never questioned that they were different. Ma believed with absolute certainty—and still may, if you ask her, though she's dispensed with the gloves and traded the straight skirt and pumps for a purple sweat suit and Velcro-closured walking shoes—that if you wore white gloves, if you kept your knees together and dressed like a lady, you could get away with just about anything.

Let me tell you a story, another true one.

It had to be around 1960, so Ma was about fifty and I was probably ten-ish. My mother still worked the PBX board in the rotunda of the old San Mateo County Courthouse. It was the kind of old-fashioned telephone exchange that had long cords—gray with red bits woven through—that pulled up from a table console and had brass plugs at the end. The kind we saw on TV when Lily Tomlin, as Ernestine, pursed not just her lips but her entire face and spoke into her headset her "gracious" *hello*. Seated at the console, Ma, along with two other women, would pull those plugs up from the horizontal board and shove them into the vertical wall of small, brass-rimmed holes that rose from the console and were marked with extension numbers. The call was the plug; the hole was the call's destination. The match made the connection.

Some of the details of this particular day are hazy; some are as clear as clean glass. I don't know why I'm at my mother's workplace. And I don't know why we're in the elevator, since, if she had been working, we could have gone right out the big glass, brass-trimmed doors that led from the first-floor rotunda out to the wide concrete steps down to Main Street. But I see Ma with her ever-so-slightly-greenish, brown-tinted hair wearing a yellow dress (which has a black pattern on it that looks suspiciously like the pattern on the wallpaper in our stairway at home). The skirt of the dress is slim, the bodice cap-sleeved. The wide neckline has a split, rolled collar that buttons with one large black button on the left. Her waist is belted, a thin black patent leather belt. Her shoes and bag match her belt. Her handbag is slipped over her left arm, her wrist-length white gloves are gathered in her right hand. The elevator doors slide open and a young man in a gray suit holds the door back with his hand so it won't close on us. We enter one at a time, Ma first, and we turn to face the front. The doors close. I am to the right and slightly behind my mother who stands center-car. The young man is to her left and just behind her. She smiles a warm "Thank you" after he asks for and pushes the button for our floor.

I am sneaking peeks at him behind my mother's back. He can't see me, I'm certain, and, when he does turn his head in my direction, I drop my gaze to the floor. It is the first time I remember looking at someone or something and having a perception that did not somehow include my mother. Evidently, it was my inkling: that instant when I first realized that a young man (or an old boy) might be . . . interesting. Nobody speaks. The old elevator makes its aged complaint in the silence around us. My mother takes her compact out of her purse and pats at her nose with the flat puff, then at that indented space between her lower lip and chin. She checks the mirror, flips the compact shut, drops it back into her bag, and snaps the latch closed. The small maple-walled box we are riding in gives its customary jostle and is just about to settle at its destination floor when my mother farts, and it is not a ladylike fluff. Not a surprise-us-all toot. Or a poot. Or a whistle or a pop. Not a sound that could be mistaken for anything but what it is: a cheek-slapping, moist and slippery horn blast that goes on and on until it finally loses steam, whimpers and dies wetly out. There occurs one of those moments of stunned silence and stopped time that we all have experienced when nobody has even yet begun to think. The elevator doors open and my mother, head erect, eyes straight ahead, strides out of the car and into the granite-floored lobby, pulling her white gloves over her fingers and smoothing them down onto her palms brusquely as if nothing at all has transpired. There's another pause—a nanosecond probably—before she notices that I am not beside her. She spins around with an annoyed look on her freshly powdered face. I'm in the elevator and I can't move. The young man is holding the door for me, the door repeatedly bumping against his hand in an effort to fulfill its repetitive destiny and close. His lips are taut. I already know what's going to happen and there's nothing I can do to stop it. "Renée!" she says, her voice rising. She looks at me in disgust while she draws out and wavers that schwa of the first syllable and snaps the second as though it is a third glove to be yanked into place. There's a marked crescendo at the end. She repeats the name with a different emphasis: "Renée," she says this time, drawing out the second syllable in a melisma of utter horror. Her arms drop to her sides, her bag slides from her crooked elbow to her hand. Then she says it: "Have a little *couth*, Renée," she says. "Say 'excuse me' to the man and come along." She turns and takes a few steps forward on the polished floor, moving towards the bank of glass doors to the outside world. For the first time in my life, I do not know where my allegiance lies. With my mother? Or with my own, new perception of the possibility of something of importance outside of her? The balance, of course, topples in an instant; I can't look at the young man, nor do I say *excuse me*, but I do come along. I walk blindly in a straight line towards my mother who has just reached one of the wide doors, the sunlight magnifying their horizontal brass releases. She pushes the bar and holds the door open. I walk out behind her. And as far as I can remember the incident is never addressed again until I'm an adult when she denies it happened. The funny thing, though, is that even in my alarm, even in the at-that-point most humiliating moment of my life, I can see that it is funny. I'd been living, say a decade or so, with my mother's sense of humor, and my mother is a funny woman. But it was also the beginning of other-consciousness. A bit of differentiation. A smidgen of individuation. The world got bigger. Minglement happened. Both my mother and I were manifestations of minglement right then: Ma was "a lady" who farted in elevators and blamed her young daughter, not a traditional category, and I had one foot in the child-world and one in that of adolescence, a place that harbors humiliation in cartloads.

Humans operate on multiple, complex levels. We don't have binary minds. Our actions and their degrees of effectiveness and/or appearance exist on multiple continuums—imaginary, yes, but conceptually pretty sound. Beyond over-simplification there is the gray area, all those mixed impulses, those aggregate, sometimes conflicting presentations and articulations, those effects that are the amalgam *minglement*. The strengths of nature and nurture and accident. The ones that move us forward. The most interesting ones to interact with.

In poetry, human endeavor that it is, I see the continuum of possibility this way: three animals, none human, in full-body profile, nose, so to speak, to tail: first, at the far left, an indigo bunting (bird; approximately five inches in length, seven-to-nine inch wingspan, weighing approximately half an ounce: male in breeding plumage: brilliant blue); then, in the center, a smallish African elephant (mammal, height at shoulder: ten feet, weight: about eleven thousand pounds, gray); and lastly, far right, a ruby-throated hummingbird (bird: approximately three to four inches in length, three to four inches in wingspan, weighing from less than one-tenth to less than a quarter of an ounce). The bright blue bunting is traditional verse; the elephant is the bulk of what we know, the gray area of hybrid poems and spin-offs; and the hummingbird, with its fiery green and iridescent red, is the radically experimental end of the continuum. And even then, within *American Hybrid*, fractal-like within the elephant itself, we have fuzzy-edged representatives of the same three designations: Reginald Shepherd's stunning poem, "Direction of Fall," might tip towards the traditional/lyric end of the hybridic spectrum ("And then this ruined sky again. Memory / came like migratory birds calling *reaper, reaper, / reaper*, hungry ghosts threshing distance // at the extremity of private sound . . ."); certainly the poem examined and quoted earlier, Ann Lauterbach's "After Mahler," with its step-system of transmogrification, might hit mid-spectrum; and Stacy Doris's excerpt from "Cheerleader's Guide to the World: Council Book," which leaps out of the verbal, periodically, into the iconographic to include her irreproducible, at least here by me, *x*, *o* lines, and arrow diagrams of various cheerleading moves, and then back again to verbal moves such as this one that follows immediately upon a diagram, "This is about Our Country and Our Culture / since even before they were Ours. // That's why it sandwiches Popol Vuh Paterson / Tibetan Dead Jigme Lingpa Pindar // Rah rah:" and breaks with only visual warning, once again, into another, a different diagram—surely this might be a move towards what could be considered the experimental.

Of course, as Swensen says in her introduction (xxv), ". . . [H]ybridity is . . . in itself no guarantee of excellence, and the decentralizing influences . . . make it harder to achieve consensus or even to maintain stable critical criteria; instead, these factors put more responsibility on individual readers to make their own assessments, which can in turn create stronger readers in that they must become more aware of and refine their own criteria." The burden, then, falls from the writer to the reader, fairly enough, to make out what she sees—hence the expedience and genuine helpfulness of the categories.

Swensen gives, as well, a superb overview of the perceived historical poetic bi-partism, and it is interesting, an intelligent and concise overview of poetry and its schools and schisms. The anthology contains more than seventy poets, and several pieces by each poet, each set prefaced with a short introduction by the editors: an insightful paragraph on how to approach the work and narrow the category by technique and/or effect, and a paragraph of biography.

Swensen and St. John considered for inclusion only poets who, at the time they began reading for the anthology, had already published a minimum of three volumes and so we have examples from familiar names such as John Ashbery, Albert Goldbarth, Jorie Graham, Lyn Hejinian, Brenda Hillman, Fanny Howe, Alice Notley, Keith and Rosmarie Waldrop, and Marjorie Welish, along with others both equally and less well-known. St. John points out that, ironically, their criteria for inclusion "excluded many of those younger poets whose work [they'd] first looked to as models of hybridization." He adds that "their anthology is yet to come" (xxviii). I look forward to this addition with both glee and impatience.

But *American Hybrid* as it stands is a sturdy, fascinating, and useful volume, a foundational collection. A great read and a fabulous text that, as I read more deeply, makes me fall in love with it. It's a desert island book. Included is work by poets I was already acquainted with as well as a few poets who were brand new to me. I rediscovered poets I recalled, mistakenly, as being landlocked in airtight categories, for instance the marvelous poet, James Galvin, whom I had earlier pegged as tightly mainstream and who I found now "exploding his modes of making sense" and ". . . leaving the relationships among his lines and phrases ever more open-ended" (130). Approaches run the gamut within the anthology from the edgy minimalism of Rae Armantrout to Mei-Mei Berssenbrugge's arty, maximal lines (which were so long that the editors had them printed landscape on the page). I found non sequiturs, visible cross-outs, play (as in *theater*) formatting, integrated photographs, variations on the use of white space, of typography, of line lengths, punctuations, stanza formats, dividing symbols, disruptions of syntax and meaning. Marvelous lexical tip-offs in the poet introductions gave me articulations to hold on to while I read the pages that followed: *indeterminancy, abstract lyricism, fractured sensibilities, philosophical speculation, loose referentiality, unstable pronouns.* This is happy-making, freeing language, and intelligent reading and observation.

And it is proof, as well, that our poetry has taken a deluxe turn towards what can happen naturally; that, as Michael Burkard says in "We Have to Talk About Another Book": "We don't have to make a sentence if we don't want to." "Our poetry," says St. John, "should be as various as the natural world, as rich and peculiar in its potential articulations." He is, he says, ". . . persuaded by the idea of an American poetry based on plurality, not purity" (xxviii). Me too.

Like language itself, the nature of poetic output has become fluid, unfixed. We are writing, now, poems that feel their way—or seem to feel their way—through the writer, from experience, through imagination and association, rather than through the predetermined form. We borrow from, expand upon, react to—combining in some way, shape, or form—all the time. We are what we take in and process directly or indirectly: a little nature, a little nurture, a whim, an impulse, a cogent plan. "'Like species,' Forrest Gander writes, 'poems are not invented, but develop out of a kind of discourse, each poet tensed against another's poetics, in conversation . . .'"(137). ". . . [E]verything is relational," says Mei-Mei Berssenbrugge (57). Our artistic receptors function under the pressure of what we know or suspect. We are the gray area personified and it's a fine thing that the poem, as human endeavor, has been recognized, as Swensen puts it, to be ". . . increasing the expressive potential of language itself—while also remaining committed to the emotional spectra of lived experience" (xxi).

The AICR newsletter quoted at the beginning of this essay put it beautifully: ". . . [M]ove over apples and bananas . . . ," it said. Move over dichotomy of *traditional* and *experimental.* Blatantly or subtly, we've got mongrel fruit. And surprises. The skirts of poetic convention are being lifted and they're flashing a new bit of intelligence and éclat. We need to broaden our language in order to keep up. *American Hybrid: A Norton Anthology of New Poetry* is here to help us do that.

WRITING ON THE BRINK:
PERIPHERAL VISION AND THE PERSONAL POEM

*'Glorious, stirring sight!' murmured
Toad. . . . 'The Poetry of motion! The real
way to travel! The only way to travel!
Here today—in next week tomorrow! Villages skipped, towns and cities jumped—
always somebody else's horizons! O bliss!
O poop-poop! Oh my! Oh my!'*

Kenneth Grahame
The Wind in the Willows

The Poetry of Motion

If a good personal poem is, as I believe it must be, a thing in motion, a thing
on its way to some place that beckons or threatens, then Toad has it right.
Look closely at what he has to say. He's talking about poetry.

One of the difficulties in personal poetry is that autobiography has often
been confused with what may be called *the personal*. I'll define the two this
way: *The personal* is what you have become, what you are in transience or may
be becoming; *autobiography*—which may or may not be factual—is what you
did, what you do, or what you *already* knew about yourself before the poem
began. The personal is an open mode, and dynamic; the autobiographical is a
closed mode that relates a done thing and is static. It's that which figures beyond such a static state I'm arguing for—that which is peripheral to the autobiographical: the personal.

I'm drawn to what flutters nebulously at the corner of my eye—just outside my certain sight. I want a share in what I am routinely denied, or only
suspect exists: I want to move with the poem in the act of becoming or of en-

countering motion. I long for a glimpse of what is beginning to occur, both in the margins, the periphery of the poem, and in a life.

It is all too easy to locate, however, what pretends to be the personal in poems. If we have been curious at all, we have met with a plethora of books and workshops that pronounce the personal as accessible through memory via vivid visual recall, colorful concrete or figurative imagination, or through forthright accusation—more workshops than we can shake an eraser at that tell us to "write what we know." We have myriad contemporary poems of precedent to look to. But don't let me mislead you: I am in full support of recall, imagination, and the occasional sharp-toothed and bitter accusation. It's just that contemporary poems are so often, so utterly, chock full of the *pretend* personal that somewhere along the compositional line, or perhaps even before, the poem as art/artefact, and as peripheral playing field, has been lost. Though verse-looking pieces such as these may seem personal to their authors, and, perhaps, their authors' loved ones, they leave me—and I would assume many other readers as well—on the outside of a poem behind glass: full-frontal and me not caring too darn much. These poems, then, make of themselves a means of telling what we can know—in its raw, factual or pseudo-factual state—rather than a means to suspect or intuit the consequences of what we do not know.

My bias for such mystery, however, by no means precludes autobiography within the confines of such an idealized poem. In fact, in most cases, something like autobiography must be present in order to ground the less-than-concrete. But I, as a reader, want to be allowed in there with the autobiographical—into a space built into the poem in which I may interact with it—as opposed to my being relegated to mere observer, to Peeping Thomasina. The head-on, other-side-of-the-glass sort of peeping serves no purpose as far as I can see except to transmit literal information (the way your refrigerator manual might, step-by-step, tell you how and how often to vacuum your coils). And of course, the obvious (or not so obvious) exception, the thrill of voyeurism. I'm greedier than that. I want to be lured *and* compelled. And I want *in*. I need to see some movement from the corner of my eye and get curious, want to know what it might be, what fleeting, unnamable, shapeless-but-in-motion thing—acknowledged but uncertain—is skirting my certainties and may, for all I know, be lingering threateningly, or downright dangerously, at the edge of my vision, at the brink of my recognition, making up some unknowable bulk of the periphery of my, or the writer's, precarious life. Now, that stuff out *there* has the potential to contain something that could directly and immediately affect life as I know it, or, at minimum, my perception of it. That's what's urgent. That's what I find interesting.

The philosopher Suzanne Langer puts her slant on it this way:

> A work of art . . . is more than an 'arrangement' of giv-
> en things—even qualitative things. Something emerges . . .
> which was not there before. . . .

The motion *is* the emergence. That place that wasn't there before? That's
where I want to go.

Here Today—In Next Week Tomorrow!

The built-in space within the poem I seek is the field on which such mystery's
action may take place. And I find that one of the primary spacemakers of such
energizing territory is time.

Tess Gallagher speaks of "deep time," and the term seems marvelously apt. Muriel Rukeyser, when she wrote of a "multiple time sense" within a
poem, was talking, I'm certain, of the same phenomenon. They're both describing a sort of simultaneity in which all the poet's considered "times" coexist—so that, despite our common perception, time is presented not as a
merely linear, countable passage, is not unidirectional as we tend to assume,
is, in fact, not directional at all, but is instead dimensional. Gallagher spoke
of those "psychic spaces in the poem that expand the time dimension of the
poetic structure," and so, when she, in another place, says that "the photograph is the enemy of poetry," she speaks exactly to both our points—
the static photograph cannot address time in its expanded sense. The only
time-motion that might occur because of such an isolated prompt—that
photograph—is in the space between a predisposed viewer and the artefact
of the picture itself which can merely hold a concrete subject captive. The
field of interplay is not of the photograph, not built into the print itself. It
can't be. The photo is a single micro-moment shot dead. The predisposed
viewer may make connections, but it is not the photo or the static poem
that embodies them; it is the viewer her- or himself. Those connections are
not written into, or inherent in, the art/artefact. The photo is clean of dimension and is time-locked.

Eavan Boland, in an essay in *Partisan Review,* stated beautifully that
"[T]here is a foreground and a background. Or, to put it another way, a poem
is an assembly of perspectives."

I propose that when those perspectives are spread across time, the good poem is possible. When they are not, the poem is likely to aspire to photo-graph-ness rather than poem-ness. The interplay of those perspectives can be the key that opens up the poem to deep time and, therefore, psychic space—my peripheral playing field.

Villages Skipped, Towns and Cities Jumped! . . .

That area past where you already know yourself to be, past what you—at the very least—are, is the resonance-making territory that lifts the poem off the page. What do you carry that others cannot see? What hovers about you? What is elliptical? Leap-frogs, if you will? With the right lens, the right field, the poem is much more than quantifiable or externally qualifiable informa-tion; it can be offset by the poem's abstract subject which functions as a lens through which to re-view the traceable material of the poem. Langer says, "The total result is much more than a literal statement. . . ." You can't explain your way there. The leap must be made in order to arrive.

In Stephen Dunn's essay, "The Good, the Not So Good," he places my concerns precisely.

> The good poem allows us to believe we have a soul. In the presence of a good poem we remember/discover the soul has an appetite, and that that appetite is for emotional veracity and for the unsayable.

Note it's the unsayable, not the *unspeakable*. The unspeakable falls within the purlieu of autobiography. Not the unspeakable to shock the reader, for the cur-rent market value of a rotten life, but the *ineffable*—that which resides in mys-tery, in uncertainty and reminds us "we have a soul." In Dunn's short prose works, *Riffs and Reciprocities*, he makes it even plainer: "It's only about unin-teresting things that we can be certain." And "[c]ertainty is what we feel when we know a little less than enough." Platitudinal? Perhaps. But correct, none-theless, understandable, and marvelously useful in assessing a poem's ambi-tion. It is in the space made accessible by uncertainty that the energy of a good poem resides. It reverberates there; it moves. It demands my attention, and the answering is less important than my own cloud of unknowing in which my *becoming* takes place. Thomas Disch focuses on the same concept, but more brutally and more practically: "Nothing so sustains a poet as an irresolvable di-lemma." Irresolvable? My cup of proverbial poetry tea. And how to do this? How to open the poem up? Dunn gives us an answer.

> The good poem 'lets in' the unruly, the difficult, the un-
> formed—in a sense, the unmanageable—and is able to
> make an environment for them. The more the imagination
> can accommodate, the more chaos the poet is equal to, ob-
> viously the richer the poem.

I do want the richer poem. I want unruliness within an identifiable environment. I want the poem that absolutely buzzes with that torque between the
known and the unknown.

Dunn again:

> The good poem simultaneously reveals and conceals. It is in
> this sense that it is mysterious.

And Langer:

> A work of art is a composition of tensions and resolutions,
> balance and unbalance, rhythmic coherence, a precarious
> yet continuous unity.

And the unity is the enclosure of the good poem, its environment. Order vs
disorder. Ease vs uneasiness. There are ways to accomplish this: ". . . [R]efuse
beauty, refuse paradise and ease. . . ," Jane Hirshfield insists. "Poems are excursions into belief and doubt. . . ." To that one, I propose this qualification:
The good ones make those excursions simultaneously, and the tensions thereof are the catalysts of thought and urgency and resonance.

In a nifty little book called *Approaches to Writing*, Paul Horgan, a two-
time winner of the Pulitzer Prize for History, says

> Much of our writing now seems to be propped up by a foun-
> dation of earnest observation rather than by one of intui-
> tive identity, or all-enduring, communion with mankind.
> To put it another way, let us say that we are living in the age
> of case history.

Therein lies my point. A better poem, in its movement, transfers energy to the
reader, and if, as Rukeyser believes, "human energy may be defined as consciousness, the capacity to make change in existing conditions," then the case
history lacks the essential energy for such an exchange. The case history is anecdote, is information, data of the autobiographical sort.

One of the prevalent confusions, and what seems often to be the source of flatness, claustrophobia, and exclusion in the poem, is an issue of *truth*—and what we mean when we use that word. Urgency, meaningfulness, and movement are seldom the by-products of truth-as-fact. "It happened." "She really did that." "But that's how I felt." All facts, no doubt. Yet confession itself is neither always noble nor is it necessarily art. Facts, or editorials on them, are not enough.

The poet's dilemma is this: Good art seldom has the same shape as life. We need to go past the seemingly true, past the factual or seemingly factual, beyond the narrative, if there is one, into poem-ness. Of course, it's a frightening thing to do, and there's the risk, I suppose, of real disruption in doing so, but, until we understand the stakes, we'll continue to be trapped in photograph-ness, and, in all likelihood, we'll leave the reader out of the action.

I recently returned to Ted Mooney's 1981 novel, *Easy Travel to Other Planets*, and, by chance, reread the back cover: "His novel is about communication. The place is a world . . . where people who can't talk to each other suffer from a disease called 'information sickness'"—a world, say the poetry world, where the unsayable is replaced by information or even the unspeakable. Here I must call up Suzanne Langer's "fundamental distinction between the informative and the evocative use of words"—the body-knowledge, the sensation of the work. Not reportage by any means, not even insight necessarily, but movement towards what might become insightful: realism wrought by uncertainty.

For many reasons, psychological and social, some writers believe that "risk-taking" involves the telling of secrets. That seems to me entirely too *post facto*, too static, too late. Real risk, I believe, lies in the task of discovering new secrets.

Thomas Disch describes poem-seeming verse this way: "[T]here are no formal challenges, no musicality, no effort to find the *mot juste* or the telling epithet. There is simply candor. . . ." A matter of engaging in factual autobiography. I like a poem that engages relations rather than relation*ships*. A past, a present, and a presumed future. When the muse is the mere self in the spotlight, trouble hangs over our heads. When art takes the light and the self steps into the background, I figure something interesting is likely to happen. Resonance and consequence travel beyond the reported, beyond the enacted, beyond the tellable to something that speaks. Not resolution, but a stab at confrontation. The actions of the past are over; their repercussions are, in all likelihood, not. They're still percussing.

A work of art . . . is neither a confessional nor a frozen tan-

trum; it is a developed metaphor, a non-discursive symbol
that articulates what is verbally ineffable—the logic of consciousness itself.

That's Langer. It speaks to the photograph-ness I spoke of earlier. "The logic
of consciousness itself"—that's where we live despite our attempts to simpli-
fy, quantify, and to name. And Heller:

> . . . [T]he poet's possession of his experience is different from
> the possession of him by the experience. The poet's view is
> somewhat more spacious, large, aerial; his experience is seen
> in an open context, its energy, its quality is felt.

In the poem that has achieved poem-ness, the reader suspects more than she
has been told. In the poem that has achieved poem-ness, the poem has gotten bigger than the poet. That's the constant warning: If the poem is merely
as large as the poet, the poem has failed. The poem that makes room for the
reader might be conceived as a poem, not only of inclusiveness, but of transcendence, or, perhaps even, a series of transcendences. It transcends the past,
the now, and the poet.

Somebody Else's Horizons

In poet Jane Cooper's foreward to Rukeyser's *The Life of Poetry*, she states that
Rukeyser "liked to say that poems are meeting-places. . . ." Dunn puts it this
way: "The personal is what matters. . . . And the expansion of what the personal means. . . ." A fusion of concerns. Dana Gioia puts it under a colder
light: "Good poetry . . . actively seeks [its readers'] imaginative and intellectual collaboration by assuming and exploiting a common frame of reference."
    Exploitation. It's a word with a nasty connotation. Like *manipulation.*
But the truth we must work with is this: Good art is most often manipulation via exploitation. It is *directive.* Not *didactic,* but *directive.* Contrary to a
frighteningly common belief that poetry can mean anything the reader wants
it to, a good poem cannot. The good poet will have defined the arena and directed the reader's attention and emotions—manipulated the art via the common "frame[s] of reference" in order to achieve a desired effect. It's what we
do as poets. Or, at least, what I think we should attempt.
    Let's take a look at Dunn's "The Sudden Light and the Trees" from his
Landscape at the End of the Century.

Syracuse, 1969

My neighbor was a biker, a pusher, a dog
and wife beater.
In bad dreams I killed him

and once, in the consequential light of day,
I called the Humane Society
about Blue, his dog. They took her away

and I readied myself, a baseball bat
inside my door.

At this point, we know the degree of this narrator's involvement—and that his participation in this narrative was prompted by, according to his "facts," justified fear. The baseball bat becomes an emblem of his fear. The word *fear* or its synonyms have not yet been used.

That night I heard his wife scream

and I couldn't help it, that pathetic
relief; her again, not me.

We have moved from the autobiographical to, I believe, a startling confession. Something has opened up, has begun to resonate and it is enough for the reader to grab on to. The autobiographical then continues:

It would be years before I'd understand

why victims cling and forgive. I plugged in
the Sleep-Sound and it crashed
like the ocean all the way to sleep.

One afternoon I found him
on the stoop,
a pistol in his hand, waiting,

he said, for me.

The tension that was posited earlier has come to fruition. Because of our ear-

lier purchase at the point of confession, our stakes are higher than they might
have otherwise been. And then another surprise: We move from the image of
a potentially powerful weapon to this:

> A sparrow had gotten in
> to our common basement.
> Could he have permission
>
> to shoot it? The bullets, he explained,
> might go through the floor.

That small brown bird is an interesting and sudden deflation of our expectations and will remain so until fourteen lines later when the gun once again
takes the foreground.

> I said I'd catch it, wait, give me
>
> a few minutes and, clear-eyed, brilliantly
> afraid, I trapped it
> with a pillow.

It's an interesting story and a story that has opened itself up beyond its prin-
cipals. The sparrow now has taken its place—and that place and its significance will grow.

> I remember how it felt
>
> when I got it in my hand, and how it burst
> that hand open
> when I took it outside, a strength
>
> that must have come out of hopelessness
> and the sudden light
> and the trees.

Look who owns that verb *burst*! Look who owns that *hopelessness*! Suddenly—
and in the same sentence as the narrator's "remember," "felt," and "got"— the
sparrow takes on the active, forceful role and now, in that beautifully calculated shift, that fragile, menaced bird embodies all the narrator's emotions to
that point: his "clear-eyed," brilliant fear. The earlier, prevailing emotion is
now finally named, creating a real tension with the speaker's earlier culpabil-

ities. And the bird, right then, surprises us once more, but this time with its forcefulness: The sparrow "burst[s]" the human hand open. It is the explosion we have been waiting for all along, but placed, now, in a receptacle, a symbol, if you will, and in a manner that opens the poem to a broader-than-autobiographical reading.

Let's go on to the poem's end:

> And I remember
>
> the way he slapped the gun against
>   his open palm,
> kept slapping it, and wouldn't speak.

The poem, despite its clear nod to real or seeming autobiography in its date/placement line (again, factual or not), despite its simple and elegant form, despite its absolute specificity of narrative, speaks for what is human in the larger sense. That final stanza is a real coup—the gun and that participle—as though the slapping continues in its arena of tense silence right up to the present telling. Time here, and its careful arrangement in this poem, has opened up more than just inclusion. It has made an imagistic impact that holds tight long after the reading of the poem has been completed.

Thomas Disch, one of my favorite critics, asks these crucial, albeit delightfully inflated, questions:

> Do the figures of the tale engage in actions that have an import beyond the bogs of Romance, beyond even the uplands of domestic tragedy? That is, do their personal fates come to have an emblematic reference to the larger patterns of history?

Dunn's do.

The plot, even in its anecdotal form, is startling—a point Dunn argues for both by example and, in his prose, elsewhere, articulation. And so much has been internalized via emblem—the baseball bat, the sparrow, the gun, as well as its menacing participle. But the bird's usurpation of the verb *burst*, and the *slapping* of the biker's gun are, as Langer gracefully puts it, ". . . outward showing[s] of inward nature[s]. . . ." By the end of the poem, the reader has assimilated the movement and the images—the torque between threat and the strength inherent in "hopelessness" are at work against each other. If, as Paul Horgan says, "Every act of art is an act of alteration," and I believe good art is, then "The Sudden Light and the Trees" is art. The speaker is changed,

is *complicit*, and the reader has, no doubt, reached a point of invited identification, participation, and is alerted and altered by that. The poem is an enactment and a contemplation of the continuing tensions involved. Dunn catches exquisitely—and surprisingly—John Berger's "ambiguity of experience."
Nothing here is flat or simple. Dunn's poem accomplishes much and renders
my world and my experience wider and clearer. My life is increased.

Oh, Bliss

I do ask a lot. I know that. But it's my prerogative to seek the grail-poem.
I want ambition, eloquence, music, accomplishment. I want what Langer
wants: ". . . not statement but *poesis*." I want the time to be deep time; I want
the lines to be taut, meaningful units, not prose that's been whacked into
the shape of what a poem might look like; I want tension; I want meaning
beyond information; and I want to be included in discovery. Time, torque,
truth in its broader sense, and transcendence—too much to ask from a poem?
I want to be able, as high school teacher Frank McNabb refers to it, to "read
the lines, read between the lines, and read beyond the lines." And I want the
poem to pay off after such scrutiny.

  Facts aren't enough. In fact, I propose that facts, by themselves, are inevitably an impoverished commodity. Muir states it exquisitely: "Exact knowledge is only a fragment of the knowledge we need in order to live." He says,

> . . . [I]t is thought, the capacity for . . . thought, together
> with one's ideal intuition of what the art can be, which al-
> lows poetry on occasion to emerge from our all too common
> private preoccupations into those universal statements that
> . . . compose the art's final justification.

Toad, says, "Oh my! Oh my!" And yes. That would be it.

WORKS CONSULTED

Boland, Eavan. "In Perspective." *Partisan Review* #2, Spring 1993. 316.

Disch, Thomas M. *The Castle of Indolence: On Poetry, Poets, and Poetasters.* New York: Picador, 1995.

Dunn, Stephen. *Landscape at the End of the Century.* New York: Norton, 1991. *Walking Light.* New York: Norton, 1993. "Reciprocities." *Southern Review*, Winter 1997. 91-102.

Gallagher, Tess. *A Concert of Tenses: Essays on Poetry.* Ann Arbor: University of Michigan Press, 1986.

Gioia, Dana. *Can Poetry Matter?* St. Paul: Graywolf, 1992.

Grahame, Kenneth. *The Wind in the Willows.* New York: Dell, 1969.

Heller, Michael. "Poetry Without Credentials." *The Ohio Review*, Number 28. 94-102.

Hirshfield, Jane. "Facing the Lion: The Way of Shadow and Light in Some Twentieth-Century Poems." *Facing the Lion: Writers on Life and Craft.* Kurt Brown, ed. Boston: Beacon, 1996. 14-32.

Horgan, Paul. *Approaches to Writing.* Middletown, CT: Wesleyan, 1988.

Langer, Suzanne K. *Feeling and Form.* New York: Scribner's Sons, 1953. *Problems of Art.* New York: Scribner's Sons, 1957.

McNabb, Frank. "Teacher to Teacher: Approach and Reflection." *Starting With Delight*, No. 1 (Spring 1993) Newsletter of the Geraldine R. Dodge Poetry Program: 3.

Mooney, Ted. *Easy Travel To Other Planets.* New York: Ballantine, 1983.

Muir, Edwin. *The Estate of Poetry.* St. Paul: Graywolf, 1993.

Rukeyser, Muriel. *The Life of Poetry.* Ashfield, MA: Paris Press, 1966.

UT PICTURA POESIS: THE PAINTING
IN THE POEM, OR SIMPLE
PERSPECTIVE FOR POETS: A MINI-ESSAY

> *Painting is a philosophical enterprise*
> *that doesn't always ways involve paint.*
> Howard Halle, Art Critic

Introduction

I've been thinking for some time now about movement and its various in-carnations in poetry. A mind is happied by movement, I think. And, if not happied, then at least engaged. Even in sleep the mind moves. We call that *dreaming.*

When we read, the eye and the mind come together to move in concert: ". . .Written language materializes thought into form. . . ."[1] So, in the case of reading, to quote Charles Tomlinson in an essay called "The Poet as Paint-er," "It is the mind sees. . . ."[2] And what it sees, or what the reader experienc-es when some part or parts of a poem carry more visual or verbal weight than others, is a metaphor of spacial relation which produces in the reader a sensa-tion of movement.

I'm describing a facet of perspective—simple artist's perspective analo-gous to that in painting. Like paintings, poems may have a foreground and a background. The eye/mind is first drawn to—and therefore attention is fo-cused on—the foreground; that foreground is then experienced in relation to

---

[1]Johanna Drucker and William Gass, *The Dual Muse: The Writer as Artist, the Artist as Writer* (Philadelphia: John Benjamins Publishing Company, 1997) 103.
[2]Charles Tomlinson, "The Poet as Painter," *Poets on Painters: Essays on the Art of Painting by Twentieth-Century Poets*, ed. J. D. McClatchy (Berkeley: University of California Press, 1998) 284.

the background. This mind's eye, in the case of poetry, works like a zoom lens: Zoom in, zoom out. Focus, travel, focus. Move up, move back.[3] It's my theory that although some readers may not have articulated it, may not have consciously acknowledged it, they have experienced that shifting, that change of focus—not a quick cut isolated from context (though this too is activated by some poetic strategies), but a sense of relativity through ". . . an imaginative reorientation of the presentation in depth."[4] That reorientation is the interim process of changing focus, the following of what readers "see" when the mind's eye, that lens, is in the process of moving toward and perceiving foreground and background in sequence.

Perspective, then, acts as an organizing principle that determines a form of structured perception, a manifest, chosen focus—Wyndham Lewis made a powerful point when he said "Art is the expression of an enormous preference."[5] What is foregrounded is privileged, is singled out, is *preferred* by focus. A writer pulls material to the foreground or pushes it into the background, and chooses to do that either knowingly or by default—but chooses it nevertheless. José Ortega y Gasset insists, "Movement implies a mover."[6] In the instance of poetry, that mover—that manipulator of perception, the depositor of the verbal catalyst that initiates the sense of movement—is the poet.

The methods are many, but foregrounding can easily be achieved by sharp, precise visuals and/or a voice at peak performance; backgrounding can be achieved through rendering language flat and even, through fuzzy visuals or abstraction, through equalizing, in a leveling-out, of materials that might have otherwise been set forth as unequal parts.

The Difference Between Poem and Painting

Thomas Munro, in *The Arts and Their Interrelations*, handily divides the arts into categories: "The Space Arts," which include painting, sculpture, and architecture, and "The Time Arts," poetry and music[7] (and, of course, we could add film to that set). He describes The Space Arts as arts of simultaneous perception and The Time Arts as arts of successive perception. Lessing,

---

[3]Somewhat like scene and narrative in fiction. In scene, action takes place up close; you can see the details clearly. In narrative, there is more distance between the reader and the "what happens." The details are vaguer, less well defined, further away.

[4]Andrew Paul Ushenko, *Dynamics of Art* (Bloomington: Indiana University Press, 1953) 90.

[5]Marshall McLuhan and Parker, Harley, *Through the Vanishing Point: space in poetry and painting* (NY: Harper & Row, Publishers, 1968) 125.

[6]José Ortega y Gasset, "On Point of View in the Arts," *Writers on Artists*, ed. Daniel Halpern, trans. Paul Snodgrass and Joseph Frank (San Francisco: North Point Press, 1988) 376.

[7]Thomas Munro, *The Arts and Their Interrelations* (NY: The Liberal Arts Press, 1951).

in *Laocoön*, concurs: ". . . [T]here is . . . this essential difference between them [poetry and painting]: In the one case the action is *visible and progressive*, its different parts occurring one after the other in a sequence of time, and in the other the action is *visible and stationary*, its different parts developing in co-existence in space."[8]

What occurs in poetry is, of course, sequential. Over time, a poem accrues both melody (or sound-object) and information. The eye sees only words, and sees them as a jerky elephant parade of black signs across the page: small unit small unit small unit. But the effect is one of wholeness. Information accrues, with a writer's skill, smoothly. Image accrues, and meaning (probably) accrues.

The painting, however, is not only self-contained in time and space, it is simultaneous; all of its aspects exist concurrently at the time of viewing. All the paint is in place at once, before the eye, and it is conceivable that the entire canvas—at least the relationships of its elements—could be comprehended in a one look. (We know, of course, that, when taking a closer look, the eye isolates and inspects—but the whole is visible on a single surface, a body prepared to be taken in as a unit.)

As a friend, a fellow poet, says, "Art ain't easy." It takes more than mere paint and a unified surface, more than just words on a page or a series of pages to achieve the status of art. The trick for any artist is to make art move beyond the physical boundaries of the artefact. Gertrude Stein addresses the issue in painting this way: "There it is and it has to look like people or objects or landscapes. Besides that it must not completely only exist in its frame. It must have its own life. And yet it may not move nor imitate movement, not really, nor must it stay still. It must not only be in its frame, but it must not, only, be in its frame."[9] The painting must extend beyond its frame; the poem must mean—and offer experience of—more than it says.

Poem Type and Extrapolation

The Barron's guide, *Perspective and Composition*, in their Art Handbook series, states that the basic concepts of rational perspective are ". . . based on drawing [read: writing] from a single point of view which represents the eye [mind] of the observer [reader]."[10] John Berger puts it far more succinctly and beauti-

---

[8]Gotthold Ephraim Lessing, *Laocoön*, trans. Edward Allen McCormick (NY: Johns Hopkins University Press, 1984) 77.
[9]Tomlinson, 104.
[10]Parramòn's Editorial Team, *Perspective and Composition*, (Barron's Art Handbooks, Barron's Educational Series, Happauge, NY, 1999) 14.

fully: "Perspective makes the single eye the centre of the visible world."[11] And the travail of that single eye is what I wish to foreground in this little essay: the simplest, most basic form, the single point of view within lineated, representational work—one source of perceived movement within the conventional or near-conventional poem plane.

It's a given that you won't have to look very far to find poems to which this doesn't apply. Paintings and poems may have, of course, more than one point of view—but even then, as in the case with some of Hockney's paintings (I'm thinking of the living room scenes in which the chairs are simultaneously viewed from different angles), multiple points of view coexist without transitions on the single canvas. (Each point of view, in isolation, is a single point of view which has then been placed within a collage-like setting comprised of multiple points of view; the bottom line stays the same: No two points of view can inhabit exactly the same place at the same time. There is the possibility of blurring, and the certainty of juxtapositioning, but each, in its turn, is a single point of view. It's not a law; it's an observation.) But the painting as collage exists to be experienced, as well, as a whole; though, in truth, in the process of study analogous to reading, the eye/mind will isolate and examine. The eye will move; the mind will, through the artist's skill, be engaged and, if the artist's good, enchanted.

Types of Movement

Essential to my idea: the premise that all movement, if you experience it, is perceived movement.

In the case of poems and paintings nothing *really* moves—except the viewing eye and the reading eye with its jerky saccadic motion. It is the mind that is alive with motion in its quest to transform mental activity into information, much of it relational.

I would call this not-actually-happening movement in reading and viewing *projected* movement. The mind projects the images, the changes within those image-geographies, from the catalysts on the page or the canvas.

Subcategories of perceived movement, then, would seem to be "actual movement," and two varieties of perceived-projected movement, "apparent movement" and "affective movement."

Actual movement is literal movement. It's what we might call "real" movement, most easily described as "the displacement of objects in our en-

---

[11] John Berger, *Ways of Seeing* (London: British Broadcasting Company and Penguin Books Ltd., 1987) 16.

vironment."[12] Something physically changes its location or its location is changed by some outside force. For example, a tangible shopping cart rolls across a parking lot to smack into and dent the equally tangible fender of a new Lexus. Or a tin of string beans, having substance and weight, is knocked from the counter to the floor by the corporeal cat. Both the cart, a portion of the fender, and the tin, and in all likelihood the cat, have literally moved through space: actual movement.

Apparent movement is movement that does not physically take place; instead, the mind takes cues that set off visions in which it seems as though it does. The best examples of this I've found are those big, often red neon arrows pointing the way to parking spaces in the dimly lit lots in front of cheap motels. The "come-this-way" illuminated signs. The "over here" signs. The "you-can't-miss-it-if-you-follow-this-sign" signs. The lovely part of the experience of these signs is this question: How can you *follow* a sign that isn't actually moving? The lights that make up these siren arrows are not really in motion, though they appear to be. In reality, stationary lights "flash in sequential order" and we "see" light moving though nothing at all is changing location.[13] We "see" movement.

Affective movement, on the other hand, is experienced movement of the mind's eye in transit between foreground and background. No clear focus is achieved during affective movement; it's like the view out the fast-moving train window, but it takes place in the mind. The world outside has to read the same grouping of words in order to experience it.

These movement types play out in the arena of poem, set off by techniques put into use by the poet.

For the possibilities of the poem, I see the breakdown in a schematic:

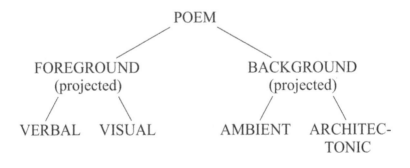

A poem may have a foreground and a background. Foregrounding, in the simple cases I'm addressing here, can be achieved through manipulation of

---

[12] "Module * Gestalt Theories of Perpetual Organization" 5.
[13] Ibid.

voice (verbal) and/or image (visual); background seems to manifest in two basic forms, ambient and architectonic. The ambient background can be a tone or a mood; the architectonic background supports the foreground in a structural way.

Foregrounding can be achieved by making one or more parts of the poem stand out from the rest either by verbal or visual immediacy. Backgrounding can be achieved through a flattening out of language—an equalizing of what might have been presented as unequal parts, or by providing a construction that places the foreground contextually.

Let's look at some examples.

In Catherine Doty's poem "Yes,"[14] the entire short poem is foregrounded by an exciting, snappy, and inviting voice.

> It's about the blood
> banging in the body,
> and the brain
> lolling in its bed
> like a happy baby.
> At your touch, the nerve,
> that volatile spook tree,
> vibrates. The lungs
> take up their work
> with a giddy vigor.
> Tremors in the joints
> and tympani,
> dust storms
> in the canister of sugar.
> The coil of ribs
> heats up, begins
> to glow. Come
> here.

The poem's short lines, its speed, its battering of b's: **b**lood, **b**anging, **b**ody, **b**rain, **b**ed, **b**aby, are all working on the reader. It's almost impossible to stop reading that first five-line sentence. By then the reader, at least this reader, is hooked and is treated to images that surprise and enhance, as well as a parade of t's that both insinuate and delight: **t**ouch, volatile spook **t**ree, vibrates, **t**remors, and **t**ympani. Not to mention the v's: ner**v**e, **v**olatile, **v**ibrates, **v**igor. Sonically tight, seductive and sexy, the poem is hot and on the boil in the foreground. Its immediacy is such that the reader is hard-pressed to look away.

---

[14]Catherine Doty, *Momentum*. (Fort Lee: CavanKerry Press, 2004) 5.

On the other hand, Anne Sexton's "Lobster,"[15] is a poem that starts out in-your-face-close and then gradually moves back. It begins: "A shoe with legs / a stone dropped from heaven /" and then removes itself slightly from the foreground by introducing a "he" between the reader and the image as the agent who makes things happen in the third and fourth lines: "he does his mournful work alone, / he is like the old prospector for gold /." You can *feel* the movement of drawing back from the stark images of the first two lines. Lines eight through ten, then, pull back even further, become vaguer, image separated from the reader by the storyteller's thrice repeated "somewhere far off," and the drawing back continues in the penultimate and the last lines, speaking of the lobster's "perfect green body // and paint it red." At that point the image is moved up again, nearly as close as the opening lines—but not quite. It's rather masterly, its sudden foregrounding and the vision moving back and back gradually until it moves forward again. This is ambient background in play: The images are pushed forward, are immediate, and the background serves to heighten the impact of the images by deemphasizing, spacially, the rest of the poem.

Stephen Dunn's wonderful poem, "The Sudden Light and the Trees,"[16] is a perfect example of architectonic backgrounding. The poem is a story. A man, the "I" in the poem, the Dunn character, has a neighbor described as "a biker, a pusher, a dog / and wife beater." A portion of their history is recounted and then the poem moves into more immediate territory with the story of a sparrow trapped in their common basement. The biker asks permission to shoot it. "The bullets, he explained, / might go through the floor./" The "I," in an uncharacteristic act of bravery, tells the biker to give him "a few minutes," catches the bird, and takes it outside. Then, instead of the speaker's agency of release, *the bird* bursts the hand holding it open, releasing itself, and, so, the sparrow has moved to the foreground, the poem zooms in, a close-up, on the bird. But what is pressed farthest into the foreground by immediacy and image is the vision that follows that scene chronologically. The "I" says ". . . And I remember // the way he slapped that gun against / his open palm, / kept slapping it, and wouldn't speak." That image, that alleged memory of persistent threat is foregrounded: That's a precisely characterized scene. Both the biker and the "I" preside in that vision, but the gun is in-your-face close and moving. That "-ing," that "slapping," the fact that "he kept slapping it" is terrifying (partially because of the poem's earlier setup). And the ongoingness of that action—that slapping, slapping of the gun and the imagined sound it makes—combined with the clarity and closeness of that final scene itself is placed in relief in relation to the structural support system of the poem.

---

[15]Anne Sexton, *The Complete Poems* (Boston: Houghton Mifflin Company, 1981) 501.
[16]Stephen Dunn, *Landscape at the End of the Century* (NY: W.W. Norton & Company, 1991) 42.

So, if those techniques of foregrounding and backgrounding work so well, why would any artist press an entire poem into a backgrounded mode? Can it even be done? I'd say that yes, it certainly can, and it can succeed. Here's why: Sometimes a manner taken on, an affectation of a flattened reality or pronouncement can be both effective, desirable, and just plain linguistically fun. Here are the first two full lines and the partial third of Mei-Mei Berssenbrugge's "Jealousy."[17]

> Attention was commanded through a simple, unadorned,
> unexplained, often decentered presence, / up to now, a margin
> of empty space like water, its surface contracting, then melting /
> along buried pipelines, where gulls gather in euphoric
> buoyancy. . . .

For all intents and purposes, she has created the aural equivalent of a basic landscape painting. It's brilliant, really. The lines seem of a consistent, gossamer-like weight, the language without high and low points. But all those three-syllable words ("Attention," "commanded," "unadorned," "unexplained," "decentered," "contracting," "euphoric," "buouancy")! Why don't they bog down, feel heavy and unwieldy? Partly because those heavy, three-syllable burdens are buoyed up by the one- and two-syllable words. And all those adjectives! those abstractions! Airy manifestations! The poem in its entirety is twenty lines long, twenty such lines, and all presented in what seems to be nearly a monotone, a buzz of background, almost like the white-noise-interference that astronomers have been known to pick up, that sonic background that finally proved to be evidence of the Big Bang.

Why Perspective Matters

Because "[w]e are never looking at just one thing; we are always looking at the relation between things and ourselves."[18]

Because "[t]he ground, or environment, is not a passive container, but active processes that influence the relationships between all of the elements in it."[19]

Because perspective translates into apparent movement and, as Dewey points out, an "organization of energies"[20] that focus the reader's own energies.

---

[17]Jorie Graham, ed., *The Best American Poetry 1990* (NY: Macmillan Publishing Company, 1990) 14.
[18]Berger 9.
[19]Felix Stalder, "From Figure/Ground to Actor—Networks: McLuhan and Latour" http://felix.openforms.com/html/mcluhan-latour.html
[20]John Dewey, *Art as Experience* (NY: G. P. Putnam's Sons, 1958) 162.

Because all of the above work to engage the reader by broadening the possibilities for resonance in the work of art.

Emphasis and de-emphasis. Foreground and background. Contrast and context. Not just tree, but tree within the forest.

Leo Stein, in *Appreciation*, tells a great story:

> When I was fourteen, my brother, who had been at college in the East, brought home some etchings—among them one of apple trees. There were plenty of apple trees all about, and to see why this etching pleased me so I took it into the orchard and compared it with the trees. Then I saw that the artist had simplified and made more evident certain characteristics of the trees themselves— . . . a matter of composition—and I improvised a definition of art: that it is nature seen in the light of its significance.[21]

His brother had "made more evident certain characteristics," had heightened their significance via those simplifications. He had, by choice, placed them in the foreground so that they played against the background of the fuller, broader context, the etching and the orchard.

And so? This is my attempt to share one way of examining the manner in which a poem might be invested with movement, how it might entice and keep a reader's attention—perspective experientially catalyzing apparent movement. It's my attempt to establish that the horizon line in painting has an equally important dynamic corollary in poetry. And to establish that, yes, poetry *is* like painting. *Ut Pictura Poesis*: the paradox of movement standing still, of depth perceived on a two-dimensional surface be it a canvas or a page, and of visions of referents conveyed by both simulacrum and verbiage moving across perceived space and time. And of the mind—if the artist is adept and the audience lucky—happied.

---

[21]Leo Stein, *Appreciation: Painting, Poetry & Prose* (Lincoln: University of Nebraska Press, 1996) 102.

CONFUSED AND CORROSIVE:

AN ESSAY/REVIEW OF BANG'S

THE BRIDE OF E AND GLÜCK'S *A VILLAGE LIFE*

I didn't bite the s.o.b. but if I had it to do over again I surely would.

I'm what? Five? Six? Seven, tops? This nightmare of a pediatric dentist drags me out of the dental chair and into his tiny waiting room where, his hairy hand clutching the back of my neck, he screams like a crazy man at my poor grandmother. I bit him, he yells, and she is not to bring me back until I can behave myself. My teeth can rot in my head. He doesn't need this crap. Goodbye. There's the door, he says, pointing with his chin. Use it. Now. Don't talk. Goodbye.

That evening my grandmother, as I suppose she must, tells my mother and that's that.

The evidence is in: I am incorrigible and a matter of great shame to those who would otherwise love me. What could I have been thinking? But after my first few words in my own defense, I know better than to continue. I'm a child of quick null-affect; it's a learned response. I am terrified of everything—in particular of those things that might set off my mother's scandal-siren, which are, of course, all things anyone might know. Back then even my childish anger turned to fear and swiftly manifested as a state of rigored silence, as a near-permanent floorward gaze, and as stomach ulcers by the time I hit double digits. I didn't bite the lying bastard. Out of terror instilled by my previous experience alone in the room with the man—he was rough and enjoyed being nasty—I refused to open my mouth. Now I had proven myself to be of inferior stock, had once again humiliated my mother, and she was going to see to it that I learned how to behave. She was going to make me into a lady, as she neatly put it, "come hell or high water, goddamnit—you got that?" The minute she could, she enrolled me in Charm School.[22] That dentist must be dead by now. I hope he gets no rest. Yes. I can hold a grudge for

---

[22] Here I have to question my memory: a seven-year old girl in Charm School? It doesn't seem right. But what did?

more than fifty years, even as its target (unrest his soul) flings itself through the afterworld and beyond.

It's difficult now, though, to even say the words *charm school* without breaking into a self-conscious chuckle—charm being something that, as far as I can see, has all but sublimed into an ambient air of unceremoniousness and a great deal of behavioral latitude.

In the fifties, however, charm was serious stuff. Charm School consisted of etiquette, of poise-making. It was white, wrist-length gloves with your dress, the hem of which culminated below your knees, in the daytime—or cheap cotton gloves when checking for dust; it was knees scrubbed raw for my age set, or nylon-hosed for the older girls, knees forced together while dangling demurely over the edge of a metal, collapsible chair. It was napkin folding, table setting, and getting in and out of the passenger seat of a 1957 Chevy without exposing one's underwear, thighs, or just generally appearing to be kin to a bushel sack of dragon fruit. Charm School meant hostess gifts and thank you notes written in elegant cursive. It meant learning how to laugh without flashing the yawning, wet tunnel of your mouth and throat. It was Keep your voice down; it was Lose gracefully. It was: Do it again. We "powdered our noses"; we didn't "have to pee." We were students of euphemism in body and speech. What we did, what we said, how we said it, and where we kept our hands while we did and said it was training for the purpose of rendering us fit for a society of the sort I have yet to experience with any regularity or ease. It was, basically, packaging. And I was only one of many being packaged, whether willingly or under duress. The expectation was era-endemic, and my mother must have rigorously economized to make it happen for me; she'd have no doubt given up cigarettes and beer and a lunch of anything but a one-slice-of-bologna-on-two-slices-of-white-with-yellow-mustard toted in to work in a greasy paper bag. She did it, as she did almost everything, with an earnest, vocal martyrdom. Yet I was almost never willfully uncooperative nor was I habitually neglectful. I was, however, staggeringly self-conscious. My mind would go blank and I could not get my body to go through the motions even by rote—for fear, I'm certain, of failure and another rousing bout of *I-work-so-goddamn-hard-and-you-can't-even-do-this-one-thing*. I dutifully read my ladies' handbook every night, the way some kids read the *Bible*. And I repeated the same months-long course three times before the sympathetic woman who ran the school suggested to my mother and her checkbook that, perhaps, she might not to want to bring me back for another go.

Bottom line? Girls like me, born in the forties, along with poets like Mary Jo Bang and Louise Glück, likely have a foundation of either ingrained or painstakingly acquired politesse to work from. A sort of benchmark of decorum to emulate or from which to vary. It's all about demeanor and bearing, and becomes a matter of degree and/or distribution in practice: aspects of presence that characterize both a person and a poem, whether by choice or by default.

Yes. A poem is an appearance and a behavior.

Mary Jo Bang's slightly skewed, energetic poems seduced me slowly over a long period of time, a poem with its legs crossed at the ankles here, a poem with a scab on its elbow there, until I succumbed fully to her curious honesty and good, troubled nature. She is complicated and funny, odd in a smart, vulnerable, internal way. She is, I discovered, metonymically speaking, someone good to spend time with: amusing and serious both, intelligent with no urge to rub a reader's face in her obvious smarts, and playful enough to toss off the white gloves when necessary and show a little panty on the jungle gym if that's what it takes. If there are insights to be found on the steep, winding tunnel-slide, she's there. She's a poet who makes acute and ofttimes surprising discoveries through trial and articulation—there's nothing grossly packaged about her. Her intuitions and craft are seamless; she's unselfconsciously sui generis. And she's willing to disregard a stray hank of hair that has tumbled out of place or the scuffed toe of a saddle oxford; she may break a hemstitch or two when she snags her skirt climbing the ladder to the monkey bars, but she's no roughneck, no cheap date either. She doesn't begrudge the effort to live consciously and with feeling. She can clean herself up later—you can almost hear her say it—but right now she's got work to do.

Her fifth book, *Elegy*, on her grief at the death of her adult son, won the 2007 National Book Critics Award in Poetry and was named a 2008 *New York Times* Notable Book. It had, as would be expected, a different cast from her previous books, but the work was not unrecognizable. It was still her intricate, captivating struggle. Her speaker, though, had grown heavy with the knowledge of loss; she was working her way, rough cuts and helplessness aside, into knowing more shadow and the questions that arise therein.

Bang's new book, *The Bride of E*, is an abecedarius that presents both the glimmerings of recovering wit, light and dark, along with the residue of her torment. She presents an Alice-in-Wonderland world of disorientation in which ideas are falling and visions are in flux. She understands about distance now, and how it both exists and is impossible to achieve. In "And as in Alice," her narrator says,

> Alice cannot be in the poem, she says, because
> She's only a metaphor for childhood
> And a poem is a metaphor already
> So we'd only have a metaphor
> Inside a metaphor. Do you see?

"They all nod," the poem continues. "They see. Except for the girl / With her head in the rabbit hole. . . ."

And how close to that vision of a Möbius remove-and-no-remove-at-all comes the end of "E is Everywhere" which flings open wide the playful E-is-also-for-Existential box that Bang is drawing from.

> And now, someone is saying, "It's amazing
> That an Australian platypus is now a curio
> On a shelf in a cabinet in a palace in Poland."
> All the while you're wondering
>
> About the man on the curb who waved at you.
> As if he knew you.
> As if you have been everywhere. As if you are existence.

And of course you are existence. Despite the "as if," there's no subjunctive there: *you are*. It's a magnificient plant of suggestion; she knows what she's doing. The ghost of the nod right there. It's all existence—and her tonal, innocent charm arises from its being observation rather than indictment.

One of the irresistible draws of Bang's work, and of her new book in particular, is that her wisdoms have not yet hardened into conclusions. There still exists for her the suspicion that her perceptions could possibly change. "The mind doesn't halt but goes halfway up," she says in "F is for Forgetting."

> The mind doesn't halt but goes halfway up
> In the elevator and then finds itself stuck.
> This is the entirety. Eternity. Made of material
> That is unlikely to change but is forever.

That "unlikely" is what may save the Bang speaker. There is still room for deliverance. There is still that possibility of liquidity, the ability to suspect. This same redemptive insight is stated even more openly in "I as in Justice":

> There is an immense power in uncertainty.
> There is that story that goes like this:
> You were a crime you didn't know had been committed.

That marvelous torquing on the image of the crime! This sense of unknowing, of being taken by surprise by yourself, keeps the poem in quickening mode. "It's the end and it isn't," she says in "O Means Mouth." "I love you except when I don't."

Bang evinces her vulnerability because the honest telling of it is part of her search. The work is neither bravada-propelled confessionalism nor is it show-offy oddballism. It is not plaintive. It is not silly-to-no-avail. But it is tender and controlled. Even in its containment it lets you experience some of the messiness of being human—because, after all, being human is a messy proposition. She is malleable and she is generous. And when she stumbles there is no shame. Her defenses—we all have them—have soft edges. She is *in medias res* on Zeno's path to a lucidity that pays off along the way but is not the end of the journey.

Louise Glück, it would seem from her poems, then, no longer stumbles; stumbling is in her past. She has traversed the charm school obstacle path, come out on the other side in charge, and is ready to tell you about the hardships she experienced and the lessons she learned on the way. She is, perhaps, a flinty Red Queen to Bang's plushier Alice. Glück, again metonymously, has seen the world and is not pleased at all.

A poet I admire greatly introduced me—this must have been in the early eighties—to Glück's work, poems that my friend admired enormously. Her own work was dense, tensile, rich with image and nuance, and immaculately set and argued, loaded with allusion and repetition and a song-like quality that seemed and still seems placenta-rich. I was awakened to another avenue of possibilities when I began to understand her genuine admiration and affection for a poet whose work differed so dramatically from her own. Glück's poems, though often magnificently lyric, seemed to me lapidary and unconditional. Her lacerative tongue made me wince, left me feeling deeply cut, the kind of magical wound that never heals. Frightening spirit in there. But powerful, mostly immaculate poems.

"Hawk's Shadow," a short piece from her second book, *The House on the Marshland*, published in 1975, was the first to leave its mark on me. Even with my terrible memory, I still clearly recall its image and the impact it made: A couple is "embracing in the road," the "I" of the embrace watching the combined, single shadow with that of a hawk hovering above with its kill in its talons. "And I thought:," the speaker says, "one shadow. Like the one we made, you holding me." I continue to experience the chill and the outrage of that image. The poem is dressed flawlessly, its suit crisp, severe, and rich-feeling. It's so sleek you know there's not even any fuzz in its pockets. The poem doesn't raise its voice; it doesn't have to. Its statement is so ruthless and so controlled that the reader knows for certain that voice has no doubt, does not even consider the fact that it emanates from a place of privilege and entitlement. A far-away place beyond question or reproach. The poem, despite the displacement inherent in the trope of hunter and prey, has eschewed euphemism for a keen truth-telling. *This is what you get if you engage.* She's simply reporting the bad news. You never get the feeling it's a warning; it's a fact. And because she knows that it will be what it is whether we understand or acknowledge it or not, I don't even think she cares much whether we listen. But there's an energy bound in such a bitter and unequivocal statement set in such a bloodless context, one that has the power of a chainsaw and the elegance of a palmed, silver and poisoned, blade. I have come to think of these cut-throat lines in her poems as her *dazzle shots*, normally a term designated for those single, on-the-mark proclamations of professional psychics, the spot-on revelations that clients (or dupes) think could not possibly have been faked, the details that convince them that everything the psychic has said and will say must also somehow be true. Glück's a master of her raw proclamations. I'm not the only one who believes she's brilliant: She's won the Pulitzer, the National Book Critics Circle Award, and the Bollingen and Wallace Stevens Awards.

But in her new book, *A Village Life*, her eleventh collection of poems, she's tried a little something new. The flap copy quotes Langdon Hammer asserting that her new work contains "the type of describing, supervising intelligence found in novels rather than poetry." Glück? The same *Glück*? But yes, at a stretch I can see what he's talking about. Though I think Hammer's description is either hyperbole or wishful thinking, I do see the evidence of a broader scope, an occasionally somewhat varied voice and pronoun, and frequently a looser line. The collection tries to ventriloquize inhabitants of the titular village. And though I find this swerve from her more fixed, precipitous mode, these loci of her slowings-down and drawings-out are only interesting assays into something less keen than what has come before. Yet, though a number of her lines may have softened, her basic nature has not. She's still at her best when she's brief. And I can still find that mesmerizing voice of superiority and certainty—and those dazzle shots that draw blood.

Early on in *A Village Life* there is a short poem entitled "First Snow" reminiscent of the dynamic displayed so bone-chillingly in her "Hawk's Shadow." An anomaly for Glück, the entire poem, rather than a single image, is couched in simile:

> Like a child, the earth's going to sleep,
> or so the story goes.
> But I'm not tired it says.
> And the mother says, You may not be tired but I'm tired—
>
> You can see it in her face, everyone can.

So the snow has to fall, sleep has to come.
Because the mother's sick to death of her life
and needs silence.

This, for my money, is Glück at her best again—the voice terse and adamant. The control rigorous—there is none of the flailing hysteria that might surround a mother-on-the-edge—yet the energy is so tightly contained it feels like a vessel ready to burst. It's not a poem of euphemism or chit-chat. Its posture is unyielding and its meaning has not been disarmed—not even by the soft shell of its simile. Its closure contains the removed-yet-obvious swipe of ill-temper: "sick to death of her life." Its gestures are not overly unbecoming, but its conduct could hardly be called *decorous*. It's a bit like watching an accident, actually. You can't pull your eyes away. And this is what I read Glück for: her ability to knock me down and leave me discombobulated in a good way. It's not that I might not ever have thought these things she says; it's that it wouldn't have occurred to me to *say* them—the magnetism of her painfully accurate edge. For anyone still struggling with appearances, this is rough stuff. The poem is perfectly set out, yes, its shoes are polished and its hem straight, but what it contains is shocking—not in content, but in articulation. At table, one might say this poem just passed wind rather dramatically and felt neither shame nor the need to say "excuse me." I'm not going to be bored with a tablemate like this one—or in this poem's presence—so I like this Red Queen. I'm fascinated by her brusqueness. The queen, it appears, has balls. It would be both a trial and a hoot to sit next to her, observing her assurance and precision as I fumbled for the right spoon and slopped soup on my chest in the process. I'd love to do it. But I wouldn't want to cross her.

She's scary, yes, but if the evidence is to be taken at face value, there is also, it seems, a great weariness growing in the work—not for the work itself but for the world. Because the Glückian speaker is already dead certain about her elevation and remove, boredom seems to have set in. The poems are riddled with participles and gerunds, their –ingy sense of ongoingness a long, single sigh that runs through the work. In her poem "Noon" alone I find *shining, wandering, getting, breaking, wandering, being, thinking, sliding, standing, being, touching, folding, being, holding,* and *telling.* That's just two pages and not an unusual configuration. The poems are as equally frequented by negatives, often in the form of contractions: *couldn't, wasn't, can't, isn't, doesn't, don't, haven't,* etc. And closures and near-closures ring with negation: ". . . life rots in the heat" ("A Corridor"), "Nothing remains of love, / only estrangement and hatred" ("Fatigue"). In "In the Plaza," the speaker tells of a man who falls in love with a young woman from across a street, projects their coming together and says yes they will become lovers, and that the woman, by committing herself to this man, will be seen by that man, then, to be of "little use." The poem closes with the line, "It hardly matters whether she lives or dies." The speaker's sense of distance and resignation is enormous, the sense of *I have removed myself from these useless endeavors* is clear.

There is one poem, though, "In the Café," the gist of which seems to have at some point deeply touched the speaker. It embodies what feels like the most obvious and personal, and apparently current, emotional information of the poems in the collection. Or it's the least guarded. The poem *starts* like this:

> It's natural to be tired of earth.
> When you've been dead this long, you'll probably be tired
>   of heaven.

It's funny. But it's not funny. It's hopeless and it's an underscore to all the *-ing*s, all those long-range ongoingnesses that populate the pages of *A Village Life*. *This is never going to end*, it tells us. And I recognize the tone. It's my mother's, the one she used when she thought I, as a child, might be working myself up to whining about something: "Goddamnit," she'd say. "You'd kick if you were in swimming." She was exhausted by the mere thought of my perceived-as-constant harangues. As in, *Goddamn it*, will you never *stop*? But of course it's true too—you kick in swimming to stay afloat, to keep your head above the water. But I knew what she meant: The world's going to be what it is no matter what. Every feeling is costly. Why waste your—and *my*—energy? Just shut up. Suck it up. *Village*'s copy says that Glück's long lines manifest "a calm omniscience." It's true, I suppose, that the voice is calm and that she believes herself omniscient, but it is a calm that intensely refutes any possible, positive, payoff of emotional investment. *This is the way it is*, the voice seems to say. *And it goes on and on and on.*

And still, for the most part, the poems are beautifully turned-out and pointed, as Glück's best poems tend to be. There is still the Glückian laceration, the truth-speaking coming from a mind that appears to be raw with angers and resignations. There is no thing unkept about this queen but her tongue. She keeps her knees together; if she's wearing anything at all, she's wearing a pair of perfect silk stockings. There is no vociferating; she isn't waving her arms like a wild woman. Her façade *seems* impenetrable.

There is no rage but the cold rage and her truths still draw blood. The only thing missing, perhaps, are her gloves. She's taken them off. She threw them away long ago.

Charm School today is either the Nelson DeMille novel about a KGB conspiracy or the sexy reality show on VH1—another species of charm school altogether, one replete with a $50,000 first prize. The first prize in our nine-teen-fifties Charm School was geared more to delayed-satisfaction thinking: When, at long last, we grew into the beautiful young women our mothers kept promising us we would become—with our peau-de-soie skin and the bearing of a purebred instead of a lame and lumpen misfit—we would have the advantage of being a lady.

And charming or not, we who have been *ladied* at some point or anoth-er are still shaped by how and what we learned and to what degree we choose to display or dispose of that knowledge. By how and when we vary, if we choose to vary, our demeanors, and by whether, over time we change or re-main the same.

I'm looking for a way to work life out; I can hold a stony, unforgiving grudge. Bang's Alice is falling down the rabbit hole. Glück's lean queen is caught in the vortex of her own severity. Whether the draw is our shared vintage and degree of experience or a more common spirit beneath the demeanor of our lives and our poems I don't know, but Bang and Glück are speaking directly to *me*. I don't want to be them—heaven knows I've got my own problems—but I want to be with them. To see how their poems are fashioned from what they have seen and know, what they may have become or may yet become. If their manners and modes, their craft and concerns, seem at opposite sides of some standard of deportment, it's a convenient dichotomy rather than an absolute one. One makes me wish to comfort her; the other makes me wince. One is confused; one corrosive. One, I'm happy to say, is making her way through a familiar and difficult world and the other appears to have arrived someplace outside that world—if I'm to take her posture to heart. But it's their devotions and elegances that charm and capture me, their ability to take—or deliver—their blows.

BASIC HEART: DEPRESSION AND THE ORDINARY

What can we do once we are ordinary?
Lynne Sharon Schwartz

Sorrow has a horizontal habit; some souls' feet are bound.
Still the black bag of night is the structure of hope. Tonight's
Concert of blue light is riddled with the infinite; your jester's
Stripped of bells—neither fool nor the absolute fire behind
That black gate. The trees read the air and, despite the meticulous
Script of your bones, you sing your savage door wide and wear
The heart, finally, as just a heart, poor vessel of all your moments.[23]

i

Writing is an act of finding out what I know, and this is what I know now:
Depression *for me* is what is ordinary. I face some aspect of it every day. Even
when the prescription drugs are working at their best, I understand the possibilities of their failure. Experience has taught me that somewhere, over my
left shoulder—always my left, I don't know why—the round-edged, faceless
thing I recognize, now, as depression is hunkering. Sometimes near, sometimes farther away, sometimes so far away I can't even see it, but, even when
it appears to have been exiled for good, I know the body's uneven tides may
drag it back in within eyeshot, within mindshot, without warning. It, or the
idea of it, is never going to go away: It is part of my basic heart. It is uneven.
It is absolutely, utterly ordinary. It is the way all the me's inside me—the writer, the
teacher, woman, wife, friend, daughter—have to live.

---

[23]Renée Ashley, "Basic Heart," *Basic Heart* (Huntsville: Texas Review Press, 2009) 50.

ii

I do not write during the bad times; I write on the upswing—but I have tried to capture what depression is, how it feels. It does not feel creative. To have depression relieved and creativity resurface—and to write about the periods during which there is neither urge nor ability to create—is both uplifting and disheartening. I revel in having my abilities returned and then use them to articulate, and for a virtual return visit to, unfeelingness and wordless abnegation. I use words, when I finally recover them, to speak of what is inexpressible—and know that, with little, sometimes no, warning, my ability to act creatively, can be smothered by the body's predilections, by its natural imbalances. It's much like having been mugged from the inside more than once and waiting for the next time. I've spent way too much time trying and failing to outwit what is housed within me.

I know of no way, really, to determine whether the writing itself has changed because of the medications, because my subject demands something different, or simply because a maturing writer's work, if she's lucky, changes. I do know that prescription drugs have both allowed me to write and prevented me from writing, that they have, at their best, opened the black gate long enough for me to experience what I'm left with when the dark thing passes: the me I might be without it. When the medications are right they lessen depression's influence, let me locate and put to use whatever thinking and writing skills I may have. I'm certain they lend me clarity and an ability to look back and sort the effects of depression—like picking stones from beans—from the parts of myself that may be more enduring. And to articulate what I find. In the midst of depression's blur, that's an impossible task. Depression—often even the effects of medication—is a subject that sets a flame beneath me and lets me see more of what I am and what I hold.

It Is Very Often As Though

We live softly damned, damnation
a small thing built into the body. All
around us: apples and auguries, poems

that speak the small prayers which keep
a weary heart singing. And when we
grasp that small music, incomplete,

approximate, fallible as the body of flesh
that lives to bear it, we can rise up, oh—
we rise and we damn near catch fire.[24]

I've always written erratically: hot for five days or maybe three or even
one, for two weeks, three weeks, then not writing at all for a month or for
many months. How much of my unevenness is depression? How much just
my basic nature? Laziness? Fear? I don't know. Depression has always been
there. My ability to concentrate is rotten, that's not new; I get up and walk
around, shake myself out as though the physical act of writing is a bodily torment. I write only when a voice or a rhythm or an image roils inside me and
I write best late at night. If I write when I don't *need* to, I write poems that
don't need to be read. When I do write, I try to see that the urgency I feel is
transferred to the poem itself, that the poem becomes a crucible for that energy. That's always the ideal, anyway.

On most days I am a sedentary person with a sluggish brain. Catch-
ing the fire of a poetic impulse is the closest I'll ever come to adventure: No
one will make a movie of my life. I lack protagonist potential. I take risks,
but on paper. I live inside my head, in the passive, noisy dark. You could sum
up most of my life in four still shots: girl/woman sitting, girl/woman lying
down. In one set she looks out towards some unnamed elsewhere, her eyes
half-closed; in the other, her eyes are shut tight.

There were a few years during high school when I walked up and down
El Camino Real, the primary road that runs the length of the San Francisco
peninsula, at night, often all night. The boil-up of adolescent fury and confusion had to go somewhere, the loneliness had to take some shape or I'd have
flown apart. Depression seemed centrifugal then. Pre-Walkman, pre-iPod, I
just walked, hoping to make eye contact with someone, to talk with anyone.
Some nights I walked all night, to Palo Alto and home again, an easy twenty
miles. Some nights to San Mateo, probably just as far but in the other direction. I was lucky: Despite the occasional eye contact and experience, I never
got badly hurt. Perhaps all this is a metaphor. I don't think so.

You could, I suppose, tap into the few peak moments of mayhem in my
life, but those are scenes, not plots, and those confrontations are short-lived.
There's drama for the moment: It tattoos the heart, and flies off until, to my
own surprise, way down the proverbial road it flies back again with its needles
and pain, a homing thing. But I am most often a bystander, seldom as innocent as I would like, and, well, at least once, the blatant instigator, though I
didn't know it at the time, of disaster.

And I manage to remember very little about most things. I remember

---

[24]Ibid., 56.

sensations, emotions, likes and dislikes. I remember holding back, constantly choking down my impulse to react. I have honed forgetting and silence into
near perfections. They make my life more manageable. But I do remember a
handful of incidents, quite visually. How reliable are those visions? I don't know.
But I will swear to them. And it goes without saying that anything I say now is
at least partially untrue: a part-lie by omission, by emphasis, angle of approach,
or memory's failure. In that, thank god, I am like any other narrator.

My road to prescription drug therapy is long and full of shadows, if not
periodically potholed with some real ankle-breakers. The backstory, of course,
is longer than the real subject of this essay, the story itself.

iii

The medications themselves are mostly a blur.

I remember the first was from a G.P. I trusted. How many years ago? At
least fifteen. She understood my problem and in a comradely way prescribed
a pair of medications she admitted was old even then, but one that had gotten her through medical school, and she was well into her thirties by the time
I saw her. Those pills, whatever they were, made a zombie out of me—speech-
less, thoughtless. I waited for it to pass; it didn't. By the time I figured out I
had to stop them, the doctor had gone off to Central America, I think, to become a missionary. Then other G.P.s, other pills; nobody back then seemed
interested in monitoring the effects of the medications they prescribed. The
first I recall by name is Paxil. That worked for a while, though my weight sky-
rocketed, but its good effects gradually petered out. Then, with my current
doctor, a woman fastidious in monitoring my reactions, Prozac; then Prozac
with a Wellbutrin chaser; then Celexa, which made my heart beat so hard I
thought it would explode in my chest; then Lamictal, which gave me a rash;
then Ultram; then Wellbutrin SR 200 once a day, then twice a day; then
Wellbutrin XL 300. And now a new one: Cymbalta. And here is the body's
fickleness once more: The first dose at sixty mg knocked me on my back; I
slept for three days. Then half a dose and the change made me hopeful for
. . . I don't know . . . maybe a week? ten days? Then the slide down began
again and back to the sixty. I've been good for a number of months. I'd like
to think I'll be this good forever—I consider myself in serviceable condition,
sometimes darn good condition. But I know better than to count on it. The
body, like the language we use to talk about it, is fluid.

iv

The mind, I think, is less so, and my reason for resisting psychotherapy has been, probably at least at first, conditioning. I managed to live through crisis periods without it. I've convinced myself that being marginally functional rather than miserable is a victory. I'm not brave enough to want to open the doors to the past. I have held so much in for so long the pressure inside might be too great: I could fly apart and never come back. Why put in jeopardy the progress I've made on my own? And why court grief? Intellectually, I know better—so what keeps me from psychoanalysis now? Some of it's money. And maybe, if I'm kinder than I think, I'm trying not to add to the ways in which I've humiliated my mother. Probably it's my passivity. I've worked out a lot of stuff. But not everything.

So when I finally come to this woman who can really help me, I say what I've always said: "Hi-I-don't-want-to-talk-I-only-want-the-pills." And then I sit down. She's surely heard this before. We just go over the basics: life, parents, husband, symptoms.

Mine is a blue-collar, when we're lucky, family. When I am born my mother is thirty-nine, my father fifty. In 1949, the late-baby phenomenon is not common. People we don't know think my parents are my grandparents— and these are the rules set down by the parent who speaks: *Don't ask anybody's business, don't tell anybody ours. Curiosity killed the goddamn cat. Don't get involved. You've got problems? Keep them to yourself—that's what I had to do. I turned out fine. I raised you, didn't I?*

My father is born in Kansas in 1902. That's really about all I know of his early life. He dropped out of grade school. As an adult: a lumber man in Santa Cruz, California, an ice man in San Francisco, a something-or-other at the airport, a worker in a suburban ball bearing factory. There are allusions—not made by him—to a lost love, and a first and second wife. Ma's his third. He's thin, he's bent. He's not strong. His color is always poor. He's ill: Part of his stomach has been removed. He drinks Schlitz (when he can afford it), and a bottle of Gallo port is hidden beside his workbench in the garage.

My mother is born in San Francisco, probably around 1911. Somewhere along the line, her own mother has lied to the stepfathers about her daughter's age—to the daughter as well—to make herself seem younger. At least this is what I'm told. And there was the Depression, the furnace ripped out of the wall; leaving school to get a job; there's the restaurant, with allusions to bootlegging in the basement and a whorehouse upstairs. Ma's father is a Spanish Jew who converts to Catholicism; his name is very common; he's a drummer, a traveling salesman, but I have no idea what he sells. I do not know my mother's mother's name, but perhaps I do—I remember seeing one on the marble in the columbarium by my father's death-condo when I visit California briefly with my second husband. Though that may have been her mother's mother. As children, Ma and her baby brother are shipped out each summer to relatives in the country. Ma continues to see the train pull away from the station near the orchards, leaving her and her beloved younger brother in the agricultural dust and, when she does, she cries. At ninety-four, she still calls out for her own mother when she is feverish and alone and telephoning me from three thousand miles away. She is angry about her life. Everything about it has been wrong.

I'm born in 1949. And this is the rope ladder I climb down. My DNA.

v

When I'm eight, I drown. We go to Disneyland though we can't afford it. I hear the discussion through the heating vent: Children from happy families go to Disneyland, so we do. We are at a motel, one of those long strip motels that were the fashion in the '50s. I am in the shallow end of the pool with my plastic, blow-up ring snugged up into my armpits. My mother is on a chaise longue to my left; my father is on a chaise longue next to her. They don't seem to see each other. I'm bored, I'm hot, the tension between my parents is giving me a headache, not that I can articulate this at the time—then, it's simply a fact of existence: We are trying to be together, so I have a headache. The subtext of my life is *If you are perfect, I will love you.* The sun's hot and the water's cold but there are other kids in the pool obviously doing all the right things. I want to be one of them: I pop up and try a handstand on the pool's floor. I've done it a half-dozen times before and I can do it, so I do. This time, however, the plastic ring slides along my body, up to and around my calves and ankles, holding my feet in the air above the water and my head below. I recall struggling to right myself, to get my head above the literal water, and that's the last I remember before I die. I have never known such nothingness since and the memory of that absolute void has stayed with me for fifty years. I often long for it: Nothing. It's impossible to imagine unless you've known it and come back: It is painless and placeless. There is no one there you are likely to disappoint; there is no one there at all, not even you. The next thing I remember is walking past the foot of one of the double beds in our motel room. My father is by the window wringing out his leather wallet and peeling his dollar bills apart and laying them on the radiator to dry. My mother is between the beds, sitting on the edge of one, then standing up; her arms are moving fast in the air about her. She is furious. I have embarrassed them in front of all those people, made a scene, a fuss, and my father, who does not know how to swim, has had to jump in and pull me out. Everybody was watching. I'm inconsiderate, thoughtless. Selfish. He could have drowned. It's forty years before I wonder why my mother, who swam at Fleishhacker Pool as a kid in San Francisco, didn't give him a hand. As far as I know I was dead; I keep this as a reference point. Some years ago, in a rare visit to Ma's, I found a black and white postcard of that motel. I can tell you which room door was ours. I can show you where I stood on my hands in the pool when I died.

She throws his ass out, I think, after he wrecks the last car, the green Nash, in Sausalito . . . or is that the time she drags me to San Francisco on the train and lies to the conductor about my age to get a cheaper ticket and we are gone for days—she shows him!—living in a hotel on Powell and charging everything to the credit card?

By the time I'm in fifth or sixth grade, he's living in a shack behind the Oasis Bar, an old building with a mission façade that faces the railroad tracks. Mine is a tri-partite world set within three square blocks. Our house on Flynn faces away from that world. The street behind us—James St.?—is where my school is. And past the school, past the whole length of the green playing field, and past the enormous warehouse of some manufacturer, is Charter Street, the tracks running its length, and the Oasis Bar. I am not supposed to go see him after school but I do sometimes. I have no idea what we talk about. He probably sweeps some change off his dresser top, walks into the bar, buys me a soda and gets himself another beer, and when he returns we sit on the edge of the perfectly made bed in that dark, low-ceilinged room— and we drink instead of talk. We can hear the jukebox from the bar. If that isn't the way it is, well . . . I can imagine nothing else. When she finds out, it's another tune altogether, however: Get off your duff and do something if you're bored. Pick yourself up, dust off your behind and keep moving or you are weak (a moral judgment) or a bum. It's a given there's one bum in the family already, and she took care of him, didn't she? Nobody is going to be weak in her house. She says: There's no such thing as depression: just laziness and dereliction. He's a goddamn drunk. Have a little pride.

When he is sixty-seven and I am sixteen, my mother and I live on the other side of town and he lives in a small cabin in the woods about an hour away. He shoots himself in the head at my mother's house. He's come for Easter; I start the fight because, I say, he was drunk when my girlfriend and I picked him up—and how could he? When I come home from my rage-filled, cathartic drive after the yelling (mine), they are taking him, on a stretcher, from the house. They have to tilt the thing to make it out the front door and around the corner of the narrow porch; they nearly dump him over the railing. I am standing on the grass in the dark with the neighbors trying to make sense of what is going on.

In my twenties I ask (at great expense, because I know she'll never let me hear the end of it) to borrow some money to "see someone." I need help. I'm in crisis. I've been in college and out again, married and divorced, had other bad, sometimes violent, live-in relationships, myriad failures circle my feet. As far as I can see, unless someone helps me straighten myself out, I am done for. My life is a rat's nest; I have thrown it away.

> And lo! she was wacky as a toad and
>   would not move from her bed,
>
> blinked a lightless room, shades
>   down like blades, o! weeks, she
>
> thought in couplets, two burps:
>   The world folds up again—set
>
> the awful world away—it lived
>   in a place beneath the bed, it
>
> lived in a place above the bed,
>   her lines, when she had lines,
>
> when she had poems—she had
>   no poems—black ducks running,
>
> stoats and swine, so down she'd never
>   rise, o! ask, help anything me[25]

It takes her only a moment to say *no*—No, she isn't "giving" me money to give to some shrink who is going to tell me that she's done everything wrong. I simply am not bright enough to work it out myself at the time. I understand neither the state in which she lives her life nor how hard it is for her to keep redefining the world in order to keep herself on top of it. And besides, she's worked on the switchboard of a big county hospital and it is common knowledge that all psychiatrists' pants are too short and they are crazy themselves to boot. I'm not blaming her for my failure to get help. We were both doing the best we could, the same thing we always did and continue to do: What

---

[25]Renée Ashley, "What Is Not a White Deer Running," *The View from the Body* (NY: Black Lawrence Press, 2016) 10.

we need to do to stay alive. But, in a rash moment in my mid-fifties, I tell her that I am taking antidepressants. She says, "Well, it runs on both sides of the family." I remind her of what she said when I was a kid: no such thing, laziness, dereliction. "Yes, of course, that's what I said," she says, "but you know what I meant." Her tone speaks whole worlds of impatience.

vi

My depression, as a middle-aged adult is non-spectacular, a dark weight. It takes the form of acedia, of lethargy, inertia. A spiritlessness and disengagement varying from deadening—shapeless, muscleless, Gary Larson's "Far Side" depiction of the boneless chicken ranch—to manageable. In my youth, melancholy, yes, and wild frustration, but seldom now. Now a resignation, a leaning-into, a wish to simply melt away, a longing to simply let the body's liquors follow gravity's dictate and mingle, at the minutest level, with the dirt below. And in the throes I can find no meaning unless darkness itself is a meaning.

I am told that depression is anger turned inward. And perhaps so. But yelling, all those outward manifestations of anger, have not worked for me in the past and are not available to me in the present. A few times, in my youth, I gave breaking things a shot, a plate here, a cup, but destruction releases nothing for me except the additional bereavement of loss and a huge sense of foolishness. Instead, I eat it. My default mode is to shut up and shut down. I am so busy trying to please, so busy quashing any impulse that may run counter to what is allowed that I no longer recognize what it is I really want or feel. Once after a visit to my mother—in my forties, I think—I remained virtually silent for nearly three weeks. I wasn't being surly: The thought/speech producing mechanism had simply closed up shop. What was there to say? Nothing—there was nothing at all to say. Don't question, don't argue, don't explain—and if you yell at me you don't love me. Don't say a word except in delight or gratitude.

The urge towards suicide? I don't think it's due to example, though that's certainly there.

Escape was on my mind long before my father carried through with his—and the answer to his mess, made clear, by Ma, at the time, is, once the floor and walls are cleaned up, ignore it. Don't talk about it. It is so not talked about that we don't even have to talk about not talking about it.

> Where the bullet broke the skull there is a hole. A small
> hole. Almost neat. And you are lying on your back. The

skull is still, your hands. The box you lie in, still. For the
first time I see the whole of you. For the first time you are
not walking away, your bent back a wall of going away.
And I have nothing to tell you. And nothing to hold back.
The world is still out here. You are still alone. The women
of your life still don't know how to say goodbye. And when
the whole world of you is ash of ash, thirty years behind the
marble wall, you begin to speak to me: Bullets, you say, are
nothing. Ash is nothing. You say: Look how your blood is
the bearer of such news.[26]

He dies when I'm nearly seventeen. I write a short essay about it at
thirty-four. At fifty-one, he begins to pop up in my poems. No one's more
surprised than I am. And he's lingering. That thing in the heart again. A
seventeen-year locust.

In the arrogance of the body I know you,
tunnel I stumble through (room I sleep in).

In this way, we died both. (One speaks over
white paper, the other swept like sand beneath

a sea.) You are the poem I keep writing.
Dear Sir, I still carry your gun in my hand.[27]

This is where chemistry and calamity collide.
Does wishing for death count? Because I'm absolutely certain I do that.
But wishing probably doesn't count. And if I'm honest, neither does the night
I sit at the side of the tracks. I don't think I am in high school yet. I am wait-
ing for the train; I am miles from home. The despair is nameless except for
loneliness or *desperation* and those may be products of hindsight. That night
I believe I'd give anything not to feel the way I've felt for so long. The train,
of course, doesn't come. When the sky breaks into its morning palette, I walk
home, wash my hair, and go to school. Would I have done it? I don't think so.
But I can't really know. Decisions are made in an instant.

---

[26]Ashley, "Father Poem," *Basic Heart* (Huntsville: Texas Review Press, 2009) 22.
[27]*View*, "Six Lines in the First Person Addressing the Second," 57.

vii

I used to think she was the bad guy, he was the victim. After marrying my own older-man-alcoholic, my second husband, I'm not so sure anymore. At least not as dogmatically, arrogantly certain. I understand a little more about disappointment now. And, besides, my story turned out a lot better. Yes, I married my father, a kind, quiet alcoholic fourteen years my senior who, for ten years out of our twenty-five, let me believe he was dying. Maybe he was. But I was incorrigibly stupid. And, because of my inaptitude for acting on my anger, I stayed on and we came through it. I know what a fuzzy bastard truth is. And mine isn't the only story.

viii

When the slide down begins, and I am able to recognize it as such, I am terrified—the prospects of another wrong prescription drug, or of just another disappointment, or perhaps of running out of possibilities, of having run through the entire medicine cabinet of the industry and coming up depressed. Depression with no outlook for its lifting? That's where I was when the train didn't come—but it has come for more than just a couple of others I know.

The Suicides

I won't name them for you, or count them,
each one a door, and the house fallen down.
A wall is a small, simple history. And falling
is everywhere. Imagine the hinged eyes close

or are closed—no, sleep is nothing like
the death. Still, no one dies of bullets
or the belt slung around the neck. No one
dies in the black wade of the sea, not one

by the train, the insatiable train—but
the blurred curve of space about the body,
the space of the body itself, its prodigal
boundary, think of that. What dies before

the heavy body follows? Rattle the skull,
the breath, the will. The walls are sighing.

There is a violent wind kissing the latch.
And there are days I do not know my name.[28]

My grace: that the chemicals make me erratic even in wanting to die and that am far too cowardly and afraid of pain to kill myself now. I am nearly certain of this. But I will nonetheless die one of these days by my hand, another's hand, or no hand at all.

It is as simple as this: No thing surrendered
in the woods last night. Everything surrenders.[29]

So, while I still have choice, I, in a manner of speaking, choose.

The pills didn't help. And they helped.
The writing blew away. The life laid down

and sang a low melody distorted by the sun.
And continued. The life swallowed

the sun and went on. Out there, the highway
had a voice like birds in a cavern. Out there,

the timberland burned like another tongue.
(The birds would not trill. The flame gave no

light.) And nothing from the news was
willing to save her. The relic was her self, old

fingerbone, divided, horizontal. When
the second illness leaned over her, a dark

tumbled to its side, a snippet of light let in.
When that second illness hunkered down, enough

glimmer blew through to see—then dark
like a lever to raise her. The choice of default,
of omission, of *take the air in, then let it go*.[30]

---

[28] *Basic Heart*, 22.
[29] *View*, 37.
[30] Ibid., "Raise Her," 12.

ix

The house is white and has a great many rooms of varying sizes and contours. Its rugs are threadbare and many of the doors are swollen shut. The windows are cracked and cloudy. There is no other house in view. Some days, the sky is the color of a storm; the wind can be humorless. The black gate swings back and forth, open and shut. So far there is no latch that can hold it for long. When it swings, anything can come in or can leave, and the swinging is at the mercy of the weather, ordinary weather. A bent nail, a hammer. A bottle of pills. Right now the dark thing is far away.

A POSSIBILITY OF MEMOIR

You are considering writing a memoir. Who knows why. Because you're up to your gills in memoirs, the thousands of memoirs published in the last decade or so by people younger, less captivating, or less clever than you? Or maybe you just read the *Book Review* every week and the rise of the creative nonfiction genre itself piqued your interest. Or, more likely, the memoir deluge has simply given you permission—and the true parts of your life are at least as engaging as that guy's whose book sold about a zillion copies before he was exposed as having misrepresented the facts. Or, wait. There was more than one of those guys. Pick one. Or pick the woman who fabricated a cool, edgy existence from a pretty comfortable perch. Or, perhaps more honestly—think about it now—you're simply being directed by your obsessions. And you are your own obsession. Parts of you, you might feel, seem to be disappearing and you need to further explore who you think you might be before you really do vanish. Middle-age, late middle-age, old age, or an exceptional youth or youthful narcissism is driving your bus. Listen, you're me one way or another. You've got a ticket. What the hell. Why not?

There will be an obstacle, of course. There are always obstacles. Your personal obstacle is an impressively incomplete set of memories. Compared to other people, even those who would never consider writing a memoir, you remember almost nothing. And the recollections you think you *do* have are in all likelihood peppered with memory's failings. You can't remember a single date, except for your birthday and your mother's birthday, to save yourself. And you have no one who is willing to tell you the truth about what really happened at any given time during any given phase of your life. The few who would know are dead or are liars. So, with a paucity of credible events—and a rotten imagination to boot—how do you write a memoir? Isn't a memoir a retelling of what really happened to you?

What happened to you, you know now, in the fifties, sixties, and even the seventies, was dampered (an understatement no one will call you on) by the five basic, ground-into-the-bone tenets of your matriarchal household: One, Don't tell the neighbors. Two, Don't ask questions. Three, Don't get involved in anybody's business. (This includes not attending funerals. Nobody's death is your business. The funeral ban, being yet another manifestation of the proscription against attending anyone's family gatherings even though you're invited, because—and you are reminded of this constantly—you'd be intruding. It adds up to a small-world logic that includes the prohibition of inviting anyone to your own family events—those three heavily scripted and awesomely horrible holidays—Thanksgiving, Christmas, and Easter—because, if anyone were to accept your invitation, *they'd* be intruding.) Number four is a compound imperative: Act happy, act grateful. And five: Should you feel anything other than happy and/or grateful, keep it to yourself.

You also are aware that because, until you were an adult and checked out bits of the wider world, your external-to-the-family role models were limited to your way-too-brief classroom observations of your teachers (very well behaved, indeed, except for that one grade school art teacher who, even back then, wore too many petticoats, no hose, and had quite a reputation—as well as a Jaguar XKE). You simply didn't know what people other than your own *did*.

You read books, of course: *Dodsworth* by Sinclair Lewis was one of your sixth grade book reports. It was about divorce, and it had a dark green, sticky library binding with the title, all capitals deeply impressed in gummy white, that ran perpendicular to the length of the spine. The pages were yellowed with age even then, and there were lots of them. You looked good carrying that book. You looked like you could handle just about anything. And though divorce never blossomed in your parents' lives, all the attendant screaming, slamming, and crying disputes and separations had, and that was close enough. The book had been an anomalous addition to the sixth grade reading list, but your teacher had understood, and her name is gone now—you just can't believe it—but you did know it for a very long time; she was an older, short, squat woman who was very kind to you for some reason you still do not understand and who scared the hell out of all the other students. Her gray hair was pulled tight against her head; her breasts hung over what served as her waist. You loved her. You knew she would keep you safe. And keep you from having any real fun. And you feel sick, ungrateful, and shamed at having forgotten her name.

Apparently, though—and, actually, much to your relief—in your reading you find there's likely a valid reason for your dearth of recall. You read somewhere—and you wish you could remember where (you so *hate* it when you do that)—that children who are brought up to do only what they *should* do have poor memories—not *bad* memories in the way you think of *bad dreams*, but poor memories, memory *processes* that are faulty, their vaults of recall themselves either sparsely populated or inaccessible. And you were a child who did what you were told. You were too good even for your own good. You were so good you stunk of good and the other kids could smell it on you. You even bored yourself. You were afraid of everything. And you had been drilled since birth on the consequences of being anything other than perfectly present and publicly invisible by a parent so angered by any form of shame that her fury would never in this lifetime be assuaged if you were caught doing something . . . untowards. You knew that you would be reminded of it over and over again (up until you passed on to the next world and into and beyond the world after that should there be one), of the great upset you had caused her; you would be faced, once again, with your own inevitable humiliation and indelible disgrace due to that fact that you had (once again) persecuted your generous parent with your selfish behaviors.

When you think in terms of *event*, you recognize with telegraphic clarity the turning points that contributed to your feelings about the world and yourself—these, in chronological order and spread throughout your first thirty-two years. Of course, there is a front- and backstory to each, but, for now, just the removed-from-their-contexts basics: First, you threatened to call the police. Second, you drowned. Third, your father killed himself and you were complicit. And fourth, you left.

And at the time of the first, you were way too young to realize you'd taken a stand or that you'd remember it later. You have no idea what year it was. Regarding the second: You know the year, 1957, only because, for some reason, you are able to visualize the year in white in the upper right-hand corner of the blue-skied cover of the souvenir booklet from Disneyland. You have the feeling, though, that you have somehow conflated a photograph of yourself, your fat eight-year-old, dour-faced self in your string-tied sunsuit, in front of Cinderella's castle—was it her castle? or some other woman's castle?—with whatever was really on the front cover, probably just the castle itself. And Tinker Bell. And you've forgotten the date of the third, your father's suicide, if you'd ever remembered it, and you don't think you did. Your current husband probably remembers the date of the fourth; he's good like that. You're not.

Yes, of course somewhere amidst all that growing-up was the whole virginity thing—and, yes, you did have some (virginity, that is)—but losing it was unremarkable. You remember thinking, "Oh." And there was marriage number one, as well, but in fact, you're a little vague on that one too, though you do remember a couple of funny stories (funny after the fact, no doubt—but, no, the thing with the frozen chicken really *was* funny. How that chicken slid across the linoleum, hit that metal strip where the carpet began, became airborne and walloped him in his own little package of Texas gizzards still seems impossible and, yet, somehow, full of light and grace).

It's an interesting idea: After all, what *should* you remember? And *if* you should, then what's the *why* behind that obligation? Someday you may figure some of that out, but, you feel, at least for now, an obligation to yourself to dig a little deeper into what you do remember on the chance of unearthing a few fragments of things you presently do not.

You know, in the way one knows *facts*, that your mother would not recognize your life were you to write it down. In your daydream about this— based partially on experience, partially on the imaginative leap that would allow you to show it to her at all—she'd read it and say, "Hey, honey, this is about a girl who lived around here. She's just about your age. Did you know her?" And to keep the peace you'd have to say "No, Ma. No, I didn't. She doesn't ring a bell at all."

After all, your mother has been rewriting your life since you began living it. She's not evil. She just honestly prefers her version of everything, including your life, as you should see it, for its impact on her own. When she's feeling particularly in-the-world and generous, she'll admit that. She, you have understood for a long time, believes fantasy is more practical than reality. And she is a practical woman; she has had to be. You call it her "Betty Boop," her "Oh! *Really?*" persona. And she is a master teller-of-tales on at least two matters: one, her victimhood during the Great Depression and her marriage to your father, and two, your life. She's so good that she believes her own stories.

For example, the day you received your acceptance letter from San Francisco State University—and you were well into your twenties at that point— your mother called her friend from the kitchen phone and said: "Hey, Elsie," and then without taking a breath, "my daughter was just accepted at *Stanford!*" And she smiled at you as though you should have been thrilled, the sticky beige receiver pressed against her ear, her head nodding yes, yes, the coiled cord dangling down against her jaw and looping back up again near her elbow. You were still in the kitchen! Still had the freshly torn-open envelope and the magical letter in your hand, had not even set it down yet, when she made the call. You were still taking it in. When you asked her why she said *Stanford*, she said warmly, "Well, you know what I meant."

When you were probably about fifty, married (again), and visiting your mother on the West Coast with your best friend from your life on the East Coast, you sat in the adjacent room—the two of them were watching "Golden Girls"—and you heard your mother tell your best friend how difficult it had been to find the money to put you through Stanford. Your friend knew the first Stanford story, the one about Elsie—she knows just about everything about you that you know. Later she told you that, when she heard your mother say how tough it was, she just nodded dumbfoundedly. What was there to say? You did nothing, when you heard it yourself but lean your forehead against the wall you were facing and sigh. It's a fact that you attended SFSU for both undergraduate and graduate degrees. You have the paperwork somewhere. You remember the faces of your instructors and the classes you took. You took out student loans and worked full-time on campus as an assistant to a succession of professors, and as a secretary in the English office where you learned to drink eight-to-twelve cups of coffee in five hours, and as a clerk in the campus library where you were continually being shhhh-ed, and off-campus as a writer's assistant and a ghost writer of ESL textbooks in a Victorian house on a steep hill on the other side of the city. That writer had an enormous, old black Labrador whom you loved, and whom you walked on those precipitous hills, and whose name you have forgotten—which seems strange because you adore dogs and usually remember their names. The woman-you-worked-for's last name is gone too, though you remember her first name and that of her husband. You remember their huge, warm kitchen and that, after a couple of years working with her in her tiny upstairs office, you quit when she became pregnant. She was nearly unbearable before she became pregnant, and, although you were always happy to walk the dog, you weren't doing babies.

The story comes back around to this, the foundational part of your mother's stories: There's always some, often negligible, bit of truth in her inventions. *Stanford* and *San Francisco* both start with an *s*, they're within fifty miles of each other. So, except for the many reiterations of blatant untruths, it's an understandable—or at least conceivable—slip. Sort of. And you did live at home most of that time. You attended college, and, it's true: Paying someone's way through college is grueling. Always that little notch or two of truth in a story's belt because of which a listener will not discard the speaker's credibility without deeper examination. When you returned East from that West Coast visit with your friend, you laughingly told your boss, at the philanthropical foundation at which you worked, the story of your mother and your friend and your two now-classic Stanford stories. He looked at you quizzically. He put his hand on your shoulder and asked you, maybe only half-kidding (he had very kindly taken you and your mother to lunch years before on one of her three East Coast trips): "Are you sure you didn't *go* to Stanford?"

The Stanford stories are one thing, but, akin to the notches in your mother's truth-belt, there were also some instances of real shared experience, though bizarre and unlikely, on which you had based a great deal of hope.

You were in bed. It was late. You lived on Flynn Street in Redwood Village. The front door was painted hot pink. You were . . . what? Eight? Nine? Your mother and father were in the front upstairs bedroom in their separate twin beds; the bathroom was between their room and your own—you were in your double bed—and there was one more room, a room designated as your playroom, beyond that. That third room was inaccessible without passing through your bedroom. A dead end on the second story. That night, as on most nights, you were hiding under your covers with the radio on, listening to country western music with the sound turned way, way down. When you heard the front door latch open and click closed again, you figured you must have fallen asleep and not known it. You'd done that before. Your father must have gone out. That must be him coming back in, you thought. So, you pulled your head out from beneath the blankets so you could give him your co-conspirator's smile when he poked his head in your room to see you sleeping. You heard the footsteps come up the carpeted staircase that ended in front of the bathroom, but they went the other way, directly into your parents' room. And there was an odd pause; then the footsteps came back towards you—he remembered you!—through the hall. A man who was not your father, who wore a light-colored trench coat and brimmed hat came into your room. His hands were in his pockets; he stopped, looked around, but clearly you weren't what he was looking for. You don't remember his face at all. He stared in your direction from the foot of your bed, but he was looking beyond you, as if you weren't even there, as if the walls had fallen away. Then he turned—he seemed disappointed and you felt bad for him—and walked on into the playroom. You just lay there in bed, looking in his direction, waiting for him to return. A few minutes later, your mother came into your room. She asked calmly, "Did you hear something?" and you said, "Yes." Then she said, "Did you see someone?" and you nodded and said, "Yes," again. It was odd, but you were neither scared nor unnerved though you had never seen that man before, though the circumstances were odd and new. "Tell me what you saw," your mother said, and you did and when your description fell short of what she wanted to hear, she asked, "What was he wearing?" and you told her. She told you the same man had entered her room, gazed about unseeingly, then turned and walked into yours. She hesitated, then went ahead and checked the playroom; the window was locked; no one was there. She told you to go back to sleep, and, without waking your father, she went downstairs in her nightgown for coffee and a cigarette.

Another time, your father was taking an afternoon nap; your mother was doing whatever mothers in the fifties did downstairs, so it must have been a Saturday because she worked during the week. You were in your playroom doing whatever an only child like yourself would do; most likely you were in the closet with the door closed talking to an imaginary person on the telephone you had drawn on the wall with a pencil. A pay phone. You heard your mother come upstairs and go into her bedroom. Then, way too quickly, you heard her footsteps in your bedroom and then in the playroom. You threw the closet door open before she could catch you talking to no one, and she took your hand and, serious but not alarmed, said "Come with me."

She led you into her bedroom and pointed to your father. He was curled up, facing the wall, on top of the faded green chenille bedspread, sleeping in his gray work clothes. Above him was a roiling cloud of green and yellow light. It was punctuated with sparkling pinpoints of brighter yellow light and was hovering there, maybe three or four feet above him. It was just about the length of his curled body. Your mother said, "Do you see it?" and you answered, "Yes." The two of you stood a moment longer, then your mother took your shoulders in her hands and turned you back towards your own room and the two of you went about your business.

Many years later, during two rare moments of apparent camaraderie, your mother and you talked about those two instances. *Wasn't it odd? Why weren't we frightened? Did you ever see anything like that again?* You had that experience in common. You thought that was kind of cool.

Now your mother is ninety-seven. She is not in the least senile. You think she may have been in her seventies when she told you, "No. Neither of those things ever happened."

Your life perceptions are very often made up of: There's *this* and then there's *that*.

Sometimes when you look at these pairings of experience, they appear to be examples of those trick-the-eye-and-mind drawings: You're a duck, no you're a rabbit; you're a young lady, no you're an old hag; you're a vase, no you're two people kissing. If a life at all, then a sort of life in dualities. But in an odd way, the experience is rather like the strange man in your room and the green cloud above your father: You don't question it—you question very little, in fact, as a rule. There's not a lot of tension between the two versions; they just are. The *this* and the *that* are just givens.

Action, you've come to understand, isn't always the immediately observable kind—because what happens to you may be internal, a reaction or product of what, however apparently forgotten, may have engaged you on the outside at some point. It's an internal action called *change*. Change often has to stew. Perhaps the catalyst fades; you don't believe that kind of alteration does.

You think of yourself, not as a poet or a novelist or even a writer-of-essays—writing books is something you do, not who you are—but as the accretion, the resulting aggregate of your experiences, internal and external, and of your neuroses and humors, of your psychological bruises and baggage, of your triumphs however small, of your interest in remembered events in terms of and through their accuracies and their perjuries. Your discoveries come through the act of articulation. In the process of exploring through writing who you might be, you're likely to discover, as well, some forgotten things that may make you smile, and, equally as likely, some things you don't want to know. You'll add them to those you already recognize and accept or have difficulty with—another of those dualities. You're a duck, you're a rabbit. A young woman, an old hag. You're like him; you're like her. Your sixth grade teacher's name was Kennedy. Mrs. Kennedy. How could you have forgotten that? You'll have to trust that your memoir can be made as mutable as a life and as the varied perceptions of a life, that who you find you are is what happened to you, and that you're allowed to write about it whatever the conventions of a given genre may be. This is your life, you'll be saying to your reader. This is one draft of your life.

HER VERY WORST MEAL AND HOW IT WAS MUCH LIKE THE THREE FAT MEN —ONE OF WHOM WAS WEARING A BERET—SHE SAW TODAY

A daydream is a meal at which images are eaten.
W. H. Auden

She eats for comfort. She eats for camaraderie. She eats out of boredom, habit, convenience, and, even occasionally, hunger. She eats to procrastinate. She eats too much. She eats too fast. There's very little she chooses not to eat—though, on that one hand, blackeyed peas are a major unfavorite (that's a first-husband story, but she would never have liked them anyway). Lemongrass, all things perfumy-tasting, she finds unpleasant. Gin. Though she could choke it all down if the need arose. Who knows . . . they might taste better than they did when she was younger. They might be fine. And fine is just fine. She doesn't need fancy or expensive, she doesn't need great. She just needs to get through the day.

And on the other hand, there are foods she is drawn to. Grapefruit. Spicy red beans with or without rice. Fresh purple figs. White bean soup. And cake. Chicken chili. Mangoes. And bread. Pepper Jack cheese. And cheddar. Hamburgers. Turkey sandwiches. Horseradish sauce on rare roast beef. Or Tabasco. Manwich Sloppy Joes. She's had roasted lamb and thought it was delicious until she pictured the lamb. Frozen pot pies, chicken best. Corn dogs! Beets. Potstickers. Ramen noodles. Sweet and sour. She's allergic to peanuts and that's a damn shame, because peanut butter *is* love. Tacos! She adores tuna casserole concocted with frozen peas and canned cream of mushroom soup (especially if the egg noodles are the really wide ones) topped with potato chips which are smooshed and crunchy. Apricots. Liverwurst. Lima beans cooked in plain tap water just with chopped onion (dehydrated is fine) and maybe, but not necessarily, a hambone. Fish fingers. TV dinners (Salisbury steak or fried chicken best, Banquet brand, the cheap ones: a staple of her childhood). She's not fussy, not particular. You can't say she's indiscriminate, however—because she won't eat those blackeyed peas.

Perhaps you could call her *open-endedly-barely-discriminate* or maybe *generous-in-her-tastes-despite-biases-but-also-taking-into-consideration-the circumstances.* In all likelihood, she'll eat it, whatever it is, even if she bitches about it during or afterwards. She's a good-time eater and a bad-time eater— her mother's response to any tension (there was always tension) was "Have a sandwich," and she did. She doesn't send food back. She chews and she swallows and she does it again.

The upshot? Food, for her, is mostly forgettable. One obvious exception might be the sashimi she could barely choke down when a kind college professor, a generous woman who was trying to widen the unworldly girl's experience, took her out to lunch. The professor did the ordering; the girl's stomach rose and threatened to spill with every bite. But she bit. And she kept it down. To not do so would have been unforgivable.

But on just about any day, Wendy's is or would be great. Never a problem: Just give her some Asian-Style Boneless Chicken Wings and a chocolate Frosty. Or the quotidian paradox: the Diet Coke Frosty float. She'll be happy. A Burger King burger and a medium Diet Coke runs a close second.

She considers herself an *easy* eater. And she thinks her friends do too. But easy isn't how one man in particular sees it. He has been stricken by the vast spectrum of her unfussiness for years. And so, through him, she was made aware of the *what-was-exceptional*: her most notable meal, her absolute worst plate of food ever.

Which she simply chose not to eat.

And she thought nothing of that decision until the above, unnamed man, after having already distanced himself from his plate with a moan of dismay so loud, and a strangled look of such complete revulsion, that the whole table he sat at in the refectory—maybe twenty adults?— turned their attention down the long board towards him. At that moment, she had just been sitting down at the table next to the crucible of their curiosity. She was about to dig in.

And she still has trouble understanding how that mild meal of leftovers could have been as revolting as it genuinely was. When she thinks of it, she thinks of it euphemistically as *Stuff in Sauce*—a mélange of leftover breakfast meats along with some potato. But not hash. She *likes* hash. This was a kind of maudlin stew of leftovers. And she knows leftovers to be a proud tribe and worthy—and these appeared to be perfectly fine leftovers until they were *gla-céd*, it seemed, in some sort of . . . gray, translucent medium, something that resembled a reduction of dirty bucket water. It was viscous, shiny, and the only taste it had was somewhere between dust and phlegm, something she could only at the time call *Oh-Christ-No-I-Can't-Eat-That*. The shining misery of the gravy had penetrated the meat scraps and clung—some mysterious, probably chemical (and perhaps dangerous) adhesion had taken place. She'd tried scraping it off, but each pass left only a slightly thinner, somewhat more roughened-up and ghastly-looking sheath of bucket-gray slime on the meat. There wasn't a chance in hell of saving a piece of over-cooked potato. She worked diligently at the larger bits of meat, though, and with good faith, but finally had to concede defeat: The dish was clearly a product of some bad wizard and, as she watched it congeal, she was certain it developed a supernatural aura of smugness.

After she had finally sighed and settled her flatware on her plate, leveraged it out a bit towards the center of the table, and reached for her cup of black tea, she realized her seatmate had been studying her intently as she'd tried to salvage her bacon. Then he said to the air that hung over the table in front of them both: "Even *she* won't eat it—well, that proves it."

She was taken aback only a bit. She wasn't sure what it proved, but she wasn't willing to eat what was on her plate just to *disprove* it.

Something in her, though, had been jostled at the recognition that a dish prepared to be *eaten* could be so utterly inedible. An anomaly had, without any effort on her part, lifted itself from her slough of blind habit and presented itself in an uncustomary glow. A little bit like an insight. She gave a small mental gasp, but had no idea what she should do with the light given off by the information.

So today she was driving to the market—it was either throw something quick together for dinner or pick up a pizza again, she hadn't yet decided—when she saw the backs of three fat men walking at the side of the non-residential, no-sidewalk, low-rent-exurban road, and she had a feeling of déjà vu. All three of the men wore what appeared to be identical light gray business suits. The fabric seemed a little shiny but it may have just been the sun. The middle man, an inch or two shorter than the others, was wearing a black beret. She could tell from the backs of their heads, all three were balding. They wore black shoes, their cuffs swept their dusty heels, and they walked in extremely close proximity to one another, as though they had their arms around one another's waists. She felt it again, that sensation she'd had at the refectory table: a recognition rising above her vast daily midden of preoccupation and mindlessness. It was as though a proverbial fog had suddenly lifted. Those men did not belong; they were aliens in any way one might choose to define the word, or they had slipped, perhaps, from an alternate version of Lewis Carroll (Tweedle Dum, Tweedle Dee, and . . .Tweedle Three?), or, more realistically, they were out-of-town (or out-of-work) real estate men—from an office with an unfortunate dress code—assessing the dried-mud, acre-plus lot in front of the low, cinder block building that housed the defunct mechanic's shop and the hut behind which had served for not too long as a dog-grooming parlor. The point being: They stood out. They were what made that day different. They were anomalous and snagged her attention. *They made her look. They made her think.*

She was late getting to the market. She'd forgotten what she'd gone for. She bought a Diet Coke in a small, plastic bottle, drank it in the car in the parking lot while she watched the seagulls circle the Chinese restaurant, and went home. She ate hummus and ginger snaps for dinner. She still sees the men in her mind.

Imagine, then, the upshots of such recognition: contingency and its seatmate opportunity arranged around thought like this: anomaly and image, and the banquet of possibilities thereof—a quote from Auden's *The Dyer's Hand*, some appalling gravy, and three fat men—one of whom was wearing a beret—who just did not belong.

DAMN SAD STORIES: AN ESSAY/REVIEW OF GUEST'S *ONE MORE THEORY ABOUT HAPPINESS: A MEMOIR* AND LEMON'S *HAPPY: A MEMOIR*

Really, poets and happiness? It's an improbable coupling under any circumstances let alone with the staggering somatic blows—Guest's near-total paralysis and Lemon's series of strokes and seizures—that are chronicled in these memoirs. Yet, a poet's penchant for precision leaves words like *happy* and *happiness* begging—each bordering on meaninglessness until the poet tips it over, examines its undersides, and tells us what he finds there. Both Guest and Lemon are exceptional, though contrastive, examiners and articulators. They're not new to recording their stories. They're celebrated poets, young and male, both with multiple books and awards already behind them; they're intuitive and they're smart. They know how to happify a book and snag a reader with the hook of irony.

The poet Jane Kenyon, who suffered from severe depression and died of leukemia in 1995 at the age of forty-seven, set out what I am certain is the fundamental nature of happiness in a poem called exactly that: "Happiness." It's written head-on, but in a poet's head-on manner, by tropes and achingly precise images masquerading as examples that wring nuanced emotions into the heart of the reader. It's an excellent lens through which to view both memoirs. Her poem begins like this:

> There's just no accounting for happiness,
> or the way it turns up like a prodigal
> who comes back to the dust at your feet
> having squandered a fortune far away.[31]

Happiness *turns up*. Happiness is the prodigal, not you. And it turns up in spite of everything, in spite of a body's infelicities. I have rarely read anything so true as this poem. To my mind, pure-and-lasting happiness is a hyper-fic-

---

[31]Jane Kenyon, *Otherwise: New & Selected Poems* (St Paul: Graywolf Press, 1996) 3.

tional telos, and it's plenty clear that illuminated moments of *impure* happiness are far more interesting—and more credible. And credibility in memoir, as we all know since the media crap-storm that stemmed from the Frey novel-cum-memoir, *A Million Little Pieces*, is not an insignificant consideration. Life rarely, if ever, takes the shape of art, but memoir is elastic and adaptable partly because of its limited focus and prose format. It's a forgiving form, and when such an abbreviated, selective *story* is constellated around a single life-altering reversal, a sense of this-then-that—of causation and consequence, as well, one would think, culpability—is not only feasible but anticipated.

Guest's *One More Theory About Happiness* is essentially his straightforward retelling of the accident in which, at twelve, he broke the third and fourth vertebrae of his neck, along with both arms, and was permanently paralyzed. The facts are carefully articulated—a bike that's old, too large, in shabby condition, loaned by a well-meaning teacher, and, it turns out, brakeless; the out-of-control ride down the steep incline of the teacher's yard; the collision with the hidden drainage ditch that throws him "over the handlebars, catapulted, tossed like a human lawn dart into the earth"; the well-meaning man next door who literally picks the young Guest up from the ground and attempts to set him on his feet, urging him "to shake it off, to get over the scare, to stand" on his own; and Guest's beautifully and briefly drawn collapse: "My head fell over," he says, "like a flower on a broken stem. My cheek rested against my chest grotesquely. Without saying another word they softly laid me on the grass again."

The details of Guest's limited recovery (he remains in a wheelchair and writes with a mouth stick) are presented vividly yet unsensationally—the torturous collar meant to immobilize his neck ("made of two stiff halves, each wrapped in a bandage-like sleeve. . . . Beneath the chin was a hard shelf. . . . When snapped together, both pieces held the neck and head still. They also held in the body's heat. . . ."), and the four long bolts screwed into his skull that stabilized his head within the halo. Whether by nature or design or both, Guest has chosen to tell his story in true Wordsworthian style; what must have been an overflow of powerful emotion now recollected in tranquility. He sticks with the past tense to keep it that way. But there's an unspoken truth, one I feel most strongly, in *One More Theory About Happiness*: It's restraint, the considerable effort Paul Guest must have made to make his heartbreaking story a sort of personal, literary Switzerland. It's admirable on a human level—and frustrating on a reader's level. Though he does let the reader inside, to revelations that skip easily over sentiment to startle: "Great grief filled me up," he tells us. "I seemed to breathe it, but what freed me was this: if my arms never worked again, never dressed myself, or combed my hair, if I depended on others to do these things for the rest of my life, I no longer had to be, or

even could be, who I once was. What I once was. I was broken. And new."
New? That's a shocking and incredible perception for a broken young boy.
How could this be? Where are the horn-blasts of his anger? of his frustration?
We see bits, tiny glimpses of these, but wouldn't these emotions have pushed
hard to make their way to the forefront of this story? Perhaps Guest did not
want to relive those feelings, though he had to have done so in writing the
book. More likely, he thought his emotions weren't the point; so, perhaps he
gave us a taste and figured we would extrapolate the rest. But, undeniably,
I have internalized his calmly written account so deeply that I've become
hysterical *for* him, and I'm projecting. But how can this have happened to
a child? It's so unfair! Of course, we do see him struggle, both physically
and psychologically—the path to adaptation is littered with painful and
disappointing setbacks. And you can't help but fall in love with the young
man who wrote this book, with its wry title and what, in my own mind,
must be its quelling of raw, unbowdlerized grief and anger in addition to his
physical pain. But he apparently really is the good boy our mothers told us to
keep a lookout for. He doesn't make waves, at least not in this memoir. His
choices are considered and deployed. His style tells me: *It's done now. This is
the story.* He does not assign blame. (There's no mention, however, of whether
his parents were as generous.) And I can't help but wonder how much of
the knowledge and maturity he attributes to his young self is a product of a
writer's confluence of memory with the gifts of adulthood. And it may not
matter in the end. Guest's good heart and sense of humor—along with his
impressive writing—deliver the story as he wanted his reader, finally, to know
it. And it's a good, horrible story. And in the end he finds poetry—and his is
fabulous poetry, funny, full of thought, and intense—and he finds love. He's
become the young man we hope moves in next door, and he has given us this
surprising and big-hearted book through which we can get to know him.

And then, of course, there's the boy our mothers told us to stay away
from. The one who not only makes waves, but is, himself, a sea full of roiling whitecaps and undertow, of unharnessed energies and misdirection. It is
no surprise that Alex Lemon chose a hyper, present-tense novelistic approach
for his memoir, *Happy*. His life had been one of extremes even before his first
stroke; what other mode could have captured the desperation of such a bitter and manic story of self-destruction and genuine psychological and physical pain?

The portrait he draws of himself is electrifying and horrifying and
brilliant. Lemon, known to his college friends as Happy, is the freshman
power-partier, baseball jock, busy womanizer, full-time boozer and salad-
bar-selection-of-drugs partaker, and is so used to being wasted that when
he suffers his first bleed from a vascular malformation in his brain stem he

seems uncertain whether it's really serious or just a particularly fucked-up day in Lemonland. Between frenzied bouts of substance abuse, he makes his way, finally, to the MRI that spells out the devastating malformation deep in his brain stem. His disbelief, his anger and horror, are made visceral for the reader. Shortly, his denial will be as well. He becomes an exaggeration of what he had been—drinking even more, taking even more drugs. And in a way it seems right, at least true to character: Out of the blue his own brain turns on this young-man-on-the-move, party-pounder, team player, and he reacts by intensifying his established pattern of abuses, behaviors laced now with a serious dose of dark introspection when he can swing it. Later he says, "I started drinking on the bus after my neurology checkup. . . . Now I'm pounding gin and whiskey and beers before games. Smoking joints in the port-a-potty. Popping pills. I don't want to be alone but I can't stand the people around me so I stay as fucked up as I can. . . . Saturday, I ate shrooms, and sipped rum in my room. . . ." He continues to play ball, convinces himself he's getting better, lies to the doctors, lies to his coach and his friends, to his mother, but he's obsessed with his condition. He starts reliving the childhood sexual abuse he suffered at the hands of an older male cousin. His fears amp up, along with his anger and resentment. He suffers another bleed. He knows he's losing himself and makes the choice to undergo an extraordinarily risky brain stem surgery to stop the bleeding. His eccentric, itinerant sculptor and art teacher mother is the only stabilizing force he knows and can finally talk to—and she sticks with him through his racking surgical convalescence— until, still severely compromised, he pushes her out of his recuperative nest, and takes up, one more time, his self-destructive lifestyle. I found myself asking why I, why any reader, shouldn't just give up on him, he's a mess and it's making me crazy. And then I realized that, as an older, and female, reader, my own lifelong-empty tank of oxytocin, the mothering hormone, and a similarly unburdened vessel of mothering instinct in general, had suddenly been filled and the juices had kicked in. I wanted to find him and smack him upside his poor damaged head and say, "Knock it off, Asshole!" and then protect him from the unfairnesses of a broken body and from himself. But— and this is the critical issue—I did not put the book down. Between the spellbinding prose and the vitality and stinging surprise of his ability to keep going, I was hooked. Lemon is a phenom, he's electric, he's dangerous, and in danger. He's extreme. And extremely talented.

In a brief epilogue, Lemon tells us he is teaching, writing, trying, still against great odds, to carry on. "There are days I can't read," he says, "days my face, my body go numb, and a couple of times each year I rush to the nearest hospital for an MRI and a new battery of tests. But after a decade of living with a black hole inside me, three years ago, I tossed out all my drugs and booze. I . . . learned to live without doing anything at all." I was shocked. It was a confession that blindsided me. Not the *booze*, but the *love*. I was relieved. And then released.

I had a friend who used to tell me, "If you want *fair*, you have to go to another booth." I tend to forget everything, but I've never forgotten that. What has happened to Paul Guest and to Alex Lemon isn't fair. But it's likely that *fairness* and *happiness* are kissing cousins. Perhaps both are things glimpsed and registered and the memory of that is what keeps us going on, waiting for the next, unexpected flash of the same. Kenyon says:

> . . . happiness is the uncle you never
> knew about, who flies a single-engine plane
> onto the grassy landing strip, hitchhikes
> into town, and inquires at every door
> until he finds you asleep midafternoon
> as you so often are during the unmerciful
> hours of your despair.[32]

Guest and Lemon have enacted their stories and despairs in character. They appear to have written their lives, both vastly different and shudderingly alike, as they believe they have lived them so far. What could be more apt in delivering the truth of character and the facts of a life to a reader and what more sobering than such damn sad stories with their nearly happy endings?

---

[32] Ibid., 3.

GOLDBARTHIA:

THE KITCHEN SINK:

NEW & SELECTED POEMS 1972-2007

BY ALBERT GOLDBARTH, A REVIEW

To enter Goldbarthian territory is to step into a land of plenty. Goldbarth is a collector of words and information and a master of connection. Once you know his work and become familiar with his sense of humor, the title of this, his second *Selected,* will lodge in your heart and chuckle there until you pass into the next world, where, if there's any fun at all, they'll still be reading Goldbarth. *The Kitchen Sink: New and Selected Poems 1972–2007* is a collection of collections on a number of levels, dazzling, enlightening, serious and elegant in its scope and intelligence—and riddled with humor both dry and out-loud-laugh-inducing.

Goldbarth's trademark is the long-lined, many-paged free verse poem—*long* meaning, as often as not, twenty-plus pages. The dilemma of choosing poems for this *Selected* must have been onerous: He could pack, maybe, sixteen such signature poems in a volume of three hundred and fifty pages with both front and back matter? Hardly what one could call a representative sampling of a body of work as vast as Goldbarth's. In his "Prefatory Note" to the volume, he states he decided "not to excerpt," a decision that eliminated the inclusion of a huge percentage of his longer works, including book-length and chapbook-length pieces. So, for a Goldbarth fan there seems to be an unusually high number of uncharacteristically short poems included in this volume. It was a reasonable editorial choice, however—and a reminder that Goldbarth isn't limited to writing on entire continents of Goldbarthian land alone; he's been known to write the small country, the state, the town, and, occasionally the single room, often the bedroom. A reminder, too, that he's as good short as he is long.

He is plenitudinous—in his interests, within his poems, and across his oeuvre, but that does not mean that he is chatty, wordy, or repetitive. He is not. His detractors—and he does have them—have been known to call him *long-winded*. He is not. Goldbarth's poems are only as long as they need to be to work their peculiar magic. His aesthetic is one of Goldbarthia, a verbal planet whose language and meaning is structured on accretion, connection, and consolidation.

So, how to write a short review of a book that touches on, despite its omissions, just about everything and the kitchen sink? Awkwardly, and with great respect, knowing nothing I can say or quote will equal the experience of reading Goldbarth for yourself.

His instinct to include only entire works is mine as well. As a Goldbarth enthusiast, I'd find excerpting a poem of his a profanation of sorts. Remove a line or snippet and a sad diminishment would result. If the poem, as a whole, didn't need that line or snippet, it wouldn't have been there in the first place. Goldbarth knows what he's doing; he is not, let's say, *full-bodied* for the sake of full-bodiedness. His poems are chock-full because his mind is; it makes connections. And his ability to distill meaning and resonance is enormous. Yes, you can give examples of his wit and his breadth, his seriousness and his depth by sampling sections and displaying them like natural crystals or thin slices of a brilliant geode, but the extraction would be anecdotal, less than a true representation of a single quadrant of the planet Goldbarthia or of a square inch of a small Goldbarthian beach. His poems are made with some *other* math. Some other physics. Not brief, usually, but definitely compressed. He has a mind that takes in everything and returns it, better and sharper for having been mulled over and conjoined by a master.

His titles are emblems; they function as more than mere labels for the poems themselves, and a selection might be one way to get across the topography of his terrain. They range from the openly encompassing ("A Continuum," "The Poem of the Praises," "Powers," "Gallery," "How the World Works: An Essay," "The Saga of Stupidity and Wonder," "Things I've Put in This Poem") to those which merely appear less openly encompassing ("The Talk Show," "Heart, Heart, Heart, Heart, Heart, Heart, Heart," "1880," "Splinter Groups at Breakfast," "Stephen Hawking, Walking," "The Jewish Poets of Arabic Spain (10th to 13th Centuries), with Chinese Poets Piping out of the Clouds (and Once an Irishman)," "'*A wooden eye. An 1884 silver dollar. A homemade explosive. A set of false teeth. And a 14-karat gold ashtray*,'" "A Photo of a Lover from My Junior Year in College," "Thermodynamics / Sumer," "The Way the Novel Functions," "Some Common Terms in Latin That Are Larger than Our Lives," "Scar / Beer / Glasses," "Whale and Bee"). See what I mean?

In "The Splinter Groups at Breakfast" (chosen rather at random—it's medium-short for Goldbarth but long—six pages—for most of us) we can see a sample grouping of topics (scanned and scooped up in a not-being-compulsive-first-glance-sort-of-way): God, vomit, masturbation, Winnebago Indians, "some poor dead dork," *Scientific American*, ouzo, retsina, the metaphoric "rump of a pony," the Pope, the Occupational Safety and Health Administration, Mali, West Africa, thermoluminescence, Rembrandt, rock-opera, turkey, the Virgin Mary, and the "varying-speed-of-light theory (VSL)." The last word of the poem is *coheres*. And the poem does.

I'll do my excerptional dirty work on his already-classic poem, featured on *Poetry Daily*'s website at one point, and aptly titled, "Library." It's an anaphoric list poem dotted with brilliant variations that keep the reader leaning into the page, in my case, in awe. It's a poem that shouldn't work, but does—because its author is a genius. I'll do the knifework, but with a cry of "I'm so terribly sorry, Mr. Goldbarth" and a certain amount of chagrin. Being a list/catalog poem, "Library" is probably the least damaged, though damaged and diminished it will be, by excerpting. It has, if I've counted correctly, one hundred and thirty-two entries and a total of two hundred and sixty-one lines (and nowhere at all so evenly dispersed as dividing by two might indicate).

It begins:

> This book saved my life.
> This book takes place on one of the two small tagalong
>   moons of Mars.

(It might be fun to note, at this point, that Goldbarth collects 1950s "outer space stuffs, toy spaceships and robots" as well as manual typewriters; see Richard Siken's excellent interview with him on this topic at https://www.poetryfoundation.org/articles/68824/albert-goldbarth-wins-mark-twain-award-for-humous-poetry. Also, a number of Goldbarth's epigraphs are from classic science fiction writer Clifford Simak.)

> This book requests its author's absolution, centuries after
>   his death.
> This book required two of the sultan's largest royal ele-
>   phants to bear it; this other book fit in a gourd.
> This book reveals The Secret Name of God, and so its
>   author is on a death list.
> This is the book I lifted high over my head, intending to
>   smash a roach in my girlfriend's bedroom; instead, my back
>   unsprung, and I toppled painfully into her bed, where
>   I stayed motionless for eight days.

The anaphora continues to entry twenty-one in which Goldbarth seems almost to jump right out of his poem:

> He was driving—evidently by some elusive, interior radar,
> since he was busy reading a book propped on the steering
> wheel.

And then dips immediately back in:

> This book picks on men.

Which is just a marvelous segue! And goes on:

> This is the split Red Sea: two *heavy* pages.
> In this book I underlined *deimos, cabochon, pelagic, hegira.*
> I wanted to use them.

Goldbarth, by the way, is everywhere in his poems, and because of entries like the one above, readers get an extra sort of meta-poem-chuckle in the process. Another example:

> This chapbook was set in type and printed by hand, by
> Larry Levis's then-wife, the poet Marcia Southwick, in 1975. It's
> 1997 now and Larry's dead—too early, way too early—and this
> elliptical, heartbreaking poem (which is, in part, exactly *about*
> too early death) keeps speaking to me from its teal-green
> cover: the way they say the nails and hair continue to grow in
> the grave.
> This book is two wings and a thorax the size of a sunflower seed.
> This book gives me a hard-on.
> This book is somewhere under those other books way over there.
> This book deflected a bullet.

You get the idea. But just part of the idea, because four entries later comes this:

> This book is by William Matthews, a *wonderful* poet, who died
> today, age fifty-five. Now Larry Levis has someone he can talk
> to.

The weave of Goldbarth's multitudes is a tight one. He invariably pulls what seems to be winging centrifugally outward back in, reins it, though never tames it, never flogs the life out of it, and still renders it cohesive. He's a sorcerer. (Remember in Disney's original *Fantasia*, the "Sorcerer's Apprentice" segment, in which Mickey, by splintering the broom-that-carried-water, multiplied, by what seemed like an order of magnitude, the number of brooms carrying water and, so, flooded the Sorcerer's quarters? All because, as the narrator in the film says, "[H]e started practicing some of the boss's best magic tricks before knowing how to control them." And the sorcerer came down and cleaned up Mickey's mess by magically pulling it all back in, by rendering the many, many brooms one broom again? Well, that's what a Goldbarth poem is like, that's who Goldbarth the poet is: the sorcerer. He is in control of all that motion. And he's showing us, in his way, that despite the fantastic activity in his poems, it is all one broom. It's Goldbarthian broom-unification theory.)

If, by some chance, you've never heard of Goldbarth despite his two National Book Critics Circle Awards, read this book. If you've heard of him, but haven't read his work, read this book. If you've read some of his work before now, read this book too. If you think you've read every bit of his work, read this book for the new poems which, in all likelihood you *haven't* read, at least not all of them. If somehow, magically, you've read all the new poems in this book, and all the older ones, buy this book anyway because it's got the best and most apt bookcover art you'll ever see. Buy the hardback; frame the dustjacket. Read the book. Then go back and read it again.

Goldbarth is a maximalist, a *sui generis* novelist, essayist, intellectual, philosopher, professor, and a serious, inherently funny poet, among a plethora of other things. He's read everything and, I swear, has remembered at least ninety-nine percent of what he's read. And he's made marvelous poetry from it.

TRUE LINES NOT MERE SENTENCES:
ON *KUROSAWA'S DOG* BY DENNIS HINRICHSEN
A REVIEW

Here's the image that spans the second, and last, section break in Hinrichsen's "Crazy Horse Mountain," which appears near the end of his new, his fifth, collection, *Kurosawa's Dog*:

Just now, the moon

*

has let fly its glass horse
over the Dakotas

It's not only a memorable image—so visual I don't think I'll *ever* forget it—but its placements are brilliant, a subtle verbal land- and skyscape of its tenor and vehicle. The sections, enjambed and tightly packed, allow for the clean separation of tenor and vehicle, of subject from verb, all three line enjambments themselves breaking at their nouns, the splitting of "the moon" from its terrestrial image "its glass horse" by a delicate little sun-like dingbat (much more delicate and suggestive than the asterisk I've used here), and "moon" hovering over "horse" as though the moon is keeping just a few steps ahead. And that only begins to point out the characteristic web of intricacies that Hinrichsen weaves into this vital and surprising book.

When you pull back a bit, you realize that this same passage is a manifestation of one of the three-step stanzas (in various formations) that Hinrichsen frequently favors and uses, as he does all his formattings, to exquisite advantage. The stanza that preceded this one:

> *hail dotting the body, rider shaken so fiercely*
> *his loose hair*
> *was the wing of a hawk . . .*

And the two that followed:

> filling the campsite with arctic light,
> though the air
> is 90, and the tent
>
> is folding like my mind
> with the wind.
> Sometimes lying down so flat

Hinrichsen's lines are true *lines* not mere sentences broken into bits—the piece is packed with image and speed. There's no rhetorical bagginess, no slack to slow the poem down or fill in the cracks; Hinrichsen makes the reader lean into each line and then even more steeply into the next without pause.

The volume is nearly bookended by "Bresson's Donkey," an allusion to Bresson's film *Au Hasard Balthazar* and the title poem, "Kurosawa's Dog," a reference to Kurosawa's *Yojimbo*. "Bresson's Donkey" begins, again with Hinrichsen's three-step stanzas, like this:

> I could believe in Jesus if there were an animal
> to be beaten
> down, all
>
> that bagpipe braying from the gut's
> spiritual core
> hauling some Boschian tower of hay

Animals, spirit, and allusion run rich throughout the volume which treats, either directly or indirectly, the death of the narrator's father; the "Boschian" allusion summons up even more visions of what is tightly packed and grotesque. The poem's about the experience of taking it in, the great abstractions that hide in the shade of emblem and metaphor. Here is the beginning of "Kurosawa's Dog":

> Even though he's dead, my father dreams repeatedly
> of the Eisenhower era.
> The clarity of fresh concrete spanning the Great Plains.

Hinrichsen has a seemingly infallible sense of formatting and use of white space. Here's the first eight lines of "Lion and Gin," a poem, as opposed to his triadic stanzas, that maintains a rigid left margin and is presented in a solid block:

> I pet my father like some big cat a hunter has set on the ground,
> though I am in Iowa now and not the Great Rift Valley
> and what I sense as tent canvas flapping, thick with waterproofing,
> is cheap cotton
> choked with starch.
> Still, he is a lion on the gurney.
> I talk a little to make sure he's dead.

Just slightly looser, these lines need their proximities; the air of his three-steps would deaden its effect. There's more here between the *here* and the *there* of the images. These lines need the rolling quality of the singular stanza unbroken by the white pause. The reader here passes through many more gates, many more levels of entry, to get to the impact point—important gates, and gates that keep throwing the reader forward because of the suspense caused by what is being withheld. Hinrichsen doesn't give the reader a chance to focus his attention outside the poem, but forces that attention with its built-in sense of urgency to reach the pay-off. The nuance and tonal coloring comes from what follows the seemingly simple subject-verb-object beginning, "I pet my father. . . ." In this short, seven-line beginning, the steps of remove, or what I call the gates, work like this: First gate: the word *like* which sets us one remove away from the thing itself. The second gate: *some big cat.* Then, moving to third gate, another remove: *a hunter.* The fourth gate, the action of that hunter, *has set on the ground*, one step further. The fifth gate: *though* which gives us a little twist in the road. Sixth gate: *I am in Iowa now.* Seventh gate: *and not the Great Rift Valley*, which twists again. Eighth gate: *and what I sense* moves us again, this time into the interior. Ninth gate: *as tent canvas flapping*, the simile that pushes us into the figurative again. Tenth gate: *thick with waterproofing*, expanding on the diversion. Eleventh gate: *is cheap cotton*, another step of diversion. And another, the twelfth gate: *choked with starch.*

Now notice that the eleventh and twelfth gates are one-to-a-line and the lines themselves are far shorter than the ones that come before. Why? Because, I'm certain, "is cheap cotton choked with starch" is *k*-sound and *ch*-sound heavy. Putting it all on a single line would draw attention to it as such ("Look how many c's I can put in a line!")—a potential bad move in a poem that's sounding natural despite its compression. Separating those two lines lets the "cheap" and the "choked" work together without tangling our tongues; it puts an emphasis on "choked" at the beginning of the twelfth line, playing beautifully into the death theme but via displacement to the "cotton." By the time we get to the thirteenth gate, that "Still," we're ready for the final turn back around to the beginning. Our ears and our attentions have been brought to a near halt by the two short lines and that "Still" is like a graceful turn to what we don't expect at the fourteenth gate: He is a "lion on the gurney." There's a little slow-down again at the fifteenth gate: "I talk a little," a little making-us-wait, and then the point of it all, and the sixteenth gate: "to make sure he's dead." A sort of periodic sentence approach to the dispersal of vital information.

That's impressive.

Hinrichsen is a masterful poet with an exquisite ear and the capability of rendering the familiar magical. The interplays—the talent and craft demonstrated in this volume—are many-layered, complex, and deeply satisfying. This is work that will hold up to the rereadings and deep scrutiny it will rightly find. Hinrichsen is superb. *Kurosawa's Dog* is a longtime companion.

WHITE PAPERS BY MARTHA COLLINS
A REVIEW

Poet, teacher, and editor Collins has followed her excellent *Blue Front*—the marvelous, horrific book about the 1909 lynching of two men, one black, one white, which her father witnessed as a young child in Cairo, Illinois—with a new volume in which her lens zooms in more tightly and she reports far more intimately. In *White Papers*, Collins examines her positioning on the racial palettes of the places she has lived. The book is deeply personal and rich with discovery and inquiry and has a feeling of collage—the poems are untitled, greatly varied in shapes and sonics and run from embodied interiorities to modes of reportage both big and small. The segments contain, like sealed vessels, her encounters, astonishments, and complicities. The first poem of the volume, whole on page one, opens, "Because my father said *Yes* / *but not in our lifetimes . . .* " and ends "Because a few years after Brown / v. Board of Education I wrote a paper / that took the position *Yes but not yet.*" True or not—though it certainly feels true—the entire book, then, is read through that lens of shared responsibility. "[T]hey lived //," she says on page three, "*in the colored section / of town* though we lived // in a city not a town it had / a downtown where we saw // them sometimes in stores / on streets at the movies we // didn't think much about / it did we lived in Iowa where // we saw them mostly saw / ourselves what did // we didn't know / where we were living." She describes, much farther on in the book, a schoolyard tree, cut down after a trio of nooses was hung from it and beatings given and taken beneath it, because it was The White Tree and a Black student had sat in its shade: "a white-trunked white- / limbed white-leafed tree // white petals sepals white / stamens pistils bees inside // a white woman pure / white body skin hair // white eyes white / lips nipples blood // white grass for the white / stones of this white dream." The narrative and the lyric segments of the piece are separated by a full page of white space divided between two pages. Apt and incredibly powerful.

I want to call *White Papers* a brave book and Collins a risk-taking poet, but those terms have been so over- and wrongly-used for poets and poems for so long that they and their synonyms no longer have any validity—they've become small and tinny, thin and cheap, meaningless amidst the tides of confession and culpability that fill so many small press pages. *White Papers*, unlike those others, is a testament towards wholeness. Collins says, ". . . [A]nd although I've gone back / and filled in some of the blanks / I'm still learning this un- / learning untying / the knot of *Yes but* re- / writing this *Yes* Yes." *White Papers* is a remarkable book, a wholly unified work—a book rather than a collection—whose object lesson is one of undividing.

ELEGY BY MARY JO BANG

A REVIEW

There's no mistaking the somber tenor of Bang's new volume of poems. The title is *Elegy*; the dedication is "For Michael Donner Van Hook, January 17, 1967 – June 21, 2004," and the first page of the first poem, "A Sonata for Four Hands," offers the reader these stark lines:

> I say Come Back and you do
> Not do what I want.

If you skip reading the book flaps (the flaps will tell you that Ms Bang has lost her son), you'll understand gradually that the speaker's grown child has died, and that her inability to comprehend the circumstances of his passing as well as the vast abstractions of *death* and *never again* has found its grounding in the poems. It seems clear that Bang, in her anguish, did not know *how not to write* these poems. She was teaching herself about the nature of grief.

This is a poetry that embodies and enacts the numbing impossibility of understanding and the ongoingness of Bang's suffering. The human experience of loss is, of course, not new, but these poems wear the hard, startling edge of inconsolable sorrow the way a blade wears its own honed edge: The grief is *of* the person. It is not merely something extra added on. Always the consummate artist, Bang gives us nothing sentimental, nothing clichéd. The poems are naked and spiky with pain.

Bang's short poem "Ode to History" appears to fill in her story:

> Had she not lain on that bed with a boy
> All those years ago, where would they be, she wondered.
> She and the child that wouldn't have been but was now
> No more. She would know nothing

> Of mothering. She would know nothing
> Of death. She would know nothing
> Of love. The three things she'd been given
> To remember. Wake me up, please, she said,
> When this life is over. Look at her—It's as if
> The windows of night have been sewn to her eyes.

It's a little masterpiece of a poem, unexcerptable, a little room that, for just an instant, seems almost to contain her pain in its closing image.

Though the poems are emotionally raw, there is nothing raw about the art. "We Took Our Places" puts forth this amazing dreamlike trope:

> The snake of time was spending itself
>
> Like an arrow in motion, aimed at a bale of hay,
> Each bale a bad day. . . .

And then the poem's closure:

> Someone shook her
> Awake and she rose and went on.

How do you write about uncontainable grief? This is exquisitely controlled writing about a loss so deep that containment cannot even be an issue. Nothing makes it bearable. Not even writing. Not even brilliant lines like these can shake off the mantle of such inadequacy. And we are made to feel her dilemma; every line is bone-hard. She has taken on, almost completely, the mannerism of the capitalized left margin, a contract with formality, a nod to control, to containment: the effort to hold down and understand the impossibility of the return she would wish for.

There are small instances where the aptitude for a dark humor evident in Bang's earlier books, here tinged with bitterness, shows through. In "A Sonata for Four Hands, II," she says,

> She was clearly a member
> Of the fiasco survivor's club
> The living often belong to.

But it's a very small handful of brief-like-lightning cracks.

Before the tragedy that preceded *Elegy*, Bang's work often pivoted on dark-humored moments like that. In *Louise in Love*, her delicious and devious poem "Captivity" begins:

> Those birds will eat anything—
> the carcass subsumed in death, the heart convulsing
> in laughter. So this is how it ends, a dart in the eye
> of Ifdom. The duck grows
> up to be a pillow, the table takes the tree
> out for a talk . . .

I say this here because though *Elegy* is pain rendered exquisitely un-exquisite, the larger body of her work has so much to offer the reader who might hesitate to enter the anguish of *Elegy*. In her previous four books, the serious lightness of Bang's darkish sensibility outweighed the darkness.

It will be interesting to see how Bang's work takes shape after *Elegy*. "There is no pretending to know /" she says later in the book, "What crawls out of the mind lying quiet / By itself in the snow of the grave grass." I have a feeling and a hope that we will find out, in time, through more of her beautiful and difficult singing.

WITHOUT WINGS BY LAURIE LAMON
A REVIEW

Laurie Lamon's second collection, *Without Wings,*—the title phrase taken from the only outright elegy in the book, an elegy for her father—continues the magical work she began in her first volume, also from CavanKerry Press, *Fork Without Hunger.* In both collections, her voice and tone are surprisingly of-a-piece, and in both, too, Lamon demonstrates an ability to vary her style and still maintain the integrity of that distinctive voice: She writes poems that hover as well as pieces that insistently hunker down. What Lamon does not do is write poems that lie docilely on the page.

The subject of absence, as both titles would have us know, is the ballast of these poems; yet they are, for the most part, pensive rather than mournful. The titles' *Without*s are loaded, and point not only to the status-aftermath of death or ruin or loss, but to absence as a place thought resides, a locus, from which the poet speaks. Though neither book feels incomplete without the other, each is enhanced when they're read sequentially—they are even unified structurally and Lamon's marvelous "Pain Thinks . . . " series bridges both volumes. *Fork Without Hunger*'s first section begins with three poems from the series; section two begins with three more; section three, three again; and section four, entitled "Coda," consists only of three of the series, a total of a dozen. *Without Wings*, the new volume, begins with an untitled forward-section consisting of four of the series' poems. Section one ends with four of the poems, as does section two. In section three there are none. Twelve poems from the series in each book but differently grouped and placed: They lead in the first volume, follow in the second, with the obvious exclusion of the final section which leaves the "Pain Thinks . . ." pieces behind as though the cycle is now complete.

My favorite of the "Pain Thinks . . ." in *Without Wings* is this short, virtuosic piece, "Pain Thinks of the Angel," that seems to rise above the page like the angel it speaks of.

> without waiting without memory
> of waiting without history closing
> its eyes Pain thinks of the angel
> without fluency & hunger nothing
> of rapture nothing of the table

The poem's lack of punctuation, use of ampersand, and absence of capital letters (with the exception of Pain personified), its resonant ambiguities, its negatives (two *withouts* in the first line! and two more to follow; then two *nothing*s) and its catalog of abstractions takes you to the place of *absence*—and just when you think you're going to float away from the lightness of it all, Lamon nails the poem down with the hard trump of the final "table." It's startling and effective. That's a poem that hovers over the page.

Her ability to make a poem hunker down on the page—a technique of a different nature, yet still true to her remarkable voice—is demonstrated beautifully by the splendid balancing of grounding and abstraction in the first stanza of her "Prime Number," its complex and compound Möbius involution, its solidity, and the lack of terminal punctuation which lets it roll down the page.

> It looks like a man wearing a shawl whose body is
> another shawl wrapped around a man who has already
> gone to his death in a subway, an office building,
> a chair beside a hospital bed—a man leaning against
> a lectern, or rising from a seat on a train that is leaving a city
> for another city; it looks like sunrise or midnight; it looks
> like prayer or hunger whose table and chair is without
> company, without the forgiveness of bread and meat;

It's a stanza from which it's difficult to escape (though who would want to?) and, despite its repetitions and density, it is spare, without excess of any kind—wonderful writing that unwinds both seductively and elegantly.

All Lamon's poems appear to be made of a dynamic stuff, a contained energy, a hard beauty honed from both craft and contemplation. The place of absence from which she writes is a place with which we're all, no doubt, woefully familiar—and yet we go eagerly with her into poem after poem, without resistance, to experience her thoughtful turns and perceptions. She helps us see better, see larger, and gives us elegant evocations so that we understand what we find there. I'm eager to see where she, with her intelligence and craft, her control, concision, and decorum, will take me next. But, for now, and even after her third volume, I'll be going back to *Without Wings* and its precursor with anticipation and a longing for more and, again more, of her beautiful same.

THE ART OF *THE ART OF:* A REVIEW OF
CHARLES BAXTER'S
THE ART OF SUBTEXT: BEYOND PLOT
AND DONALD REVELL'S
THE ART OF ATTENTION: A POET'S EYE

.

The Art of series is a new line of books reinvigorating the practice of craft and criticism. Each book will be a brief, witty, and useful exploration of fiction, nonfiction, or poetry by a writer impassioned by a singular craft issue. *The Art of* volumes will provide a series of sustained examination of key, but sometimes neglected, aspects of creative writing by some of contemporary literature's finest practitioners.

Series flyleaf

The first two books in this great little series edited by Charles Baxter—Baxter's own *The Art of Subtext* and Donald Revell's *The Art of Attention*—bode well for readers who seek accomplished, but accessible and articulate reading on the topics of the writer's craft no matter their genre of focus.

If Baxter's *The Art of Subtext: Beyond Plot* doesn't become a model text, I'll be very surprised—and disappointed in the reading-about-writing world. Baxter's a veteran literary writer—he's written four novels, four volumes of short stories, one volume of essays, and a volume of poetry; and he's edited four books. This first book of the series treats the topic of subtext with both humor and elegance. And as the book accretes meaning, the reader is drawn in as though she were reading one of Baxter's novels: She can't wait to find out what he'll say—and how he'll say it—next.

In his introduction he states:

> This brief book examines those elements that propel readers
> beyond the plot of a novel or short story into the realm of
> what haunts the imagination: the implied, the half-visible,
> and the unspoken . . . To discuss subtexts at first appears to
> be a hopelessly contradictory mission. It's like saying, 'I am
> about to show you how to show the unseen.' Or: 'I wish to
> demonstrate how to think about the unthinkable.'

There's no bravado here, no I-know-this-and-you-don't attitude. No exclu-
sional academic rhetoric. Baxter's excited about subtext and its intricacies,
and the crystalline observations that follow in the book make compulsive
reading for those of us to whom the concept of *means more than it says* is critical. Who does not want their creative work to "haunt the imagination"?

Later in the book, Baxter reinvests the old show-not-tell saw with energy and the clearest of points: "It is not that actions speak louder than words;
they speak *instead* of words." And later: "A certain kind of story does not de-
pend so much on what the characters say they want as what they actually
want but can't own up to." He's talking about that second layer, the depth
that, as he says, is the "pile-up of emotions that resists easy articulation." Oh,
what I would give to see more young writers get past that "easy articulation"!
Though I'm not saying, by any means, that this book is limited in its useful-
ness to beginners. It is not.

I'm recommending the first section, "The Art of Staging," to my poetry students—it's a brilliant little thirty-one page mini-essay on meaning more
than you say, on compression, a vital issue that most students, young and old,
neophyte and old hand, need to be aware of. And I'm recommending the entire book to everyone I know who writes or just reads seriously. I know of no
one who has thought this issue through as clearly as Baxter has. Even for those
of us who think we have the proverbial handle on the subject, Baxter will have
something valuable to offer.

Subtext is an invisible current that runs through the human character.
Baxter is here, now, to help us learn to embody that current in our literary
characters and for those who read to recognize the craft and beauty and depth
of what they're reading. Baxter uses both classics and contemporary literature
to draw his points; the "Books referred to and recommended" section at the
back will be, for a great many readers, worth the price of the book.

In *The Art of Attention: A Poet's Eye*, Donald Revell—author of ten volumes
of poetry, four volumes of translation (Rimbaud and Apollinaire), as well as a

volume of prose—assumes a volatile, opinionated, and surprisingly agreeable voice. The book cover embodies his tone iconigraphically: The title is in block caps, the i of "attention" is an exclamation point—ATTENT!ON.

Revell knows, it's clear, that he's arguing for a very specific kind of poetry in a world in which the schools of poetry are fighting for space and recognition. His is a convincing stance—not for the exclusion of the other schools, but for the inclusion of this school, what I'd call his School of Absolute Attention.

Revell argues that "poetry is a form of attention, itself the consequence of attention" and he believes that *shared* attention across time—the poet having attended to what the reader now attends to—is the source of both the artistic richness and the spiritual richness of poems. He argues for "vivid presentations, events as may be called, in Dame Julian of Norwich's word, 'showings'." "The poet's trajectory is an eyebeam, not an outline. It is a visual sequence," he states. "I am speaking of intimacy," he says,

> which is an occasion of attention. It is the intimacy of poetry that makes our art such a beautiful recourse from the disgrace and manipulations of public speech, of empty rhetoric. A poem that begins to see and then continues seeing is not deceived, nor is it deceptive. It never strays, neither into habit nor abstraction.

His is a generous vision of goodwill and participation, of visual activity and acuity that leads to the exclusion of "[p]roud mind, which loves to impose itself between appearance and reality." "[S]uch imposition," he says, "lies at the core of all bad poems. . . ." He goes on,

> The art of poetry is not about the acquisition of wiles or the deployment of strategies. Beginning in the senses, imagination senses farther, senses more.

He's talking about Blake, he's talking about Goethe:

> Again the poetry of attention is not metaphysical; it succeeds by faith alone. The opened eye will see, and light will shape the materials given freely to a poet. What need for invention? As it turns out, craft is to poetry what invention is to the imagination—not antithetical, but needless.

I've fallen down the rabbit hole—right? At this point I have to go back and read his "author biography": "He teaches at the University of Utah. . . ." But it doesn't say *what* he teaches. OK. I go online. Poets.org says he's a Professor of English and head of the Creative Writing Department. Well, OK, perhaps I'm prejudiced; perhaps I'm defensive: I teach, too, in an MFA program in creative writing. I believe in craft. How can I couch my reservations? Well, he says craft is not "antithetical, but needless." He talks about workshops, finding his central observation in a quote from Goethe: "Time 'lost in invention, internal arrangement, and combination'—sounds to me chillingly an accurate assessment of our poetry workshops on any given day." Well, yes. OK. Sometimes. But I'm hooked now; I want to know more about this man, maybe study with him, hear how in his generosity he approaches the teaching of poetry. I'd like to be in his workshop. Or at least a fly on the wall. I'd like to listen to him lecture. I'd like to hear him think. But wait: That's what I'm doing in reading this book.

My intense enjoyment of this volume, tempered with the bouts of frustration that rise and then are laid to rest like waves coming into shore— or simply are passed over by my desire to find out what he'll say next— lies in Revell's ability to carry me along with him, agreeing with point after point, and then, in his undertow, sucking my head below water with a statement that raises my poetic hackles. Yes, yes, I say, poetry is after intimacy and is a product, yes, of intense attention, but the imposition of "[p]roud mind" "lies at the core of **all** bad poems"? [emphasis mine] What? That's a darn broad statement! And, besides, I *like* mind—though I admit that "proud" mind can be a difficulty, but is it always the "core of all bad poems"? I find it hard to believe. I've read enough bad poems to be able to enumerate some other core failures of the bad-poem genre. But here's the beauty of Revell's tactic: I read along and I say, *yes, yes*, and then I come to those bits that shake me from my reverie of yes, I shake my head, snort some sort of riposte, argue silently, but then duck my head back down into the book because I can't wait to immerse myself once again in the part of the vision that *does* make so much sense to me. Do I agree with it all? No. Do I want to read on? Absolutely. Revell is a vibrant thinker, a grand articulator, and someone I want to get to know better through his book. He's *interesting*. He's not glib, he's not wholly agreeable, he's certainly not for the novice poet, and he's fascinating in his mix of eliciting *yes, yes*, and *no, no*. He knows he's baiting somebody: "Compared to the facts, arguments are incoherent, dependent, like Republicans, on discord." And he knows he's got the right goods: "Attention is a question of entirety, of being wholly present." It's an honorable and simple choice he's calling for:

> In the poetry of attention we therefore find a pious materialism. Sad and strange that these two notions—piety

and materialism—should be so generally proposed (and opposed) as antitheses. Their separation banishes the eye to a wilderness of mirrors.

"Eyesight," he insists—and I believe he is correct—"is prophetic instantly."

His Scholiums, #1—On Piety, #2—On Nonaggression, #3—"Who made the eyes but I?" make his playing field clear. "Anywhere you look, it's a love poem," he says. "The eye provides." He is calling for peace.

> To see the sovereignty of what is seen is, quietly, really to worship. And to articulate such worship in a poem Wages Peace. So a quiet poem, then, as William Carlos Williams's 'The Red Wheelbarrow' must be, among so many other things, a prayer and a call for peace.

"The open eye," Revell says near the end of the book, "is naked and Edenic." And, still, he gives me what I ask for: Yes, he says, "There is poetry outside of Eden too." And, in the section near the end of the book in which he examines some of his own poems in the light of what he has espoused throughout the earlier pages of *The Art of Attention*, he admits to having written "outside of Eden" himself. I love the faith and courage of his exploration and the humanness of his change.

He isn't saying that what he argues for is all there is. He's saying it's all we need. And I appreciate his saying so.

I like Revell *and* his book. I like the way he irritates me into articulating my own position. I like the way the book pleases me, soothes me, then baits me and pisses me off. *The Art of Attention: A Poet's Eye* is a book I will return to time and time again to find further clarification of Revell's aesthetic. And of my own.

Revell's is a far less decorous book than Baxter's, a more personal book in that way, a book to engage with, and to argue with. Surely he wants us to. He knows his "poetic is neither method nor craft; it is [his] way of being in the world." And that's something I would never argue with.

These are books informed by intelligence, insight, and, yes, attention. They're shaped by deep understanding and what I can only assume has been a long road to articulation. They're neither *Cliff Notes* for beginner writers, nor are they crib sheets for quick comprehension or facile chatter for department soirees. They're vessels for observation, personality, and insight. And I eagerly look forward to the coming volumes in the series. With the Baxter and the Revell to go by, I expect lively, varied, and engaging erudition along with singular personalities to engage with. They'll be, I'm pretty sure, smart books by smart writers, and smart readers will rejoice to have them.

WE MAD CLIMB SHAKY LADDERS

BY PAMELA SPIRO WAGNER

A REVIEW

With an Introduction and Commentary by Mary B. O'Malley, MD, PhD, Pamela Spiro Wagner's psychiatrist, this surprising book from CavanKerry Press's Laurel Books—dedicated to exploring "the many poignant issues associated with confronting serious physical and/or psychological illness"—defies the mandates handed down to so many readers of poetry: that poems not be read with the author's biography in mind; that a reader can never assume that the speaker of a poem is the author; that the poem is the poem and the life is the life, and assumptions about the twain meeting are made only by novices and the generally naïve. *We Mad Climb Shaky Ladders*, however, is constructed to compel its readers to ignore these injunctions, to use the background information included in the book to enter the work as it is meant to be entered. This is a hybrid collection by design, document as well as art: There is a Forward by the poet Baron Wormser, in addition to the Introduction by Dr. O'Malley; and the poems themselves are presented in tandem with commentaries, also written by Dr. O'Malley. Ms Spiro Wagner's extraordinarily eloquent Dedications tell the reader much about the writer as well.

Here is what we learn: The poems in this collection were written over a twenty-five year period by an intelligent woman who has, since the onset of mental illness in adolescence, suffered from paranoid schizophrenia as well as narcolepsy, and whose brain has suffered "erosions" from Lyme Disease spirochetes—these plus the many side-effects of treatment (electroconvulsive therapies, psychoactive drugs), the various and potholed byways of serious mental disturbance. We learn, too, that Spiro Wagner believes she is evil, believes that her eye contact can and has caused others harm, that the world itself is menacing, riddled with threat and follow-through. We learn that her psychiatrist claims to be able to assess her mental state during a given visit by how much eye contact Spiro Wagner is willing to make, and that voices only she can hear lead her to harm herself and that she deeply fears harming others; that she attended medical school for a year and a half, but, because of her illness, had to drop out. And that she has an identical twin sister, Carolyn Spiro, a psychiatrist, and that together they wrote *Divided Minds: Twin Sisters and Their Journey Through Schizophrenia* (St. Martin's Press, 2005).

The background and contextual information work to deepen the power of the poems. The reader, after taking in the initial prose amendments, has something like a steady-state awareness of Spiro Wagner's mental condition and the tenor of her life, the constant precarious nature of her hours. So, for the reader, behind every unit of meaning in the poems there's a background hum of understanding, an, at least, approximate comprehension of the intensity and fear and confusion with which the poet's experience is laden. Every morpheme, then, in a poem is played out against that backdrop of understanding and is emotionally contextualized. Meaning is augmented, its emotional edges amplified and sharpened.

Spiro Wagner is a talented poet whose craft, if her health allows, and I certainly hope it does, will sharpen as well, will allow her gift to unfold further. Most often, in the poems themselves, there is some beautiful transparency made even more vibrant by our having the knowledge exterior to the poems. "Poem That Can Forget But Not Forgive," a great phrase-of-a-title, begins "This poem is afraid / because I am afraid" and the reader who is convinced by the speaker's circumstances is persuaded that her fear is justified. The poem ends: "This poem is sad as water, poor as sand. / This poem wants to live well / but it doesn't know how." Lovely and powerful in itself, but when you know the writer's circumstances, you can imagine just how sad water can be, just how poor sand. It's a marvelous dual image, and the history we are given magnifies our experience of it. Interestingly, the note provided by Dr. O'Malley before this poem reads: "The next poem explores a voice that Pam did not have as a child and still feels is beyond her authority." How smart of the poet to give that voice to the poem! How cleanly and well she articulates her need! She got there and was able to take the reader with her. One step removed from her own voice, she was able to voice her heartbreak—and transparently, exquisitely. And we understand even more fully her fear: It's a fear that's strong and palpable enough to lodge in a reader's own chest and formidable enough to render her mute until the recognition of that terror fades just enough to let her get past it. When she relives it, rereads it again, she'll own it all over again. And she will read it again—because this is painfully effective work that functions on its own terms: within a context that demands attention, and using the reader's own emotional knowledge, her own ability to recognize and balance the measure of human pain therein.

Are all the poems as transparent, as artful as the lines quoted above? No. Nor is every line in any given poem. Sometimes a poem will go off on a small prosy spree; sometimes, though seldom, it will just go off. *But* when Spiro Wagner hits, she really hits. Lines like "I knew then all the sharp vowels of fear" ("Fusion") and the collection's title, the brilliant sentence that drew me without hesitation to the book in the first place, *We Mad Climb Shaky Ladders*, are apt and dazzling tropes and rich in the mouth.

One of my favorite pieces in the collection is "Word Salad," a strong, self-contained poem that does break away from the pattern of hybrid dependency and uses a definition in the epigraph position to help the reader comprehend the context and explain the dynamic of the language:

'Word salad,' a term used for the completely disjointed, incomprehensible language sometimes seen in schizophrenia.

Unpinned, words scatter, moths in the night.
The sense of things loses hold, demurs.
Everything means. Numbers soldier
with colors and directions, four by four
in a pinwheel: this is the secret wisdom.
I inscribe it on sacred sheets of paper.
The Oxford dictionary holds not a candle.
The self reduced to a cipher, a scribble,
the Eye is all, with a Freemason's lash,
and twenty-six runic hieroglyphs to share
how a stitch in time saved the cat
and if a messy rock gathers no stones,
clams must surely be lifted higher
by the same rising boats. Why, why not throw
glass tomes at grass huts? It is a question
of propriety: grass is too dignified to lie down
before gloss. Whirligig! How to pull the center
back into the world? It would take all
the OED to recapture the moths, all Harcourt's
English Grammar to pin them again.

The poem stands strong on its own, yes, but Dr. O'Malley's notes, again, enhance the degree of its emotional resonance.

The random feels not so random to the person in the midst of disorganized thought. Important meaning melts into mental chaos, but each word still carries a feeling of deep impact.

'Everything means . . .' What is interesting is again that the emotions carry the words. Meaning comes first and meaning continues despite the fact that the words fail.

What Dr. O'Malley articulates here is exactly what I sensed as I read the poem. With help from O'Malley, who knows the poem's core material from the outside, Spiro Wagner was able to help me know its matter even more deeply from the inside.

What one experiences in this book is a vision of a fine poet determined to flower in poisoned soil. It's a document of both psychological and artistic poignancy and fascination. And though I see the book's potential for being picked up out of mere curiosity or the equivalent of rubbernecking, I believe the good reader will be both challenged and changed by the art and the experience it embodies. This isn't a book to read for its chronicle of madness; it's a book to read for the art of humanity amidst it.

Pamela Spiro Wagner's feelings and her insights have made their hard way through the chaos of illness and articulation to us—and they are not the pourings-out of a novice writer or a self-indulgent one. Her control, over time, seems as profound as her circumstances seem troubled. "We are given different blessings, / " she says. "Mine is to write." "Come in, come in!" she asks. I have. And I will again.

BUNNY NOIR

I am at least thirty-five, not a kid anymore. I've held a variety of jobs: car hop, burger flipper, salesperson, envelope stuffer, telephone operator, off-set press operator, bindery worker, gas station attendant, gal Friday, bookstore clerk, tutor, researcher, ghost writer, secretary and ipso facto editor for non-profit electric power research, as well as secretary for a company that, if I remember correctly, made titanium replacement knees. I have been a duster-of-battleship-filters. And once, I transcribed some tapes for the singer Connie Francis on an old manual typewriter in her unfinished basement; the tin table that was my sole working surface had one leg stove in, and the old cassette recorder I was transcribing from crashed to the concrete every time I swung the carriage.

Now I work in The Cheese Shop located in the larger of two small strip malls that constitute the town center of my mountain borough. I do this be-cause I've discovered through long experience that driving over the moun-tain and busting my bum adjuncting at state colleges doesn't pay my bills. I can, however, just make ends meet by driving a very short way down the mountain, wearing an apron, wielding a knife, working odd and very long hours, and by being always—even on my scrupulously scrubbed and cologne-daubed days off—identifiable by a heady miasma of Stilton. I work, as they say, *under the table*, because the shop is an ambitious ven-ture for this town and is barely making it, because I'll work all night and into the day and then the night again because the women who own the shop are friends of a friend, because they really need the help, because the work is easy compared to some and seems to have nothing to do with my real life which, at the time, is not so easy, and because I just plain need the money.

I've been on the East coast about three years. I know just a few folks in town, but the handful I know are willing to come in and buy cheese for the pleasure of seeing me in an apron. They like to watch me struggle with the big wheels of Jarlsburg, the crocks of mozzarella. They like to see me wrestle the plastic wrap, fumble the knife, and cut the tips of the fingers off my plastic gloves.

The experience is a proverbial cheese roller coaster ride every day: Gruyère, Danish Blue, Gorgonzola, French Brie and domestic, goat and buffalo cheeses, herbed and herbless soft cheeses, Vermont Cheddar, English Cheddar, Gouda, Swiss, often a rather handsome, layered Huntsman, and champagne, jalapeño, bacon, port, vegetable, and salmon spreads. Patés, mousses, relishes, you get the idea. And now, during the Easter season, we have a selection of domestic cheddars in spring-type shapes, sealed in painted wax: white geese with yellow bills and red bows, pink-eyed rabbits crouched in tufts of green grass, cows with black spots and cows with brown spots, and Easter eggs decorated like . . . Easter eggs.

Hannah White is a real estate woman, and my favorite customer. She brings her clients into the shop in a genial selling effort to introduce them to the town's one posh point. She tells them, "Look! Look at this! It's a little store, isn't it? Upscale. Convenient." She smiles like the fabulous saleswoman she is. "I have them cater my parties," she says. "The patés are perfect, the peppers are roasted in the back of the store, and the spreads are delicious, particularly the sundried tomato, but stay away from the Florentine—it gets watery unless you use it the same day." Then she points to me and says, "This lady here behind the counter is a published author," in a voice that makes it clear, even to browsing strangers, that I'm another funny sort of cheese, a domestic that may, if they're very lucky, have an interesting shelf life while they're around. The intro is a good ice-breaker and everyone laughs because they don't know whether to believe her or not because—and we all know this to be true—all books are written by dead white men. "Really?" they ask, and I say, "Uh huh." So, now they've met a woman who can, if she's very careful, use both hands at once and can speak the local language. I'm good for the cheese business. I'm not wild about cheese, myself, but they love me here in these small, fragrant quarters. The incongruity and my consistent ineptness somehow cheer us all.

The store is narrow and long, like a railroad flat or a Victorian shotgun house. The front door is aligned almost perfectly with the beaded curtain at the back that goes into the cramped work area, storage, and kitchen, and which, in turn, is directly aligned with the back door that leads to the dumpster and the low yellow hill beyond that which gathers blown trash. As you enter, bells strung from the center of the door rattle against the glass. To your right are the big clear glass bins of pita chips, bagel chips, and wine crackers. There's the display for the jelly beans, lollipops, and chocolate foil-covered kittens. The refrigerated cases continue from that point and reach nearly all the way back to the beaded curtain. To your left, narrow shelves line the walls, crammed precariously with jars of delicacies (brandied cherries, pickled gherkins, flavored oils, salsas made with fruit and not with fruit, and olive pastes, anchovies, coffee concentrates, teas, and imported vinegars), kitchen accoutrements (British tea pots made to resemble either Westminster Abbey or a tobacconist's shop, hand-thrown potteries, wine glasses, cheese knives, cheese wires, cheese graters of at least a dozen sorts, spread knives, measuring cups, demitasses, and French press coffee pots, along with occasional sets of European-seeming pot holders and tea towels) and, interlaced throughout them all, my favorites, the stuffed teddies and bunnies and monkeys and dogs. Cramped as the store is, however, if you were to open all the doors, and your arm were true, you could throw a mozzarella ball straight through from front door to garbage pit and give it a fleeting glimpse of the store's entire inventory on the way.

Easter is two weeks away. I've had three days straight off during which I've worked on my moody novel in the five-by-five furnace room of our house on the main road of town. I've been living in a shadowy, imaginary place, but out in the world, in the strip mall lot, the sun is bright, the sky is blue with just a suspicion of cloud. I'm rested, pleased with the work I've done in the last somewhat claustrophobic half-week. I park the car, glance in the windows of the video store, the drug store, and the closed Chinese take-out with the notice from the health department taped to the front door. A modest crowd has gathered in front of The Cheese Store and a small boy in blue corduroy overalls and a striped tee-shirt is throwing a crying fit and banging his head against the glass of the front window. His apparent mother is reading and re-reading—out loud—the poster in the window:

Meet the Easter Bunny
2:00 pm Saturday

I remember now: The boss's son, the college basketball star and physics major is going to dress up like the rabbit and pass out candy to the kids who come by. I look at my watch: It's 2:10. The kids around me swarm like termites and the headbanger stops long enough for me to slip past him and through the doorway.

There's a palpable tension in the air inside thickening the already dense scents of cheese, coffee, and chocolate. I make my way past two customers, who seem to be buying time in front of the glass cases, and into the back room. The rattle of the bead curtain makes a dull, dry sound, something like a low fire in dry grass. There is shredded cellophane everywhere and, now, a marshmallow chick is holding strong to the bottom of my shoe. Linden, the boss, is at the small workspace. Before her are piled masses of mismatched papers: bills from vendors, orders, menus, borough reports. Her small, pointy elbows are on the desk, her head with her short-cropped hair is in her hands. There's music coming through the speakers: Someone is singing about the Easter Bunny to the tune of "I've Been Working on the Railroad" and there's a base line accompanying the music. Linden's one-word-like growl, an approximation of an exclamation she learned from a mystery novel and has been quoting roughly ever since: "Shit-fuck-god-damn-kid-shit-oh-mother-crap." She hasn't looked up yet. To her right, draped over a chair and another mass of unruly papers is the body of the rented bunny costume, a pair of bunny-hand mittens the size of large pizzas, and two, maybe, sixteen-inch long bunny booties. On the floor beside that is the largest head I have ever seen in my life with two upright ears that could stand in for the pickets in a picket fence. Georgia, the other, even more diminutive, partner, is leaning against the door of the giant fridge, thin arms crossed, with a *Well-what-are-you-going-to-do-now-Miss-Smarty?* look on her face. The kitchen is ringing with unspoken *I told you so*'s.

You could cut the air with a cheese knife.

There's a voice from the front of the store, Mary, the high school girl they've hired for the holiday, a tinge of panic in her voice. "People are starting to leave . . . "

In front of me Linden has one last snort of grief, "Son of a bitch." She looks up at me and before I can say, "Hey, what's up?" she says "Get in the suit."

I turn but there's no one behind me. She can't have been talking to me. What did she say? *Those aren't your boots? Where is the loot? The question is moot? Ain't life a hoot? Get to the root? Did you hear that toot?* "What?" I say, puzzled.

"Get in the suit." It's the tone of voice a person uses when he's told his dog three times to "Sit" and the dog has merely stared off into the distance standing on all fours, his tongue dangling from his mouth.

"Suit?" It's dawning on me now what she's really saying. I scan the area. This has never happened before: I am the tallest person in the room.

Linden is pointing her chin toward the flaccid, furry thing on the chair to her right. "Get in the suit," she says again.

I'm laughing now. "I can't get in the suit!" I look around again. "Where's Simon? He's supposed to be in the suit."

"Simon's . . . " I don't hear the rest.

The voice from the front of the store has thinly threaded the back room with panic now. I hear the word *going* and the words *losing customers*. And then, clearly, a frustrated young Mary shouts, "At least get some goddamned candy out there!"

"Just until he comes," Linden says to me. "He'll be here any minute."

So I get in the suit—which is intended for a giant. I am 5'2" when I correct my posture. The neckline, supposed to be up close to the neck base is below my clavicle and sagging. The arms are easily eight inches too long. When I slide on the bunny-mittens, the sleeves bunch up above the wrists and nearly eliminate any flexibility I might have otherwise had. The legs are . . . a nightmare: Because my own legs are so short, there are none. My bunny-crotch is dragging on the floor. I push up the puddles of fluffy legs and step into the bunny feet. I shuffle, can't take a normal step: My ankles are bound by the reach of my bunny-crotch, my feet will fall off if I lift them from the floor.

Linden grabs the enormous head, crawls up on her desk chair, stands, and drops it over my head. It settles awkwardly and with an echo inside. It is, maybe, papier-mâché, something like that. It is a universe unto itself. I'm looking through a mesh screen at the bunny's mouth, but I have to look up to do it. I have no peripheral vision. I can't see down, can't see the floor or my giant, flopping feet. So I waddle towards the beaded curtain and the public area of the store, legless and nearly armless, and, for all intents and purposes, blind. Linden loops a basket handle over one of my stumpy arms and says, "Go!" and starts pushing me down the main aisle, and then stands back, her little hands on her nearly existent hips. She calls from behind and I turn and feel only the faintest dreamlike resistance and then hear glass breaking. Linden says, "Forget it. Just keep going!" and all the way up the aisle I hear packages and hard goods being swept off shelves. It is a long, long walk; the room has tripled in length since I arrived. I hear the bells on the front door jingle when my bunny face smacks the glass and it seems, at the time, like the sound of freedom. I push it open and hobble out. The door closes behind me with a whiffly sound.

The basket on my arm is being pulled sidewalk-ways by children reaching for candy. It's fun for a while. I'm pulled this way and that. I'm petted and cooed at. I'm not supposed to say a word and I don't. But it's amazing. These kids are willing to see what they want to see despite the fact that it's just me in this deranged get-up.

After the initial flurry of kids, a little blonde girl in a crisp dress approaches—I can just make out the look on her face and it's already unpleasant. I hold the basket out to her. Unfortunately, it's empty, but I can't see that from inside my bunny head. She stomps her foot, shakes with fury, and screams "Bad Bunny!" I think, at the time, she sounds like a furious Joan Crawford. "Bad, bad Bunny!" I'm offering, it appears, a basket of nothing. I do the best I can. I waddle over and knock on the window of the store, hold the basket up, and within moments Mary has come out and given me a refill but by the time I turn around, restocked, the little blonde girl is gone. Bad bunny, I think. Bad bunny, bad bunny. I'm going to use that some day.

Mary has refilled my basket twice now with the cheap, hard candies they're giving away before I'm tackled from the rear. A small boy has evidently seen me from a distance and started running. He hits me at the back of my invisible knees as he throws his arms around my Bunny-middle and I buckle but do not fall. He's screaming in paroxysms of joy: "E-e-e-e-easter Bunny!" and he's not grabbing for the basket full of candy, he's grabbing for me. I turn and squat down so I can see him. He's quite beautiful, this little boy: dark, almost black hair, enormous brown eyes. I'm thinking maybe kids aren't so bad, this genuine thrill in the air, this love, this non-greedy appreciation. He grabs me a second time, but this time a bit less enthusiastically, and then his arms drop heavily to his side; the corners of his mouth drop nearly as far. His voice is filled with heart-rending sorrow. "You're not real," he says to me. He backs away and, for a fraction of a second, I am heartbroken for him, poor child, disillusioned, disappointed, beautiful child. Then, something I have always suspected but never articulated presses the air from my lungs and there is no Bunny left in me. I am something large and cumbersome, amorphous, awkward, and hurt. I hear myself say it, but am both astonished and appalled that I am real enough to do so. I step forward and grasp the young boy's shoulders firmly in my fingerless hands. It is some pissy matron's voice I hear echo in the cavern of mâché rabbit's head. "I may not be the Easter Bunny," the voice says, "but I'm *real*."

It doesn't faze the kid. He has already written me off—had, in fact, written me off before I'd finished my half-protest/half-plea. His disgust is more real than I am. His attention is elsewhere at this point: his mother's pocketbook, the suckers he snatched from my basket as he turned away.

So, when the Harleys pull into the lot with their sun-lit flashes of chrome and their loud, reverberating mechanical growls, I'm relieved of being the center of attention.

Until, of course, the three of them, men of the black-leather-and-bandanna-club-emblem-on-the-backs-of-their-jackets type, come rolling up to me. There's a radio on one bike, blasting country western music, and I, for a moment, wonder if I should be frightened, but, somehow, the idea of three tough-guy bikers shaking down an Easter Bunny seems a bit far-fetched. The two to my left get off their bikes, give the stands a kick, and park them there by the curb, illegally. They head for Dairy Queen leaving the third guy right there in front of me. He can't seem to take his eyes off of me. He's still on his bike, engine and radio running, and he's smiling. He has clearly, in his past, had a good experience with a very large rabbit.

He turns off the bike but leaves the radio on and shouts to me over some tune with a good beat. "You dance?"

I don't believe I've heard him right. Between the giant head having its own weather system, my blindness, and this startling address from the not-bad-looking biker, I'm thinking neither quickly nor clearly.

He gets off his bike and comes closer. "Dance?" he says into my screen.

I shake my head no. I can't tell whether it's just my head moving inside the globe of the bunny head or whether the bunny head has, too, acknowledged his question. I hold my basket out towards him, offering candy.

He smiles. "No thanks," he says. "I'm diabetic."

We stand there looking at each other, both seemingly smitten with what we've found in front of us, but, as far as I can tell, anyone who was standing around for a different kind of bunny-attention has fled. Nobody inside the store shows concern, nobody's coming out to see if I'm being bothered by the man or the seismic interruption. I just stand there swinging my basket while he rocks back and forth to the music. Then, he moves up next to me, bends his knees a bit, bumps his hip against the approximate area of mine, and says, "It's easy. Look." His right boot moves to the side and then his left slides over to meet it.

I like bikes. I like to dance. I'm forgetting this guy doesn't see me at all. I'm thinking: Cool! But the truth is, this dude's trying to pick up the Easter Bunny. I set my basket down on the sidewalk. I can do this. Or at least I can try: The limited step the bunny crotch allows me, the floppy, dangerous feet, all not good, but I do it. Then he leads me into a similar movement to the left when the left foot, which follows the right, touches the sidewalk beside the right—and he claps his hands. We're not quite dancing to the music, but it's OK. There I am: no legs, stunted arms, a head I can barely balance—"Weebles wobble but they don't fall down." I'm starting to like it. By the time we get to the "move back" part, despite my handicaps, I'm getting very good.

When I do take the time, between moves, to look around, I see we've drawn a small crowd, adults and children, ten, maybe twelve in all. Cars slow down as they pass in the lot.

It doesn't take long before the biker and I gather steam and are sliding to the beat. People are laughing and clapping; the biker's smiling hugely. It's great! We're moving to the right, to the left, to the back; we're rocking forward, rocking back, stepping and turning. Periodically, when I see a mom or a child looking bewildered, I point to the basket on the sidewalk with my fingerless hand, telling them, silently, to help themselves.

And way, way too soon, the other two bikers return, each with an enormous paper cup with Dennis the Menace on the side. They're slurping something thick through straws. I can see their cheeks and throats struggle to suck it up. And then they're leaning up against the window of The Cheese Shop and watching me and my man.

We finish our dance and, again way too soon, his friends finish their drinks and toss their cups into the refuse bin next to a half-barrel of pansies. My biker waits a moment while he watches them move towards their bikes and then he bends at the waist, lifts and kisses my paw, and remounts his own shiny Harley. As he pulls away, he mouths "Thank you for the dance."

They're long gone before the police arrive. Someone has reported a disturbance. When the tall cop asks me about the men and the music, I put my face grill as close to his face as I'm able. "I can't take my head off," I say, "but there was no problem. They were fine."

"Friends?" he asks.

I give him a quick, muffled summary, the cop shakes his head, leaves, half-laughing, and then Linden, who evidently has neither seen nor heard any of this comes out to tell me it's time to come in. I've been out on the sidewalk doing bunny-duty for an hour and a half. That's sufficient. But she doesn't let me take off my head until we get to the back of the store.

The next few days are unremarkable except that I begin to develop a taste for cheese and the roasted peppers. When the customers come in, I listen to their stories, mostly secondhand, about the drunken rabbit and the bikers. A long-haired, lithe young woman says she heard the police had to rough them up. I just shake my head. I don't know: I saw nothing, know nothing. Shrug my shoulders. "I just can't imagine . . . ," I say.

I'm dying to confess, or to make up stories too: how the Easter Bunny wielded a wire cheese cutter and scared off the bad guys, or how the Bunny just leaned over, whispered something in one of the bikers' ears and those bad bikers fled. I want to tell them the bikers ate too much candy, got stomach aches, and had to go home to their mothers. Nobody mentions to me that the Bunny had no legs or that its arms were severely compromised; nobody tells me the Bunny danced brilliantly considering the circumstances—which stinks. But these are the stories myths are made of and when they laugh and ask who was in the suit I just smile and say I have no idea. It was my day off. They must have hired a professional, I say. I was home writing my moody novel in the cramped furnace room, but, I tell them, these stories that I've been hearing are great. I can't believe I missed it all. Maybe, I tell them, I'll write about this. What do you think? I say. A noir children's book? A cautionary tale like *Struwwelpeter*? Or how about a sestina or a villanelle about some cheese, some bikers, and a very bad, bad bunny?

DEAR GHOSTS, BY TESS GALLAGHER

A REVIEW

Dear Ghosts, is as apt as a title can be. The poems in Tess Gallagher's eighth volume mark a new stage in the trajectory of a lifetime's work and are dedicated:

> *to the ghosts*
> *in and out of the flesh*
> *who accompany me*
> *with such tenderness, such ferocity*

And tenderness and ferocity both thrive in these new poems.

Gallagher is defining her place in a world that is becoming, for her, both smaller and larger at once. The dead and the living fill these pages, but the dead abound: two husbands, a father, a mother; a dead finch, a junco, a hummingbird, and a waitress with "eyes like a drowned cat"; as well as Gallagher's confrontation with her own mortality, her cancer, her multiple surgeries, her survival. And the living? The voice of a woman who has contemplated and approached the distances between the living and the dead with dignity and poise. It's rare that an author's photograph on a book is of any value beyond that of satisfying a reader's curiosity, but the one on the back flap of *Dear Ghosts,* is clearly a message. In earlier incarnations, Gallagher's photos have boasted surprisingly long, thick, strong-looking dark hair, much like the manes of the horses she so loves; in *Dear Ghosts,* the photo is of a woman with no hair at all—or with so little that it cannot matter. It's a shock—if not to Gallagher, who, in "The Women of Auschwitz," tells of having her long hair cut and her head shaved during her illness, then to the reader who has followed her work in poetry (she has also published books of essays, short stories, and poetry translations) for decades. Gallagher says in that poem, "I make visible the bare altar / of the skull." And she does.

The book itself, though, is not a shock at all. Instead, it is a smooth transition, part of Gallagher's lengthy and articulate continuum. It has been fourteen years since *Moon Crossing Bridge*, the book of poems that I believe fulfilled her earlier promise, and was published after the death of her second husband, writer Raymond Carver. That book was airless with pain, loss, and the spectacles that image conjures; the final line of "Yes," in that 1992 volume, captured the breadth of that book, captured its paradox, exactly as though the book itself were speaking. It said, "I gleam," and, then perhaps six spaces farther on, "I mourn."

The themes in this new volume are the same and are different, more encompassing, more embracing: mortality, illness, Ireland, war, loss, and women deep in the solace of other women, the poems and approaches themselves noticeably more expansive, inclusive—many of her lines looser and longer as well. Even the book itself is lengthy: one hundred and forty pages, long for a volume that isn't a *Selected* or *Collected*. Yet Gallagher has not buried her knack for voice and rhythm; it is not only evident, but perhaps stronger than ever—from the bright statement in the dark poem "The Dogs of Bucharest": "But the oxygen of poetry is its own happy / contagion . . . " to the axe-edged address from "Eternal":

> Only human.
> Bullet. Bullet. Bullet.
> Dead. Only dead.
> Are you with me?

Gallagher is writing as well and, perhaps, even more deeply than ever before.

She has honed an already fine ability to juxtapose the abstract and the concrete, to ground the abstract in such a way that the reader questions neither the speaker's authority nor her sincerity. The pairings are both confident and vibrant. The beginning of the first stanza of "Fire Starter":

> The seen caresses the unseen.
> Two eagles, like twin palms in shadow-play
> flex an opening in sky . . .

She's brilliant at this. Here: the image first, the telling to come. The beginning of the second stanza:

> It's WWII. My father
> is a pipe-fitter in the Bremerton shipyards.
> For a year I am an only child running

into the winter glare. But before my father goes
to the shipyard, my mother
lets me see him, in recollection, leave the bed in darkness
to work another job.

And the third:

He slips from the warmth not to wake us.
Soon, like a thief who belongs, he enters,
one after the other, the neighborhood houses, before
the families are up. He gathers
what he needs to lay the fire
in each stove, then strikes a match
to set it going, so when they rise
from sleep, the house will have the chill off
and a fire crackling. Such work is his . . .

The reader, of course, cannot help but recall Hayden's "Those Winter Sundays"
and the fire-building there—but this poem doesn't try to be another classic
in the Hayden manner. Gallagher has used a different recording device: The
scene is broader, the distance greater. A lesser poet would have dived right in to
the narrative, into "her story," but Gallagher, so often the master, sets the image up to precede the story and, because of that finesse, the entire narrative is
read through the lens of that first mesmerizing set of images. It's a brilliant tac-
tical maneuver. At the very end of the poem, "The sweet wood-smoke nostal-
gia of democracy / hangs over the town" echoing the "shadow play" of the first
stanza and its "[t]wo eagles, like twin palms" in that "opening sky."

A gift for image seized and compounded is a joy. The incorporation of
humor, the distinct projection to the external while never leaving the realm
of the meaningful internal, those are traits of a special kind of talent. The second stanza of five in "My Unopened Life," the first poem of the volume:

Hadn't I done well enough with the life
I'd seized, sure as a cat with
its mouthful of bird, bird with its
belly full of worm, worm like an acrobat of darkness
keeping its moist nose to the earth, soaring
perpetually into the darkness without so much as
the obvious question: why all this darkness?
And even in the belly of the bird: *why
only darkness?*

The telescoping image is not only delightful but pressed into double, triple, or quadruple duty in the last stanza of the poem which continues the trope and its tightly managed themes and draws the poem to a close neatly and resonantly.

> So are we each lit briefly by engulfments
> of space like the worm in the beak
> of the bird, yielding to sudden corridors
> of light-into-light, never asking: *why*
> *tell me why*
> > *all this light?*

Tenderness and ferocity. Lightness and darkness and the power wrought between the two. Gallagher is a poet of the numen and of the telos, of the ghosts, and of the earthly experiences that bind them all so tightly together. In *Dear Ghosts,* Gallagher gleams. And she mourns. Beautifully.

SELECTED POEMS BY FANNY HOWE
A REVIEW

The efforts to comprehend both the earthly life and the life of the spirit, as well as the attempt to locate God in the midst of the quotidian, are united at the center of Howe's *Selected Poems*—and the resulting marriage is the hub of all that matters on the small, clean pages that comprise this collection. Howe's speaker isn't coy. She makes her beliefs clear: The seeking, the finding, and the not-finding are inextricable, and are built-in—not adjunct to, but *integral* to, the life of the body and of the complications of living.

In "The Nursery" the idea is vibrantly evident:

> One in one, we slept together
>   all sculpture
>   of two figures welded.
> But the infant's fingers
> squeezed & kneaded
>   me, as if to show
> the Lord won't crush what moves
> on its own. . . .

And, in "Introduction to the World," she states " . . . The grace of God / Places a person in the truth / And is always expressed as a taste in the mouth /." "*Human* was God's secret name," she says in "O'Clock." "Daily," she says in "The Quietist," "says 'divine.'"

And the concept of unities is woven throughout in other contexts as well. You can see hints of it above: "One in one," "two figures welded." Howe speaks of sorrow, which "can be a home to stand on so / And see far to: another earth, a place I might know." And in "Robeson Street," the impossibility of parsing, of fragmenting, is stated even more blatantly: "Three hundred and twenty eight more days / are due this year and even with that many lives / I'd still have only one history."

The manner in which Howe manifests these totalities is surprising: In short segments of well-spaced, short lines, these serial poems can easily tease or frustrate the unwary or arrogant reader. Their meticulous compressions lend themselves, often, to Dickinsonian ambiguities, the same heightened sense of intelligence and play. The fifth section of "The Vineyard" sets one instance out beautifully.

> All night the rain
>
> Pelts the big leaves
> Kids are in peril skidding
> In puddles cars turn over

Are the kids "skidding / In puddles"? or are the puddles where the "cars turn over"? The consistent left-margin capitalizations and the absence of line-end punctuations leave the reader suspended between the two possibilities. And that's where Howe wants you: in the land between the questions and the answers. The section ends like this:

> In each landscape weights and shapes
> Repeat the Father's name: *Not-this-Not-that*

Not-this-not-that. Not-here-not-there. It's all one long *one*.

Between the unembellished disclosures, the sometimes nearly telegraphic elisions, and the erasures of boundaries, the reader is conscripted into the human spirit-searching of these not-quite-narratives and not-quite monologues and/or meditations. The material of the poems is the life and the quest, certainly, but the real matter, the *what-matters-most*, is captured in the spaces where those two things rub together, the crevices where the frictions create philosophical heat.

This is not easy reading. There are uncrowded pages; lots of white space; words, primarily, of few syllables; lines of short duration; and whole serial poems themselves that appear to be small, single pieces headed not even by a title but by an asterisk or some small symbol. On the first few read-throughs I approached Howe's work naïvely. And the work does not allow for naïveté.

In 1991, in an article in *The New York Times Book Review*, Mark Strand warned readers that they had to "slow down for poetry." I think that, until now, I didn't realize just *how* slowly a reader sometimes has to go. Howe's work is not indecipherable by any means, but it is dense and thought-worthy and necessitates a slow, careful read. Or any number of slow, careful reads.

Howe is a religious poet who does not write conventionally religious poetry, neither the popular gauzy verse of worship nor the didactic verse of definition; her poems are too deeply rooted in and controlled by the body's life to be called religious poetry *per se*. Her poems are the poems of the seeking, of the obvious incorporation.

"Half of every experience," she says near the end of the collection, "is lack of experience." The concrete and the abstract are of one thing. What you know and what you don't know are of one thing; you still have only "one history." And in the face of this indivisibility, Howe, in "Lines Out to Silence," tells us how she manages:

> Now theology is necessary
> for the way there are these holes & questions

" . . . [T]he world in my eyes / is hardly a certainty," she says near the beginning of the volume; and " . . . [N]o answers, please, to any of my questions," near the end. She knows how she must live and where—a special, difficult kind of wisdom: "—not here—not there—but always between."

In her *Selected Poems*, she'll take you to that between place. You'll find assertions and questions, yes; not missing information, but mystery encoded and unembellished, a life alluded to, pondered and pressed into the service of the line and the poem and the discovery that is the selected poetic oeuvre, so far, of Fanny Howe.

LINE OR NO LINE: AN ESSAY/REVIEW OF LONGENBACH'S *THE ART OF THE POETIC LINE* AND MCDOWELL AND RZICZNEK'S *THE ROSE METAL PRESS FIELD GUIDE TO PROSE POETRY*

The older I get, the more obvious some patterns of human response become. My neural webs—much like the worldwide one, another web taking up a lot of real estate in the foreground of my thoughts—make connections between my observations, my perceptions and experience, and thrust those recognitions forward in the mind-queue where they, more often than not, meet up with others of a similar bent. The connections mingle and multiply, and the dynamics repeat themselves, until fractals begin to look like cleanly sliced pieces of cake. And so I see, too, that this connecting and compounding has many correspondences with the small-world paradigm, otherwise known as the human web, manifested so aptly in *Six Degrees of Kevin Bacon* on the internet, and which appears to be a spin-off of John Guare's play, *Six Degrees of Separation,* which no doubt had its genesis in the 1929 short story "Chains" by the Hungarian writer Frigyes Karinthy, who *Wikipedia* identifies as the "first proponent of the six degrees of separation concept." And these three manners of web—the neural, the world wide, and the human—call forth, almost against my will, a linguistic connection to yet another, much less complex, but still apropos, system of webbing: the one which exists between the toes of ducks.

And having none of these exactly in hand, I am nevertheless web-rich. And I can feel another association forming. So now, along with these two books on the nature of line and no-line in poetry, Longenbach's *The Art of the Poetic Line* and McDowell and Rzicznek's *The Rose Metal Press Field Guide to Prose Poetry*—the first a paradoxically tiny but encyclopedic compendium of techniques for poetic lineation, and the second, a selection of personal essays on non-lineated or prose poetry—the anecdote of my personal, but long-gone, duck seems both apt and felicitous. And then, the duck having been added to the mix, my mother must follow close behind.

My mother is ninety-nine and lives alone, three thousand miles from where I reside. She still lives in the same house I'm about to tell you about, and we have no other family to speak of. So, obviously, I keep waiting for *the call* from a stranger. I've gotten plenty of calls, but, so far, not *the* call. As time moves on, the expectation becomes more charged with certainty, and the certainty more charged with resignation. The anticipation has been, in a way, renting out a large part of my conscious mind for over twenty years; it has, in fact, earned tenure, while I have not, and, under different circumstances this would be tragic, but with the long-now of the current state of affairs, frankly, the horrification factor is losing its edge. All that she will allow to be done for her has been done. She's made her choices by default; she will not budge. It's not that she's senile; she's not. She's stubborn and angry and will stick to her life-choice guns until no life exists for the choice to determine. I know that sounds hard-hearted, but the being-held-in-suspension has worn down my ability to feel. She must feel it herself, though I suspect that in her case she experiences it as a sense of abandonment and terror. She has always been the metaphorical long-haul trucker in the shiny, new eighteen-wheeler with mud flaps and a bottomless tank of fuel. And though she is somewhat diminished, she's still holding on to that trucker attitude and she's rolling her eighteen wheels in neutral and on her own terms downhill towards eternity.

The poor duck, the actual duck, on the other hand, came into my life late one afternoon, did its brief, surprising work, and exited the morning afterward. Ma was fifty-two or -three back then. Almost a decade younger than I am now and, for all intents and purposes, a single mother of one. She still worked full-time at the county courthouse as a PBX operator and she maintained her brittle thread of sanity by steady, predictable patterns of behavior and boatloads of cultivated aloneness disguised as self-denial.

I was in the very early throes of high school. We had just moved from an apartment on the other side of town to the almost equally as small, two-bedroom, one-bath house on Hillview Avenue, nearer the high school and the courthouse. The bathroom, with a footprint just slightly larger than that of the bathtub conjoined with a phone booth, was just through the archway from the living room and on the right. It opened into what could only be called a small *fainting room*, though surely it was *not* a fainting room because the house was a bungalow, one old, stucco story but neither dignified nor old enough to have a genuine fainting room. Ma, when we first moved in, had ordered, extravagantly, an olive green nylon, multi-level loop, wall-to-wall carpet for every room except the kitchen and bathroom. And below that archway was a lumpy carpet seam right where, for some odd architectural reason, the hardwood floor dropped down on the living room side a full three-quarters of an inch. An old maroon sofa covered in a gristly, rayon frisé that engraved its fibrous, paisley-like pattern on your cheek as soon as you fell asleep there hunkered in the living room. That sofa was pushed back against the synthetic ecru drapes, which, when drawn, nearly covered the picture window. There were two mismatched chairs on the other outside wall, perpendicular to the sofa. One was a low, masculine piece, my mother, sometime in a past so distant it was before my remembering, had re-upholstered in a peony-leaf green fabric, nubby, but patternless. By this point, though, the chair had faded and was softened by age and use. Its arms were very low along the seat cushion, straight and upholstered, and ended with what looked a little like curled fists carved in dark wood. There was an ottoman that matched, its brown feet four echoes of those dark fists. The chair had been my father's—Ma'd thrown him out for the last time close to a decade before but held on to the chair. The other chair Ma'd picked up at the local auction house, an almost delicate wingback covered in a pinwale corduroy somewhere between pink and red, with a medallion of iris quilted into the center of its back. It had been uncomfortable when she brought it home, eighty percent of the chair poking precariously out of the trunk of her little white Opel Kadett, tied in with some small gauge, hemp twine that someone at the auction house must have given her, and it had not gotten more comfortable with age. Ma tended to sit sideways on the sofa, feet up on the seat cushions as though it were a chaise and her head propped between the sofa back and curtain-covered wall on a pillow she'd bring out from her bedroom.

The house was small enough that when I sat at the end of the sofa next to the front door, I could see a sliver of bathroom on the tub side. A narrow strip of porcelain, aluminum runner, and glass enclosure. But if I sat in the green chair, I could see a slightly larger slice of the same scene. There was never anything much to see in that sliver and slice, but I was constantly aware of it because such proximity reinforced the notion of being entirely too close, of having no privacy, no place to go to get away. Of needing to shut the door. But even with the bathroom door closed, anyone could hear every jostle, breath, and displacement that transpired in that bright and claustrophobic room (someone long before we had moved in had installed a primitive skylight with chicken wire in the glass high above the small sink whose scaly pipes Ma had concealed with a tiny formica sink-surround from Sears). The toilet was tucked into a just-barely-toilet-sized rectangular alcove to the right of the sink and flimsy wire shelves were suspended between two peeling fake-chrome poles, one on each side of the tank, which stretched loosely from floor to ceiling. They always held the same inventory: a box of tissues, Ma's liniments and emulsions, a compact of pale face powder, the long plastic tube of black mascara, a small cut-glass dish that seemed always to have three mostly-used-up bright red lipsticks, plus a couple of hair brushes and a rat-tailed comb, my pimple creams, pHisoHex, and multiple mouthwashes. There was also a white china poodle whose poofy fur parts had obviously been extruded from a garlic press and who was chained delicately to two little poodles of exactly the same design. The mother poodle tended to fall over because her little china feet could get no steady purchase on the widely-spaced wire shelves. So, most of the time all three dogs were on their sides, apparently dead or sleeping, in the bathroom glare. The most interesting part, for the rare visitor, was that when you hunkered down on the toilet, all that paraphernalia on the shelves behind your head shifted a bit in an unsettling way, and your knees bumped the vanity. The longer your thigh bones, the wider you had to spread your knees to settle on the toilet seat. The combination tub/shower with its glass wall and sliding glass door was along the wall on the other side; that was your vista. You could almost reach over the sink and touch it.

Perhaps now is a good time to introduce the concept of the *practical joke*.

Wikipedia: "A practical joke (also known as a prank or gag) is a mischievous trick played on a person, especially one that causes the victim to experience embarrassment, indignity, or discomfort. . . . The term 'practical' refers to the fact that the joke consists of someone doing something (a practice) instead of a verbal or written joke." There's a footnote on *prank* that led me to "Other forms of pranks involve unusual applications of everyday items like covering a room with Post-It Notes." By these definitions, then, it was the hybrid *practical prank* that I was about to court.

The afternoon of the event, my friend Holly showed up with a mallard duck decoy. I cannot for the life of me remember why she dropped by or why she had the duck or for what reason she brought it into the house. But the moment I saw that marvelous, awful duck, I knew what I was going to do. I asked if I could keep it overnight. Holly was reluctant. It wasn't her duck, she told me. "One night," I assured her. I'd bring it over to her place the next day. Honest. "What could I possibly do to the duck?" I asked her, reaching over and tapping on its hollow head with a couple of fingers. Swayed by my powerful yet specious argument, Holly handed it over and left shortly afterward. The duck was amazingly weighty for a rubber duck, but its green head and oddly yellowed bill were heavy with promise as well. Its sturdy rubber body was a nice speckly gray, its breast a little darker. It was at least life-size. It was magnificent.

Leaving the seat down, I placed him gently in the toilet bowl facing for-

ward. It was a brilliant fit—he was neither floating freely nor wedged in tightly. It was as though that duck had been created for that particular commode.
His regal, hollow, rubber head rose greenly above the white wooden seat with
the clean, white porcelain bowl below, its water sloshing as though in his
wake. His splendid bill with its apparently lifelike-from-a-distance speckled
yellow-orange-greeny color slid smoothly across the seat front, poking just
over the outer edge. It settled into the curve there so beautifully it was as
though that particular seat had been molded for that particular bill and had
been waiting for this meeting all its wooden life.

I was already laughing.

The plan hinged on my mother's predictability. Every weekday evening
between 5:20 and 5:30, she would unlock the old front door with its two
Schlage deadbolts, push it noisily open, and, keys still jangling in her hand,
toss whatever coat or sweater she had, her gloves, and her purse onto the
wing chair to her left. She'd look my way if I were in the living room reading or watching TV, a sort of weary *hello* would drop from her mouth, and
she'd stand there a moment, as though she were relieved to be home, but her
tired eyes would be scanning the room—and looking around the corners
too, I would have sworn—assessing which of my chores had not been done
or been done perfunctorily. Did she smell baked chicken? Was the smell of
warm laundry in the air? Had I vacuumed? I could see her counting off my,
admittedly, few chores, her mind clicking away like an abacus. If my infrac-
tions appeared large on a particular day, her sigh would be deep and heavy,
her shoulders would droop even lower, and she'd begin the inquisition; if they
were small, she'd sigh as though my uselessness were just one more disappointment in a lifetime of disappointments. But, always, after that, she'd head
straight for the bathroom where she would take a five-minute freshen-her-
self-up, flush, open the door, and make that sharp left back into the living
room where she'd gather up her coat, hang it in the small closet on the one,
broad-shouldered wooden hanger we owned, then come back, pick up her
purse and keys, and walk slowly back to her bedroom. Not bothering to close
her door, she'd flop heavily onto the edge of her bed and kick off her heels.
It would take approximately another five minutes for her to change from her
work clothes into some other, less-good dress, slip on some low shoes, and
head into the kitchen to conjure dinner.

Because I knew I could count on that pattern, I sat in the green chair,
the floor lamp shade angled perfectly over my open book so she wouldn't tell
me I was ruining my eyes. And I waited. I couldn't read; I was too wound-up.
I kept looking out the front window, laughing to myself—Wait! Was that her
car? I'd nearly vacuumed the green out of the carpet and had dusted the TV
screen because I knew that a dusty screen was a dead giveaway. The chicken

smelled the way chicken smells when it has another fifteen minutes to go and the fat is sizzling in the pan. I was a perfect child. This was going to be great.

I'm not really sure what I expected. I don't think I even thought that far ahead. But I certainly had expectations because my heart was beating like a hammer in my chest and I was looking forward to the night being different, to having a little fun for a change. Half of me probably acknowledged she'd catch a glimpse of the duck when she first walked into the bathroom and call out to me, "What the hell is a duck doing in the toilet?" and I'd have to restrain myself from answering, "The backstroke." But even that would have been sufficiently different, a change of some sort, if only momentary. And maybe a quarter of me thought she'd be startled by that green head looking her way and that she'd laugh and say affectionately, "Oh, Renée. You're such a nut," lift the duck from the toilet, giving it a little shake so it didn't drip on the oval, rubber-backed, shag rug, and set it in the bathtub to dry off— and not mention it again—but, still, the night would be better for that instant of genuine warmth. The other quarter of me, I'm sure, knew there was a real possibility she wouldn't notice the duck at all, she'd defile it, and I'd have to do some unpleasant duck-scrubbing before I saw Holly the next day. But in my mindless anticipation, the whole set-up just seemed funny to me: my zombie Ma, predictable, oblivious, and a big duck waiting in the toilet. How could that not be funny?

So when Ma finally turned the second key in the lock and pushed the door open, I was nonchalantly coiled up in Dad's chair pretending to read a thick book with smallish print and yellowed pages, a library book wrapped in those old covers that felt painted on and were almost always a solid, saturated color except for the title and author and Dewey Decimal System number stamped deeply in white or black onto the spine. I know it was a big book because I only took out big books. They were like anchors in another world. Ma tossed down her coat and purse and keys, gave me a look that said *I'm doing the best I can,* and walked past me and past the bathroom and turned right into her bedroom.

It was unthinkable! She *never* varied unless she thought I'd been in some way particularly abhorrent and wasn't in sight and then she might stop in the living room and do that deep-in-her-throat-controlled-fury thing that everything with ears and within walking distance of town could hear and she'd keep it up until I would come running to get my direct earful. But I was right there; she looked right at me. I was curled in Dad's chair waiting. And waiting. My face can only have been a rictus of stifled anticipation and confusion. She'd gone into her bedroom! She shouted to me from back there. Had I peeled the potatoes? And from my perfect spot in the living room I answered, "Yes." And still she didn't come out. "Good," she said after a moment. "Throw them in the water. I'll be out in a minute."

And I thought—more of a thought-scream than a thought-thought—"No! I *can't*! I'll *miss* it!" But I unwound myself from the chair and ran into the kitchen, overfilled the tri-corner Silver Seal pot with cold water, turned on the burner, put the pot on, threw both potatoes, whole, into the water, checked to make sure the splash hadn't doused the flame, and dashed back to my chair, pulled my feet up again, and picked up the book. Ma was just coming out of her bedroom. She turned into the bathroom and pulled the door closed behind her.

And nothing happened.

I straightened myself out. I moved literally to the edge of my seat—and I waited and waited and waited—and finally I gave up. Something in me acknowledged that in the not too-distant future I'd be scrubbing a decoy. Then the bowels of acoustic hell blew out. A scream, the likes of which surely must never have been heard before, cut right through my disappointment. I could hear the crashing of cheap, thin metal. Then a cabinet door flew open and struck the wall with a *crack*! I could hear a shower of breakage and then what only could have been the sound of Ma's new sink-surround being pulled away from the wall. There was a horrible human groan. And before I could even process what came next, the bathroom door flew open. Ma, the wide, dark top of a nylon stocking flapping around each foot, her big white panties pooled around her ankles, her skirt and slip bunched up like a useless life preserver around her waist, was seemingly flung from the bathroom and into the fainting room wall where she ricocheted off onto the closet door. And then, in a terrible ballet of confluences, she stepped with one foot on the opposite foot's nylon stocking, hit that seam in the carpet that covered that three-quarter-inch-drop, and she was lost. She took one off-balance step towards the living room, her shin struck the coffee table and she fell, belly against the Formica coffee table top and her face full-flat into the center sofa cushion. Her arms, which looked broken, were sticking out like . . . broken arms. And she just stayed there, her pale white behind in the air, shaking, now, as though those flailing buttocks themselves were trying to catch their breath. And my mother—in that position—cried for what seemed like a very long time.

When I was able to close my mouth, I knew there was nothing in the world I could do about what was coming. I started to laugh. I was crying at the same time. When Ma finally raised her head and moved, and I saw that her arms were not broken after all, I knew she was going to kill me, but, still, I couldn't stop. The tears were rolling down my cheeks, over my jaw, down past my clavicle, and into my bra. I tried to stop, and I'd manage for a gasp's worth, but the pressure would build—the pressure of surprise and terror both—and I'd break out again, the laughter and the bawling having merged into a kind of a howl. I tried to speak. "Oh, Ma . . . ," but my words were unintelligible. The pay-off of a lifetime, and nowhere to look and nothing to say. It was brilliant and awful. It was hilarious. It was horrible. It overshot anything I could have imagined, and every time I moved to help her to her feet and came close to her bare ass sticking up and the soles of her feet trailing those ruined hose, I thought I was going to disintegrate from the mixture of horror and astonishment. I was going to laugh so hard that I was going to die before she could kill me.

It had played out like this: Ma hadn't noticed the duck until she had pulled up, and pushed down, the usual articles of clothing, and she'd been lowering herself onto the seat when she caught, somehow, a glimpse of that green head and bright eye between her legs. She told me years later, still not laughing, her body had acted independently, had simply shot up and away. I could see it all: her reptile brain shouting *Flee! Flee!* She'd been a billiard ball speeding across green, level felt. She'd been physics and geometry. Every abrupt contact sent her helplessly shooting off in another direction until she focused her eyes and will just long enough to reach out and turn the doorknob. After a similar scenario in the fainting room, she'd taken her awkward rest where she had. And when she'd finally righted herself, and shaken off my hysterical attempts to help her, she'd said only one thing and she said it with a deadly calm: "Renée, you're a goddamned asshole." Beyond that, she didn't speak to me for a very long time.

And so, my hypothesis: that much of what we experience in human intercourse depends on a particular triad of psychological states experienced in cause-and-effect order: recognition, expectation, and reaction to variation. And poetry is a human intercourse—created by one and experienced by another.

There is much in common in *The Art of the Poetic Line* and *The Rose Metal Press Field Guide to Prose Poetry: Contemporary Poets in Discussion and Practice*— and the observations of how both lineation and its absence work on the reader—with the story of my mother and the duck. The shared matters have to do with the recognition of a pattern, the expectation, in its nuanced or not-so-nuanced forms, of continuation, and the resultant payoff set into action by the catalyst of variation.

No one I know enjoys being bored. Readers of poems recognize a pattern and then develop an expectation—unconsciously, in all likelihood, but set in place all the same. The pattern is, then, somehow altered (line "ending," syntaxes, etc.) and, the reader's expectation unmet, her interest attention is ratcheted up and the triad set in motion again.

If you are the one who is the maker, who has experienced the blind "aha!" that precedes the setting in place of the plan, the setting up of the

catalyst, you are the manipulator: Let's call her the daughter in the anecdote above. The instant the daughter saw that duck, the game was afoot. Or,
that might be the poet who suddenly has a lyric impulse. Neither plan nor
poem need be articulated before or during the "aha." The "aha" is preverbal, a
sort of understanding-but-not-yet-having-the-words-to-articulate-the-under-
standing-with moment. Articulation is a later step. On the other hand, if you
are the one on which the plan has been foisted or the one to which, in some
manner, the poem has been passed, you're either Ma or the reader. You are the
manipulatee. And of course, since, reading and writing are different manifestations of the same activity, both parties, the manipulator as well as the manipulatee, can experience surprise.

Longenbach's *The Art of the Poetic Line* is more than just the little (128
5"x 7" pages) book it appears to be. It's concise, yes, and though the font is a
reasonable size, the book is almost airlessly packed with intelligent observation on the nature and possibilities of the poetic line. It's straightforward, absolutely clear, bursting with information that will scoop up and hold the attention of a smart poet, want-to-be poet, or dedicated poetry reader.

The first sentence in Longenbach's *Preface* is this: "Poetry is the sound of
language organized in lines." I'd never heard it stated that way before. And I
thought, uh-oh, a formalist in my hand. But then came this near the end of
that same paragraph: "We wouldn't be attracted to the notion of prose poetry
if it didn't feel exciting to abandon the decorum of lines." First of all, his use
of the word *decorum* near the end of that sentence lights up, in retrospect, the
words *exciting* and *abandon* that come earlier, making those two ideas look
suddenly young and dangerous. With that first paragraph, he has defined the
parameters of his volume. In my second reading, I was better able to see the
character, or at least the persona, of the man who wrote the book. His precision and efficiency—he lacks all prissiness and/or snobbishness—is ideal for
the almost endless mutability of the reasoned line. I liked him.

Longenbach divides his book into three sections: 1) "how the power
of lineation arises from the relationship between the lines and the syntax
of a particular poem"; 2) how "the power especially of free-verse lineation
depends on the interaction of different kinds of line endings within the same
poem"; and 3) how the "relationship of lineated poems to prose" might be
considered. This ambitious triumvirate sets the reader up for the decorum
and thoroughness that is a hallmark of the book itself and Longenbach's
many, and utterly crucial for the writer of poetry, observations on line.

The basic point he makes again and again in context after context is that
"line has no identity except in relation to the other elements in the poem." He
is not being prescriptive, but descriptive; he is articulating what he sees and
how it appears to function. And what he sees in "all accomplished poetry," is

tension "between pattern and variation."

Longenbach is a great teacher, sagacious in his statements and restatements. An example from section one:

> If rhyme is jettisoned from a poem, what tactic must flex its muscles in order to keep the poetic contraption in the air? Meter. And if meter is foresworn? Line. And if line is abandoned? Syntax. And if syntax is abandoned? Diction. Sometimes it will be necessary for a poet to remember every tool in the kit; at other times it will be equally crucial to forget them, though nothing can be forgotten if it has not first been remembered.

I'm a sucker for a fabulous teacher, so how could I not be charmed by a man who has put into context now, and expanded precisely on, the "power of lineation" statement set up in his *Preface*?

Here's a great excerpt from section one, "Line and Syntax," regarding line breaks in free-verse:

> Deciding where the line should end in a free-verse poem might initially seem more mysterious than in a metered or syllabic poem, but in fact it is not: whether or not the line ending is determined by an arbitrary constraint, the line ending won't have a powerful function unless we hear it playing off the syntax in relationship to other line endings.

And this from section two, "Ending the Line":

> The purpose—the thrill—of a free verse prosody lies in the ability to shape the movement of a poem through the strategic use of different kinds of line endings. The line's control of intonation creates the expectation for meaningfulness, allowing a poem's language to wander from its more workaday organizational tasks.

And: "The drama of lineation lies in the simultaneous making and breaking of our expectations for pattern."

Isn't that fabulous? Isn't that true of what keeps us going in poetry—and elsewhere? the finessed and utterly necessary surprise?

In section three, "Poem and Prose," he says:

> We are used to thinking of prose poetry as writing that sacrifices lineation in order to partake more readily of certain aspects of prose: our attention shifts from line to sentence, and syntax must hold our attention without the additional direction of line (or meter or rhyme).

And then coming full circle:

> The effect of our more typical notion of a prose poem depends on the deletion of lineation from the formal decorum of poetry, and the absence of the line would not be interesting if we did not feel the possibility of its presence.

You should read *The Art of the Poetic Line*; it's a remarkable book. The speaker has convinced me that he is a gentleman and a scholar in very best sense. Poetry—and the line—is the deep and only subject of his book—and this within a series of books that has often, albeit delightfully so, given the author's personality its head. His is a well-packed, weighty, and generous addition to the literature dedicated to the craft of poetry.

A different nature of book altogether, *The Rose Metal Press Field Guide to Prose Poetry: Contemporary Poets in Discussion and Practice*, announces itself as a book of modest ambition: "[Our] book is here to reveal a small window on the vast and potentially limitless universe of prose poetry," and the editors mourn the fact that the term *the prose poem* "has come to define a small, justified block of writing wherein 'weird shit happens'." As do I. The "weird shit" imperative, though, must be emanating from writers who haven't read broadly enough to be aware of the gorgeous lyric and meditational, not to mention narrative, non-weird-shit prose poems out there, so I'm already convinced Rose Metal Press's objective is a commendable one. They go on:

> But the question remains, what exactly is a prose poem? There is no one correct answer. There are no two correct answers. In fact, there might not even be an accurate enough question with which to wrangle. The best we can do is call it something instead of calling it something else.

I have to disagree, though, that the question might not be sufficiently accurate: Though there may be no "correct" answers, the question itself is plenty accurate. The fact that it cannot be answered definitively is its answer.

The book's contributors were asked "to speak about the impact of the prose poem on their personal lives and aesthetics," the editors having decided early on that they didn't want some kind of "be-all-end-all pronouncement on the genre's shape and prominence, but rather to add more voices to an ongoing conversation about what the prose poem can be and do and say." The book includes thirty-four personal essays, then, on the prose poem, "all written by current practitioners and teachers of the form" and an example of a prose poem from each.

But the highlight, for me, the most fascinating and telling part of book, is in the Introduction:

> The story of the voting for the 1978 Pulitzer Prize in Poetry has been told many times, but it bears repeating here to illustrate said suspicion.[33] Two members of the three-member committee voted to award that year's prize to Mark Strand for his book of short prose musing on death, entitled *The Monument*. The third committee member, Louis Simpson, opposed the selection and ultimately kept Strand from receiving the prize. Simpson objected to Strand's collection on the grounds that it was composed of prose pieces, not lineated ones. Simpson argued that the Pulitzer Prize in Poetry was to honor excellence in verse writing, and after taking his argument to the higher-ups, the committee's selection of Strand was overturned.

I had never heard this story or, if I had, I'd forgotten it. But it took place only thirty-two years ago! Granted, that's a lifetime for some, but it explains a lot as well as anchors this sub-genre, though I'd prefer to call it a *hybrid form*, in America's literary history with a heck of a hoot. It's both awful—poor Mark Strand! poor majority of the committee!—and, still, awfully funny. The dividing line for Simpson between poetry and prose was a critical demarcation—one worth fighting for—and despite the fact that the majority, both his peers, were ready for the merger—he won! And then, twelve years later, in 1990, Charles Simic's book of "mostly prose poems" won the Pulitzer Prize.

Things have changed. And they have not changed. As the editors at Rose Metal point out, the conversation continues. And to muddy the waters even further, the first piece in the book is entitled, "Prose Poem Essay on the Prose Poem"—a short piece by the poet Bob Hicok, known best for his wildly compressed, and mostly very funny, lineated narratives. "Certain questions," he says about two-thirds of the way through "are answered best with a shrug:

---

[33]Charles Simic once wrote, "The prose poem has the unusual distinction of being regarded with suspicion not only by the usual haters of poetry, but also by many poets themselves." (*Great American Prose Poems*, David Lehman, "Introduction," p. 11.)

why write until the carriage returns? Cause it's a pumpkin and I want pie,"
which at first sounded to me like the "weird shit" the editors mentioned
earlier. But, because I know Hicok's work and his searingly dry wit, I lin-
gered, and of course he's punning on the carriage that comes for Cinderella,
zapped by her fairy godmother from a pumpkin, which will, once again, *become* pumpkin, and the carriage on a typewriter—although I did ask myself
how many readers would recognize the reference to such an antiquated device. But what's he saying, really? Simply, you do what you need to do to get
the results you want. That's pretty nifty, actually. A nice compression, a bit of
color, no imperative. The piece is sharp and goofy, and in its way definitive.
"Once upon a time there was a little bit of plot and a lotta bit of letting go of
plot," it begins. It's a piece full of silliness and significance: it *is* an ars poetica
for the hybrid form. "For instance:" Hicok says,

> there was this guy I knew in this room of needing some-
> one to look out the window and feel how the field of a prose
> poem grows, how like an acre it spreads across the page with
> the sense that we need more land to let language have its say.

I like that. It's an impulse I recognize, but can't consistently harness.

And there are other well-spoken passages in the collection—many of
which use simile well to make their point, and many, too, which touch on the
same territory as Longenbach, but with a great deal more air. "In prose poetry," Maurice Kilwein Guevara says,

> the line break is not available as an organizational unit so the
> writer depends instead on the sentence and the paragraph.
> It seems to me, for this reason, that some of the most inter-
> esting prose poems are constructed as complex electrical cir-
> cuits with breakers and relays that create multiple patterns
> of energy and surprise in the gaps between the sentences and
> the paragraphs. In this sense, a well-made prose poem, when
> it carefully uses words and when it strategically does not,
> dramatizes the velocity of a human imagination at work and
> at play and in the buzzing conversation with itself.

Less literal precision, certainly, looser, but look: a fantastic trope! The prose
poem "constructed as complex electrical circuits with breakers and relays that
create multiple patterns of energy and surprise"! I love it, and I believe it.
I can feel that; I don't have to think about it. And that sort of connective,
metaphorical recognition is something that Longenbach, both his feet firmly

on the ground of observation, does not provide. But after that initial glow, I've got questions. How is Kilwein Guevara's description of a prose poem any different from a lineated poem that exhibits velocity and imagination? A Bob Hicok poem, for instance. Hicok's work is bursting with velocity and imagination. Or what about one of James Richardson's marvelous, non-lineated "Ten Second Essays"? You'll find a velocity and imagination there as well. So I'm confused. I seem to know something more than I did about the prose poem, or know it differently, but, oddly, I'm not exactly certain what that knowledge might be.

I can see what I'm doing—and in a way it's not fair, and in another way it makes my point very well. *The Rose Metal Press Field Guide to Prose Poetry* is a book that had no greater ambition than to capture some insights and articulations by practitioners about what is admittedly a permeable, uncodified form. It is a sampling of tastes and experiences, and some of them quite interesting. Yet these writers do know what a prose poem is, even though many of their articulations are a bit swampy.

One piece that stood out in particular, though, was "Out of My Prose Poem Past," by David Lazar. In it he discusses his tastes in the context of his editorship at *Hotel Amerika*. "I tend to look for work," he says,

> that stretches my sense of what a prose poem can do, rhetorically, and I'm biased toward a sense of musicality except when the rhetoric is sharp and purposive. I like wit and distress to the point of extremis.

He *knows* what he's looking for, and that's a bit of solid ground to stand on, which is a relief, in a book that is basically about a not-knowing.

The book's title though misled me, set up an expectation and, mostly, left that expectation unfulfilled; there's more musing than guiding happening here. So I go back to trope, which seems more real than this proposed *field*. This time to Tung-Hui Hu's "It's Not in Cleveland, But I'm Getting Closer."

> [A] good prose poem makes its own envelope. It wraps and secrets words inside a block of text, rather than unfolding meaning outwards onto the page (the Latin *implicare* rather than *explicare*).

That's good. It takes the justified margins and incorporates them into the image. Nice. I see it; I understand. And yet I have those crossover questions again: Doesn't a good lineated poem also make its own envelope—if not in a rectangular visual resemblance, then in some other fashion? Figuratively? A poem is a *vessel* after all. And doesn't a good lineated poem also, and literally, secret words? Doesn't it unfold meaning outwards? I agree these are excellent criteria for a poem, but they apply to both prose and lineated forms. They are in no way singular to the prose poem.

But for this little segment from Mary Ann Samyn's "'Close to You': The Prose Poem: Some Observations," I do not have such questions.

> Perhaps this is the difference: in my lined poems, I expect to have to wait, exposed, out in the open; in my prose poems, I push a button and the elevator opens and then I go up or down, depending.

Or *did* not. Because now I have gone back to reread an earlier snippet from the same essay:

> It is not my process that differs; it's the push and pull of language. Magnets are a useful metaphor. In many of my lined poems, there is a strong sense of each line existing independently and, indeed, repelling, to some extent, the other lines. In my prose poems, the attraction is much stronger. The cohesive force holds the prose poem together and accounts for its blockiness. Yet, there is something happening sentence to sentence.

I believed the first quote was speaking about her process, different for lined poems than from prose poems, but this earlier segment posits an a priori *no*. And again, metaphor is working for me better than the prose at its face value. She is saying there's a different force to each, to lineated language and to prose. I recognize this, I do. Though I would not have come to the word *force* by myself, I understand this. I'm glad she said that. It's a true thing—and stable. I can stand there.

I wrestled with this book more than I might have, I think, because I read it immediately after Longenbach's solid-ground descriptions and evidences, his sturdy informations. Context and positioning being such makers of experience, both books were redeemed—though in fairness they should not have needed redemption—by adjusting my wrong-sighted gaze, by trying to experience both books in the spirit in which they were offered, not the personal context in which I first tried to receive them. *The Rose Metal Press Field Guide to Prose Poetry: Contemporary Poets in Discussion and Practice* is a book that, without really asking them, raises interesting questions: Can you write in an undefined form? How much does comfort have to do with form? Can you bear up under that much liberty? Can you write well enough, intuitively enough, to travel that particular *field* with guides who can only suggest where you might be and might be going, but cannot get you there? The *Field Guide* is more a book of faith than a source of information. A book of recognitions rather than of comprehensions. It's a different kind of resource.

And since I've been stewing about all these connections connecting (webs, jokes, practical and otherwise, the place of anecdotes in reviews, of secondary sources, of poetry both lineated and un-, and the recognition of the brittleness and utter importance of the role of expectation in poetry, prose, and life), I've come to the conclusion that my triad of brain-states and their interrelated dynamics are more than just present. I think they're basic.

The world has become wider since the duck, and even webbier. And so, because I can, and out of curiosity and a bit of sentimentality, I google *mallard decoy*. And as with just about everything else, the variety of decoys available surprises me. It's kind of terrifying and kind of funny. You can purchase various species in "cast poly resin," molded plastic, inflatable plastic, parachute material, and doubtless others I won't bother to find and catalog; you can buy them with weighted keels (what's a keel?), flocked heads, mechanical wings or feet or bills, remote controls (some that don't even need batteries). You can purchase a "feeder duck butt motion decoy," which is the back half of a faux mallard that wiggles in the water as though its head were submerged instead of missing, and is indistinguishable, evidently, from a live mallard butt action that takes place while its front half is feeding under water. You can buy a "landing motion duck decoy," or one with windmill-like wings that paddle like his feet, if he had feet, might. You can buy "drake mallard breast feathers intack" (sic), the "Expedite Quiver Duck Butt Mallard Drake Decoy," the "Higdon Floating Flasher Mallard Drake 6 Volt HDI-51057," or even a "Very Early Flap-o-matic Drake Mallard Duck Decoy OP." I'm rather partial to the idea of the Flap-o-matic. You can invest in beautifully carved and painted duck objets d'art not ever meant to touch water; you can buy practical carved or molded wooden ducks with either painted or glass eyes. But my duck, the duck of my acquaintance, is a collectible now, listed under "Sports Memorabilia." It's the "Tuffy-Dux," thirteen-and-a-half inch rubber mallard drake duck decoy. The one listed tonight at goantiques.com "could use a little cleaning," "has a few cracks here and there," but would be "a very nice display piece." It's in "Decent Used Condition" and hales from the mid-1900s, which is a comforting connection because so do I. There's a small, poor picture of the thing: the grayish body, the darker breast, the green head looking forward from which extends a yellowish life-sized bill. It is the duck. It could be the very same duck.

But Ma, alas, is no longer the very same Ma. Now, at nearly a hundred and still full of piss and malice, when I telephone to tell her about this review I'm writing about these books on poetry and how our duck experience connected everything—because I believe she'll think it's funny and laugh about this thing we shared so long ago—she calls me *asshole* again and tells me I'm making it up. If she doesn't remember it, it never happened. It's that simple. And I suppose simple is good at her stage of life. Yet, once again, the outcome is not what I anticipated. I am surprised and saddened that, while the rest of the world, and me with it, is opening up by cyber-proxy and experience, Ma's world is shutting down, getting smaller all the time. And I see now just how much and how often I have been adjusting my gaze so that I might understand more of the world. I have been engaged, and that engagement, in a life that includes books about poems and in poems themselves, is also a good thing. And because I know that when the impulse for a poem—prose or otherwise—comes over me, I will not know how it will end until I come to its end. And that it would be less exciting if I *did* know. I am still capable of being surprised despite knowing surprise is on its way. It's the sequence—recognition, expectation, and response to variation—that keeps me from sleeping my life away and that makes poetry such a magical—nearly inexhaustible—opportunity for variation and response, be there line or be there no line at all.

AN AESTHETIC OF ANOMALY: EDWARD TAYLOR'S
"PREFACE" TO HIS "GODS DETERMINATIONS,"
MY MOTHER AND THE TROLLEY, AND SOME THOUGHTS
ON INVOLUNTARY COMEDY

I

"The Preface" because I read it and I crack up. Not once, not just the first or the first few times. Every time. Across a lot of years. That fourteenth line. It stuns me and I laugh out loud.

This sort of thing runs in my family.

When my mother was a young woman in San Francisco, she was riding a trolley car to work; it was rush hour, the car was crowded. Ma and another woman, a stranger dressed to the proverbial nines, had had to run to make the car—Ma assured me it had been a breathy, but sure-footed, near-miss for both. And they were pole-hanging, the two of them holding on to the same brass stanchion at the outside step when, for some undiscernible reason, that second woman lost her grip. The car was moving rapidly at that point and she fell to the street. The trolley stopped. Police came. First aid people. The woman was attended to; she was not seriously injured, but, certainly, bloodied and wildly humiliated. Her clothes were ruined. And my mother couldn't stop laughing. She'd watched that unfortunate woman hit the pavement and roll like a stone, seen her come to a precarious halt perched on all fours, her previously well-dressed butt in the air doggy-style; she'd seen that fine red skirt torn and wrenched above the woman's waist, her ribbony garters white against the backs of her thighs, nipping at the dark bands of her ruined stockings, and my mother, still clinging to her shiny brass pole, couldn't stop laughing. And, by the time that woman lifted her head and began to stare, bewildered, at her own bloody palms, my mother's visceral, barroom laugh had enveloped the trolley and the fallen woman, as well as the distance between.

Ma first told me the story probably forty years after the fact, and the teary-eyed laughter began all over again. In the midst of this renewed bout, she told me that she was certain the other passengers, and the police, had believed she'd pushed the woman. She seemed to *need* to assure me that she hadn't.

I believed her.

Of course, the worst possible scenario was that those people thought she really *had* knocked the woman to the street. But probably they never thought that at all; maybe they just figured she was crazy. At the very least, though, they must have believed she was guilty of laughter at an inappropriate (not to mention an extended and amplified) moment. But both back then, when Ma first experienced what must certainly have been, for one reason or another, nasty and recriminating glances, and, forty years later, when she still felt, urgently, the need to defend herself against the old and unspoken charge—that nebulous threat of *responsibility*—she had laughed even harder.

Of course, I think her response was more complicated than a simple attack of random, misguided laughter. I believe that in those few moments it took the woman to fall, and in those corresponding few moments it took my mother to recognize that the woman *had* fallen, Ma had gotten, suddenly, in a blast of unarticulated insight, the mother of all jokes: that though we preen and strut, though we think ourselves such an elevated and sophisticated species, though we have consciousness and are conscious of our consciousness, though we theorize about the intangible and unprovable, though we manipulate all that we are possibly able on this earth, we fall down. Accidents happen even to those who dress well, and they're *funnier* when they happen to those who dress well. We, as a species, are just plain vulnerable—and all the more so because of our position as we *perceive* it within the hierarchy of the demonstrable world. You're upright and important. Then you're not. You look foolish. Or, you're in trouble. Fast, like that. That *dressed-up* woman had been taken down before anyone could figure out what happened; she had been, without a moment's warning, demoted to the *messed-up* woman. And it's not just the "messed-up" part that's funny; it's the where she came from, where she went, and how quickly she arrived there that kicked the progression into the slapstick mode. If she'd been badly hurt, as she well might have been, it would not have been funny. But she wasn't. It was a version of the pratfall—this time, a Darwinian banana peel.

It's funny. And disconcerting when it happens close to home. Ma maintains she simply got nervous. It had shocked her, she said, this woman, so much like herself, in such proximity, taking that ungraceful, *unladylike*, head-over-carcass, momentum-powered tumble into the city street. It had been a "deviation from the common rule" of trolley rides, of ladies, in fact.[34] The incident had created a disturbing sense of *dis*-ease in her. It had been an *anomaly*. It made her nervous. It made her silly. And that made her laugh.

It's much the same for me with Taylor's "Preface."

I'd read him in college. I remember being mildly thrilled that the poems included in our anthology were neither as long, nor as painful, as the Puritan prose. When I look back at my marginalia now, it tickles me—the word *imagery* appears over and over, along with snaky arrows meandering in great numbers across the tissuey pages. Clearly, it was all news to me, this idea of *imagery*. And I'd drawn a big star in the Table of Contents by "The Preface" and written in green ink, between the title and the page number, *"Who in this Bowling Alley bowld the Sun?"* And lots of green exclamation points. That's it. That's the one: Taylor's glorious fourteenth line.

And then I forgot all about him and it.

I got out of school. I had what I called, for a lot of years, a life. But that life has changed and Taylor's back in it.

And I'm thinking of how, just lately, in the midst of my laughing, someone told me that fourteenth line wasn't funny, or at least wasn't *meant* to be. It set me to wondering all over again about Ma and about laughter in what seems to be the wrong places, about what appears to be an awkward subjectivity of the laugh response.

I know that if I read that "bowling" line to Ma, in its context, in its precision, with its unexpected analogue, its aha! moment of recognition, of rightness and outrageousness, she'd be horrified. She'd laugh. She'd get nervous and she'd laugh and she'd stand back and wait for the lightning to strike while she was laughing all the harder. I know this like it's in my blood—it's what she does; it's what I do. The *whats* have clearly been in place for some time. Now, I think I'm able to see the pattern, to take those *whats* one step further: now I have an idea about why we're laughing.

Much of what I'm getting at, no doubt, hinges on our sense of vulnerability. Fred Miller Robinson, when he speaks of Poe in his book *Comic Moments*, seems to understand: "The gap between the vulnerable human and the overwhelmingly superior Other can be readily converted into a comic contradiction. . . ."[35] Readily is right. Faster than we can comprehend. And the conversion seems to have a tripartite nature: roles belonging to the vulnerable human who makes the blunder, the vulnerable human who witnesses the blunder being made, and an awareness, on at least one of those parts, of some "overwhelmingly superior Other" that supposedly presides over it all and passes judgment on it. It has to do with a sense of complicity. And all that

---

[34] *Webster's Ninth New Collegiate Dictionary* (1988).
[35] Fred Miller Robinson, *Comic Moments* (Athens: University of Georgia Press, 1992) 35.

comes together in an instant. Ma, certainly, after the fall, *experienced*, if not articulated, a vulnerability; her great Other had just totted up one more small comeuppance for the self-impressed species, and she was aware of that—just as she became aware of the presence of that other, lesser, Other, the unspoken prohibition of laughter in a potentially serious context. It all happened too quickly to perceive it as personal at first; by the time that registered, the sequence was already begun.

Only after recognition took hold did the "Oh-My-God-That's-Not-Funny" response kick in. And then, in all probability, the "Damn-Damn-Damn-That-Could-Have-Been-Me" response. And then, after looking around her, the "Oh-Boy-Someone's-In-Trouble-And-I-Think-I'm-It" response. It's part of what I'll call *the follow-up to the bringing down.*

And it's much the same in Taylor's "Preface."

Robinson attributes such a response to a "breach of decorum."[36] And Freud points out that "It seems to be generally agreed that the rediscovery of what is familiar, 'recognition', is pleasurable"[37]—which abuts beautifully with Robinson's notion of the "sympathetic element in laughter."[38] Shock. Recognition. And that troublesome sense of familiarity and complicity. Sanford Pinsker, in his excellent review of Robinson's book, talks about Freud's "'joke-work,'" meaning an exploration of the pleasure that occurs when liberated nonsense allows us to say something blasphemous, hostile, or obscene.[39] And with Taylor it is a sense of the slightly blasphemous that swats into action the sudden bringing down, which sets into motion the, shall we call it *subjective*, follow-up response.

Belief in a God or no aside, I was brought up to fear the possible Him, to, at least, consider the offenses I would commit and the potential consequences should I decide to commit them. And when I have the gall to cross that invisible line, whatever we choose to call it, wherever we choose to place it—and I do all too frequently, consciously and unconsciously, cross that line—I am programmed to step back and wait for the bolt. I get these *frissons* of dis-ease.

Taylor, for that instant, that one line, seems to have taken that sort of liberty. I witness it every time I read or recall it. I *relive* the trespass. And this in a poem of devotion, wearing its serious, devotional clothes. I witness the vulnerable poet make what feels, at the onset, like an obvious blunder, an *inappropriate* trope, and I am *complicit* in the witnessing. I get the shivers and then, down that predictable line: "Oh-My-God-Someone's-In-Trouble and . . ." And it makes

---

[36] Robinson, *Comic* 6.

[37] Sigmund Freud, *Jokes and their Relation to the Unconscious,* trans. and ed. James Strachy (NY: W.W. Norton & Co., 1960) 121.

[38] Robinson, *Comic* 7.

[39] Sanford Pinsker, Rev. of Fred Miller Robinson's *Comic Moments,* "Book Briefs," *The Georgia Review* XL-VII, No. 4 (Winter 1993) 821.

me suspect that the effect of the laughter and tension cycle is sharpened by
the perceived solemnity of the situation. In this instance, it's not so much a
matter of simply overcoming a taboo, as it is just leap-frogging that taboo for
an instant and then falling back. My reaction is prompted, I'm certain, by the
conjoining of what Robinson so rightly calls "the effect of strangeness" and
"the surprise of meaning."[40]

It's the trolley all over again.

Freud alludes to some authors who describe laughter as a "*detente,* a phenomenon of relaxation of tension"; he says that they see laughter as a "release
from constraint."[41] It must be the truth, I think: a discomfiture and a release. I
think of it as a barely man-or-woman-sized hole in the contextual fence. We're
not sure just *why* we're laughing, but we have a real sense of the tense and the
funny. We try to squeeze through. At the time, it's not articulated; it's a reflex,
an unpremeditated flight response. Then, almost immediately, at that point
of release, we experience a pall of guilt for having laughed and our tension is
heightened. And that kind of tension, in the presence of laughter, begets laughter which begets tension which begets laughter. A Möbius strip of laughter.

Who in this Bowling Alley bowld the Sun?

It's risky.

Of course, none of this would matter if Taylor's metaphor weren't so
striking, so to speak, so exactly right. If it weren't so borderline naughty in
its vehicle-to-tenor transference, in its dressing down of God. Taylor's implied
metaphor is that the pathetically human bowling alley is analogous to the
kingdom of God's creation as we can know it. It's not the sort of comparison you
hear every day. It is, in fact, an articulated—by limitation—demotion for God,
one that radiates connotations of what might be called a less-than-properly-
elevated nature. A real stopper, in fact. God, in all his presumed omnipotence,
touted as a designer of bowling alleys—and this the evidence of his glory!

And, sure, I'll grant you that what makes me laugh and what's, literally,
intentional comedy may be two different things, but that particular "surprise
of meaning" makes me laugh every time. It may be unintentional—it is *surely* unintentional—but I've got a feeling that's part of what's so darn funny.

Taylor was a Harvard graduate, a physician and an orthodox Puritan
minister in Westfield, Massachusetts, at the cusp of the seventeenth and
eighteenth centuries. His work was never published in his lifetime[42]—in fact,

---

[40] Robinson, *Comic* 5.
[41] Freud, *Jokes* 147.
[42] There are many ideas about why his work went unpublished: Though he carefully bound and preserved
his manuscripts, he ordered that his heirs never publish the poems; or he didn't order it, but the family for
one reason or another, perpetuated the story that he had; that publishing was a lowly enterprise and was
beneath him; that his work was so unorthodox (some critics consider him a closet Catholic) that he could
not have both made the work public and maintained his ecclesiastical position. It goes on. Your guess.

his manuscript wasn't even found until 1937, tucked deep into some shadowy recess of the Yale University Library. Its discovery seems to have caused quite a stir; evidently, we were a little short of American Puritan poetry. We had Anne Bradstreet, of course, and the endearingly named, but agonizingly heavy-handed, bludgeon-footed, best-selling "Day of Doom" by Michael Wigglesworth; and we had lots of prose. We had Jonathan Edwards' "Sinners in the Hands of an Angry God." That was fun. But evidently there was an open slot in the textbooks for poetry and Taylor got the job.

Certainly other poets have catalogued the world, but Taylor's panache is singular. His veritable muster of plain, worldly images, and his great show of ascending and descending energy, give us the dynamic of a struggle—not one of faith, but one of expression. We get a real taste of the Puritan dilemma and of the Puritan himself via his own perception. The world as metaphor. The metaphor as witness. Nothing intimate here, no details of the singular man or his life, nothing personal, except such as a man's relation to his God is personal. Except as a display of immense piety and frustration is personal. No art for art's sake. Taylor is earnestly, privately, and logically, in his time and by his beliefs, marking the justification of his election to his God.

"The Preface," written around 1700, is, for me, Taylor's most appealing piece. Nothing I can find in the body of work comes close. And, in turn, nothing else on its own within "The Preface" comes close to that fourteenth line. Though there is great charm and energy throughout the poem, and though the construction as a whole feeds the power of that single, brilliant line, there is little doubt that it earns its renown from that one "accurate unexpected detail."[43] Yet I love the poem in its entirety. In it, Taylor gives me pleasure. I like pleasure. And I like the little details, the sidebars, that bolster it.

So, my concern in this essay is a small one: as far as poetry goes, just this forty-four line "Preface." Not the less interesting "Prologue" that follows it. Not the interminable, abstract dialectic, "Gods Determinations Touching His Elect," that follows that. *Never* that. And more, a small concern within that small concern: my *experience* of "The Preface," and, in wonderful particular, the effects of its collocation of pedestrian, downright homely metaphors. The pleasure those metaphors lend me. And that laughter.

II

"The Preface" falls naturally into two parts. The first is characterized by awe in

---

[43] Donald Hall, "Marianne Moore: Valiant and Alien," *Their Ancient Glittering Eyes* (NY: Ticknor & Fields, 1992) 172.

the guise of an interrogatory battering, intimated and concretely annotated—the *who did it?* throughout which Taylor is nearly goofy with wonder; the second is awe once more, but in a more abstract mode, and accompanied by attribution—his answer—and the more predictable, darker didacticism. And though "The Preface" moves naturally from part to part, from question to answer, it is clear from the onset there was never any *real* question.

Puritans, officially, did not question. It's an obvious and interesting issue: Clearly a doctrine of "no doubt" in itself speaks of the possibility of doubt. It's a simple, linear, cognitive progression: In the consciousness the concept of doubt must exist in order to expunge it. Posit the concept of doubt, then wipe it out—it does not exist inside the fence of Puritanism. It's paradoxical. In fact, the whole world of Puritan paradox may be the engine that drives the adamant energy of the poem. Edmund Morgan put it this way:

> Puritanism required that a man devote his life to seeking salvation but told him he was helpless to do anything but evil. Puritanism required that he rest his whole hope in Christ but taught him that Christ would utterly reject him unless before he was born Christ had foreordained his salvation. Puritanism required that man refrain from sin but told him he would sin anyhow.[44]

And, beyond all that, it required that he praise God but did not give him the language to do so. An unenviable dilemma.

The question/answer form does lend itself to venting, though, the frustration and subsequent adamance from what Carlisle calls—despite the orthodox proscription against doubt—the "obsessively asked Puritan question: am I one of the elect?" He says that the format "revealed another of the ways in which Taylor apprehended life. . . ."[45] Perhaps. Perhaps not. Either way, the question/answer dichotomy of "The Preface," is, quite clearly, motivated by rhetoric, and, one might say, Puritanically punctuated for emphasis, each trope a fist coming down—after all, Taylor was a minister, an arguer *for* God. His poems were not inquiries; they were pure and private sermons of and for the self.

---

[44]Edmund S. Morgan, *The Puritan Dilemma: The Story of John Winthrop*, The Library of American Biography (Boston: Little, Brown, 1958) 7-8.
[45]E. F. Carlisle, "The Puritan Structure of Edward Taylor's Poetry," *American Quarterly 20* (1968) 155-56.

"The Preface" is written in a single stanza of forty-four lines, rhymed couplets of iambic pentameter. The rhetoric and its tension builds as the lines accrue, peaks at line fourteen, and then, in an enactment of the sequence of creation, grace, and the fall, spirals downward. Wild. Efficient.

Taylor begins the poem at the beginning of all beginning, his pre-creation mass, Infinity, pure God-in-the-concept, then, as the world progresses, he adds parallel, physical "evidences" of his God via his earthly metaphors and then ends with—or descends towards—the quintessentially Puritanical final trope.

The two poles of Taylor's concern are set up immediately: the "infinite" and that "nothing" which later will characterize his "nothing man." God and man, the absolute dichotomy in the Puritan mind. Insuperable. Perfect.

> Infinity, when all things it beheld,
> In Nothing, and of Nothing all did build,

Through the dense music of his repetitions, Taylor virtually renders the abstract palpable in these lines: "in" and "infinity," the "all"s, "thing/s" and "nothing," the gorgeous iambic rhyme of "beheld" and "did build." It's tight, melodic. At the same time, he sets the foundation for his "nothing" word-play—a delicious and complex depth of accrued meaning by the time the poem hits its doctrinal stride in line thirty-eight. He's moving quickly. And from this point, from this abstract, creationist realm, he moves in a swift, natural progression to one of the familiar and finite. In line three, he sets into motion his marvelous catalog of what Woolsey calls Taylor's "incorrigibly-terrestrial metaphors."[46]

> Upon what Base was fixt the Lath, wherein
> He turn'd this Globe, and riggalld it so trim?

The catalog of works has been opened. The images continue:

> Who blew the Bellows of his Furnace Vast?
> Or held the Mould wherein the world was Cast?
> Who laid its Corner Stone? Or whose Command?
> Where stand the Pillars upon which it stands?
> Who Lac'de and Fillitted the earth so fine,
> With Rivers like green Ribbons Smaragdine?
> Who made the Sea's its Selvedge, and it locks

---

[46]Stephen Alfred Woolsey, "'My Handy Works are Words and Wordiness': Edward Taylor and the Life of Language" (diss., Drew University, 1988) 236n.

> Like a Quilt Ball within a Silver Box?
> Who Spread its Canopy? Or Curtains Spun?

There's a childlike quality to these insistent questions, a humility I'm very drawn to. And a childlike repetitiveness: Who? Who? Who? That small and weak fist beating "who?" A non-censoredness. And an if-at-first-you-don't-quite-succeed interchangeability. (It's interesting, too, to note the difference between the catalog of metaphors and Taylor's similes: *like green Ribbons Smaragdine, like a Quilt Ball within a Silver Box.* These are the *poet's* editorializations, his embellishments, not God's works per attribution and they are slight and frivolous in comparison to those in the catalog of works itself.)

So, was there a plan here? the big to the little? the structural to the decorative? *Lath, furnace, mould, corner stone, pillars. Lac'de and fillitted. Selvedge, canopy, curtains.* God is a woodworker. A metalsmith. A mason. A seamstress. A weaver. Is there a considered pattern of movement? I don't think so. An arena, I think, a *locus* of domestic craftsmanship—though one which he will violate soon enough. But there does seem to be a small trade show taking place here. It's quaint, but it's not really funny yet. An expectation has been set up, however, a context of domestic artistry. It is still sober and practical. And, with this in mind, Alan B. Howard's point about the nature of Puritan perception is key in trying to deduce Taylor's intention: " . . .[A]ny suggestion that the creation might faintly resemble the bright chaos of a tradesman's fair simply did not exist for Taylor." His explanation is convincing: "[T]he imagery . . . is unified and coherent simply because each individual image exists for him only at the point at which it touches the idea of God as an enormously powerful artisan."[47] And Stanford, in the Introduction to his edition of Taylor's poems, agrees:

> Taylor saw nothing incongruous in using an image from everyday life . . . to illustrate a serious theological idea. . . . Taylor had little concern with incongruous connotations. He saw resemblances rather than differences.[48]

Daly brings it down to the level of the text itself in order to remove it once again: "In Puritan poems, symbolic correspondences occur, not at the level of the trope, but at the level of perception."[49] So, though the "tradesman's fair" is

---

[47]Alan B. Howard. "The World as Emblem: Language and Vision in the Poetry of Edward Taylor," *American Literature* 44 (Nov. 1972) 382.

[48]Donald E. Stanford, Introduction, *The Poems of Edward Taylor* (Chapel Hill: University of North Carolina Press, 1989) xxxiii.

[49]Robert Daly, *God's Altar: The World and the Flesh in Puritan Poetry* (Berkeley: University of California Press, 1978) 93.

our first perception, the deeper truth is, no doubt, the Howard-Stanford-Daly core of reasoning. Taylor is stacking up evidence like firewood. Or, more aptly, stockpiling munitions. It was his job: What God put within his purlieu, within his dim understanding, he should report, and with it he might, in his poor way, glorify God. Evidently, it's a stance adopted from Augustine of Hippo, from the Doctrine of Accommodation, which "implied that the Divine Author was employing the writer in His service. . . ."[50] Taylor was God's scribe. He functioned within, what Junkins calls, this "religio-aesthetic"; it was the *raison d'etre* of the poem.[51] God was, of course, inexpressible; there had to be a scaling down to accommodate the severely limited human capacity to comprehend, so that, even in His employ, His poets had, finally, to fail. Taylor's inability, then, to breech the gap between man and God was a just confirmation of his doctrine: The more he failed the better he was. The gap was inviolable. The homely crafts that Taylor enumerates—the structures and objects that, if all went well, protected and comforted him in the vicissitudes of an environment with a great potential for destruction—were visible and comprehensible. Survival—his physical life—depended on homely concerns. And that life—as well as his spiritual life—belonged to God. It was no more than reasonable for him to draw parallels.

There are, in fact, a drumful of theories on the dynamic of Puritan metaphor of this nature. Daly quotes Richard Baxter's "Saints' Everlasting Rest" in explanation: " . . . heavenly contemplation assisted by sensible objects."[52] Carlisle supports Taylor's method with a certain insight: That man, too, like Taylor's household metaphors, " . . . must be acted on by someone . . . ; he has no real power to 'make' or 'act' in his own salvation; God must act on him. . . ."[53] And, actually, that's a good argument. The catalog of work exists *only* to exalt God—and to stress the chasm between nothing-man and all-God. Pearce, in his *The Continuity of American Poetry*, puts it this way: Taylor "is constrained everywhere to find an earthly counterpart—however poor or dim—of the ineffably holy."[54] That constraint is abundantly clear in "The Preface."

Taylor, in fact, in his enthusiasm, bombards us with a virtual artillery of image and, I think, we must look at it on artillery's terms. Taylor never meant to offer a multiple-choice. Nor was he trying to create a pattern. He was building an arsenal of metaphors whose "force, like the army of the saints, lies

---

[50]Mason I. Lowance, Jr., "Religion in Puritan Poetry: The Doctrine of Accommodation," in Peter White, ed. *Puritan Poets and Poetics: Seventeenth-Century American Poetry in Theory and Practice* (University Park: Pennsylvania State University Press, 1985) 39.

[51]Donald Junkins, "Edward Taylor's Creative Process," *Early American Literature* 4 (1969-70), 67.

[52]Daly, *God's Altar* 59.

[53]Carlisle, "Puritan Structure," 162.

[54]Roy Harvey Pearce, *The Continuity of American Poetry* (Middletown: Wesleyan University Press, 1987) 45.

in their numbers, not in their individual will."[55] And it works. As I read, I am carried on the swell of Taylor's rhetorical energy, the stockpiling of this argument's evidence.

Puritan poets were, in their own eyes, not *creating*—the trope, evidently, was not the issue. Again, it was the perception rather than the poem as art/artifact that carried the weight. These poets were transcribing the facets of God's works which God allowed them to see. The profane indicating the sacred. It was their duty to see and to make note. Daly makes the perfect distinction:

> [This view of poetry] . . . has far more in common with the Roman notion of the poets as '*vates*,' a 'seer' who observed and utters a truth outside himself, than with the Greek notion of the poet as '*poeta*,' a 'maker' who fashions verbal artifacts finally of his own creation.[56]

What was important was not the poet's experience, but his noting of the evidence of God—and clearly no evidence was unworthy. God, supposedly, had set it up that way. "Man's reason, though dim, [was] sufficient to lead man part of the way to God, Who ha[d] ordered all things to aid such a pilgrimage."[57] So, faith was built-in according to God's plan. The Puritan's, ideally, was an art of no art. It was to " . . . contain only enough art to guide one to the truth."[58] Hence the disparities in level of tenor and vehicle—God's accommodation of man's dimness left a big gap.

The Puritans saw their world according to their Grace, according to God's condescension. Art was a devotional process—it was meant to adore, not to explore. The *telos* of the art was communion, adoration; the *telos* of the life, justification of hoped-for election, of salvation. One was merely a road to the next. Art, itself, was suspect, but useful. It smacked of human pride. Men could make nothing; only God could make. Woolsey points out the paradox once more: "Words adequate and appropriate to the situation [were] impossible to find, yet silence [was] unthinkable."[59]

For Taylor, I'm sure, despite the knowledge of ultimate futility, each image was a stab at bringing the ineffable nearer to articulation. Yet the ineffable is, by its nature, *ineffable*. And I can feel his dissatisfaction in the speed

---

[55] David Leverenz, *The Language of Puritan Feeling* (New Brunswick: Rutgers University Press, 1980) 163.
[56] Robert Daly, "The Danforths: Puritan Poets in the Woods of Arcadia," in *Puritan Poets and Poetics: Seventeenth-Century American Poetry in Theory and Practice*, Peter White, ed., 151.
[57] Daly, *God's Altar* 19.
[58] Mason I. Lowance, Jr., "Religion in Puritan Poetry: The Doctrine of Accommodation," in *Puritan Poets and Poetics: Seventeenth-Century American Poetry in Theory and Practice*, Peter White, ed., 40.
[59] Woolsey, "'My Handy Works are Words and Wordiness': Edward Taylor and the Life of Language," 98.

and lightfootedness of his catalog. Even in his inclusive view of builders and makers, despite the numbers of his "proofs," he never quite satisfied himself, I think; each time he tried again. The result is that great show of ascending energy—the urgency in the poem builds, and the power accretes, until, finally, in line fourteen, he is *nearly* out of control and he swings wild:

Who in this Bowling Alley bowld the Sun?

Ba-boom. The sudden bringing down.

Taylor has set up in us an expectation throughout what might be called his catalog of practicality, his list of metaphor-as-witness. Now he breaks the pattern, knocks us down with the anomalistic. Bowling, for that man of God, was no acknowledged trade, no practical craft. The effect on the reader is a sort of shock. Immediately the stereotypical, cacophonous, competitive, beery, smoky bowling alley we all know—a version of which was rife in the seventeenth century as well—springs to mind. This startling shift, from the craftsman's essential realm to the raucous and gamey, smacks of a Robin Williams line, an instantaneous, nearly perfect leap out of the proverbial not-previously-rocked boat. Clark Griffith suggests, perhaps, the poet was carried away by the "momentum of metaphor."[60] Yes, I think so; and it's at this line that Taylor steps onto the line of decorum, with his, let's say, most *exuberant* trope. He's desperately casting about at this point, and the poem takes in and sends back that desperate energy. The reader gets a big shot of a hyper quality that lends itself to giddiness. And it's at this point that this whole idea of metaphor and humor comes into play—of discomfiture, of the bringing down, and of the following-up reaction.

Freud says joke-work makes sense into nonsense. I believe that's what the bowling line *approaches*. I don't believe it crosses over; in fact, the comparison is so close to precisely right that the sense gets blurred for a moment: The vehicle startles—prolongs the unarticulated moment—and then crosses back over (at least for me) into the recognizable and discomfiting.

Why does that make me laugh?

Reed says, " . . . Taylor's conceits are often too extreme, . . . produce an effect that, for the modern reader, often verges on the ludicrous."[61] He's accused of "straining the link" between vehicle and tenor.[62] Blau says Taylor's metaphors can "attract the attention away from the idea which they are

[60]see Clark Griffith, "Edward Taylor and the Momentum of Metaphor," *English Literary History* 33 (1966): 459, for explanation.

[61]Michael D. Reed, "Edward Taylor's Poetry: Puritan Structure and Form," *American Literature* 46 (1974-5) 304.

[62]Kathleen Blake, "Edward Taylor's Protestant Poetic: Nontransubstantiating Metaphor," *American Literature* XLII (March 1971) 4.

supposed to convey. . . . [T]he disparity between things compared is too great for the mind to bridge with appreciation."[63] All true to some degree, I suppose, on that continuum of critical assessment. (The critics are nearly as funny as the image itself. Taylor, though he flailed in the face of the infinite, in the context of ineffability, did it brilliantly. The critics, on the other hand, are working within the realm of curtailed, finite meaning, the perfectly adequate utterance. They, too, wear their "good clothes" and they do struggle mightily to maintain their critical demeanor—which results in what often, in the case of Taylor criticism, reads like wry understatement. The contrast between those two energies, the devotional and the critical, themselves make for a laughable tickle in that neighborhood of "the effect of strangeness" and "the surprise of meaning.") Those critical demeanors, however, their foibles aside, do come close to the point. Taylor's line does at first seem to approach the territory of their commentary, and we do gear up for some sort of disapproving response. But the reasoning-out of the metaphor never takes that infinitesimal final step into the ludicrous. The metaphor itself, historically and currently, makes much too much good sense for that. But by the time we work it out, we're already laughing and have set into motion the laughter-tension loop. That gap in comprehension, however, does prolong the non-verbal moment (a moment that I believe to some degree is inherent in the processing of any good metaphor) and is what sets into motion—and contributes to the seemingly exaggerated nature of—that noisy and nervous-making follow-up to the sudden bringing down.

In fact, poetry and comedy seem to share several techniques, and, within this moment of the poem, they're all working furiously and simultaneously. Freud talks about the "technical methods of joking": "condensation, displacement, [and] indirect representation. . . ."[64] The parallels are stunning. The economy of joke work to the compression of poetry: These things take far longer to explain than it does to experience them first hand from the piece. Displacement: the dilemma of the ineffable, itself, that results in that marvelous indirect representation, the image. And Freud again: "A favorite definition of joking has long been the ability to find similarity between dissimilar things—that is, hidden similarities."[65] What else is metaphor?

At line fourteen, poetry, the image, the joke—and that laugh—have come together. But is the bowling metaphor a joke as we know it? Yes and no. I think we tend, at first thought, to think of a joke as deliberate, calculated, something told for effect. But Webster reminds us that a joke is also

[63] Herbert Blau, "Heaven's Sugar Cake: Theology and Imagery in the Poetry of Edward Taylor," *New England Quarterly* XXVI (Sept., 1953) 359.

[64] Freud, *Jokes* 95.

[65] Ibid., 11.

"the humorous or ridiculous *element* in something." Yes, absolutely: joke-like. Humorous. Comedy? *Yes, yes.* And it's all these many things going on simultaneously (compression, displacement, indirect representation, the sense of blasphemy, of witness, of complicity)—these dynamics which, in concert, heighten the stun-laugh-recognition-shame-laugh-even-harder progression. Both the catalyst and the outcome are *dis*-ease. We look for that hole in the fence: release.

And the effect of this flurry of cognitive activity is compounded by Taylor's lineation. The fourteenth line is the second of only three one-thrust, self-contained lines in "The Preface." The first two are unremarkable, his line five, "Who blew the Bellows of his Furnace Vast?," a line perfectly integrated into his interrogatory catalog of practicalities; and the second, line eight, "Where stand the Pillars upon which it stands?" All other lines in the catalog, other than fourteen, are either compound or enjambed. But in fourteen, Taylor, after setting up the expectation of a continued laundry list of banal, homely metaphors, without warning, in that one swift thrust, tosses in an anomalous figure that startles—that jarring, self-contained climax to the catalog (and a rhetorical peak to "The Preface" itself), the *Bowling Alley*. And the solid "spun"/"Sun" stressed rhyme along with that dual interrogatory lift at the line breaks heightens that sense of closure—the door of the catalog of works, along with its climactic anomaly, slams shut. All that in an instant. Ba-boom. You get mugged like a punch—all at once—so fast you don't have time to sort out your reactions. The bringing down so quickly. The absence of warning. Donald Hall's "accurate unexpected detail."[66] It's perfect.

Really perfect.

As is the evolution of the bowling alley itself in relation to the trope—though I laughed my good hard laugh even long before it occurred to me to look up its origin. The *Encyclopedia Britannica* says it "probably" began in ancient Germany as a religious ceremony. The pin (the "kegel" then) represented the heathen. You rolled a stone at it, and, if you knocked it over, you were "believed to have cleansed [yourself] of sin."[67] I love this idea just in general, but the best part is it's a perfect fit for Taylor's trope. That incredible "surprise of meaning."

But the years exacerbated the risk-factor in bowling and it is that evolution that creates the high/low, abstract/concrete discrepancy—and it added it earlier than I might have imagined. My twentieth-century notion of the smoky, beery nature of bowling alleys was closer to the encyclopedia's historical notation than I could have imagined. In 1511, King Henry VIII issued an edict declaring bowling "evil" because of its link with "dissolute places" and gambling. The edict, of course, was virtually ignored until it was

---

[66]Hall, *Glittering* 172.
[67]"Bowling," *Encyclopedia Britannica: Macropedia,* 15th ed., 1979.

rescinded in 1845, which is funny in itself. Bowling's image continued to go downhill despite the game's great popularity, and in the seventeenth century the game became "more and more . . . associated with pothouses and taverns, and the excesses of drinking and gambling by the shady characters who met there. . . ." Not just a twentieth century manifestation after all. That was news to me. Great news that made Taylor's line even funnier—the kind of funny not attributable to a historical, contextual misreading. And all the more right: the human realm as sin-filled and besmirched. Taylor knew the connotations. Stanford and Howard were no doubt correct: Taylor had one thing in mind—getting near the idea of God while acknowledging the insuperable chasm between man and the ineffable.

Nevertheless, despite any profound intention, it is the unification in the trope, the figure of the high abstract and the low concrete that really clinches the laugh. Robinson puts it this way: "What is primarily necessary for the conversion or shading into the comic is the *increased and conscious assertion of the human in the face of the Other.*"[68] And Freud takes the same idea even further:

> . . . I do not trace the comic pleasure in analogies to the contrast between the two things compared but to the difference between the two expenditures on abstraction. When an unfamiliar thing that is hard to take in, a thing that is abstract and in fact sublime in an intellectual sense, is alleged to tally with something familiar and inferior, in imagining which there is a complete absence of any expenditure on abstraction, then that abstract thing is itself unmasked as something equally inferior. The comic of comparison is thus reduced to a case of degradation.[69]

Freud quotes Herbert Spencer's "The Physiology of Laughter" (1860): "Laughter **naturally** results only when consciousness is unawares transferred from great things to small—only when there is what we may call a *descending incongruity.*"[70] It's true. And it all falls into place. *A descending incongruity. Affinity. Meiotic deflation—meiosis*: "the representation of a thing as less than it actually is in order to compel greater esteem for it."[71] It's the aesthetic for the entire catalog of works.

And it is this just-right factor that gives me my foot-stomping certainty: "The Affinity between the objects is what makes the contradictions comic."[72]

---

[68] Robinson, *Comic* 35. Emphasis mine.

[69] Freud, *Jokes* 210-11.

[70] Ibid., 146. Bold emphasis mine.

[71] The term *meiotic deflation* comes from Michael Clark's "The Honeyed Knot of Puritan Aesthetics" in *White Puritan* 77. The definition (of *meiosis*) comes from *Webster's Ninth New Collegiate Dictionary*.

[72] Robinson, *Comic* 45. Robinson is speaking of Magritte's "Le Domaine d'Arnheim."

The bowling alley is exactly right. Originally, nothing-man in his sin-sweat knocking down those unbelievers with a rock for the all-God's glory. And, later, man's realm as rife with sin and a world in which the upright fall and fall again. The precision of the parallel adds to the *dis*-ease. The recognition-laughter-tension-laughter sequence is in full motion. I think you have to love that.

Freud, arguing the same rhetorical idea in a different arena, quotes a great couple of lines from Heine: " . . . Till at last, / at last every button bursts / on my breeches of patience." It's the same equation as the bowling line, and a laugher, too, though clearly not to the same degree. The deflation is not nearly as hyperbolic. Patience, a decidedly small, human virtue, is not quite in the same high abstract category as God-the-creator. The gap is a much smaller one.

Nevertheless, Freud's explanation is apt: He says it has "a characteristic that we do not find in every good (that is to say, in every apt) analogy. [It is] to a great degree 'debasing'. . . . [It] juxtapose[s] something of a high category, something abstract (. . . 'patience') with something of a very concrete and even low kind ('breeches')."[73] And bowling is certainly the lowest of Taylor's catalog. The high. And the low. And the gap in between.

It's an interesting puzzle: God-the-maker-of-bowling-alleys bowling the sun, setting the sun loose across the sky. Kenneth Murdock, in his *Literature & Theology in Colonial New England*, gives a straightforward, actually beautiful, reading of the line. He says it has the imaginative strength of great poetry. Taylor's God was not content to fix the sun on its orbit in the firmament; he must, with a magnificent sweep of his arm, bowl it into place. The image makes him just what Taylor felt him to be—a God so great, so serenely powerful, that even the sun for him is a toy, a bowling ball, and all the material wonders of the universe are merely the appurtenances of a bowling green.[74]

It's lovely and it works, though the progression of the catalog of metaphors doesn't indicate that Taylor thought it through that far. I think, in his "momentum," he flung it out, surprised himself, and, in his singled-mindedness, said, "Wow, it's a keeper."

John Gatta, Jr. gives Taylor credit for both his serious intent and his comic achievement:

> In creating his celebrated image of God as a prize bowler
> of the universe, Taylor is actually underscoring the comic
> disparity between earthly vehicle and divine tenor, thereby
> dramatizing his awareness of the transcendent nature of his
> subject.[75]

[73]Freud, *Jokes* 85.
[74]Murdock, *Literature & Theology* 171.
[75] John Gatta, Jr., "The Comic Design of Gods Determinations," *Early American Literature* X (1975) 127.

On the money whether Taylor intended it or not.

Warren, from another angle, says " . . . the shock comes from the modernization, *the provincializing and localizing of the Infinite. . . .*"[76] It's that too. The *localizing* of the infinite—but to such an unseemly location! The unification of the ineffably sacred and unutterably profane. All dressed up and falling off the trolley. And it doesn't end there.

Taking into consideration the Christocentricity of Taylor and the Puritan penchant for puns, word games, and typological double meanings, the word *sun* in that fourteenth line begs for scrutiny.

There's the pun—and Puritans loved them: *Who in this Bowling Alley bowld the Son?* The homonym. God-the-Father setting loose His son into the world. Both as rhetorical climax and as image, this is bountifully meaningful. Christ, the son, was the bridge between nothing-man and all-God. There was no other way to breach that chasm but Christ.[77] Exactly right again. And it is startling: suddenly an issue of ontology addressed by way of a bowling alley and compounded by a pun.

Metaphor lends itself comfortably, in fact, to both the apt and the comic, though, in "serious" poetry, we—as writers—tend to quash the funny stuff, when we spot it, in order to be taken seriously. Kids, on the other hand, are more than willing to give that safety measure a miss.

There's an excellent classroom exercise for exploring metaphor that asks young students to name three categories of things: invisible things (such as love or anger), colors, and visible things (a window, a caterpillar, a brick), and to write each list in a column down the page, the three columns across the page; and then, in a Chinese menu sort of way, it directs the students to match up words, any one word or phrase from each of the columns, in the form of metaphor.

Here are the examples from the book:

Invisible things	*Colors*	*Visible things*
fear	fire-red	needle
love	black	door
memory	moon-white	star

---

[76] Austin Warren, "Edward Taylor's Poetry: Colonial Baroque," *Kenyon Review* III (Summer 1941) 361. Emphasis mine.

[77] There's a third reading of the line I can't account for. Daly states that "for the Puritans . . . the sun was frequently used as an admittedly imperfect figure for God. . . ." Whoa. Who bowled *God*? Surely this wasn't Taylor's intention; it's way out of line. Puritan doctrine didn't allow for doubt or questions of that nature. There was no *room* for doubt in Puritan theology. But the reading is available, even if after Taylor's fact, if Daly is right. I can see no indication, however, in the body of Taylor's work, that he entertained notions of this nature. My guess is, and it sounds snottier than it's intended, that Taylor hadn't read Daly. I can't account for that kind of reading any other way. I can't believe Taylor was an apostate.

Some examples from these offerings might be: love is a black door, or, love is a moon-white needle; memory is a fire-red door; fear is a black star.[78] All good, meaningful figures. But in my experience, more often, in the actual classroom dynamic, children come up with metaphors of this nature:

> Love is a caterpillar-green tennis ball.
> Hunger is an electricity-red lightning bolt.
> Death is an elephant-gray moving van.

And if you push them—after they've had their good, hard laugh—about how love is like a caterpillar-green tennis ball, they'll tell you: It's bouncy; you can see it coming; or going; sometimes it goes flat. Or hunger is a lightning bolt because it burns, or it strikes, it could kill you, or you can hear the rumble. And death is a moving van . . . Well, figure it out.

There is always that surprise of finding the "similarity between dissimilar things," those "hidden similarities." I used to tremble in fear that those young students would come up with a mixture that would stymie me, some catastrophic, from my point of view, image that allowed for no tenor-to-vehicle transference. It never happened. Some were hilarious. A few we had to reach for. But the mind leaps first. Then we look back and build bridges.

It's not so far from the bowling alley, is it? Robinson nailed it: the effect of strangeness, the surprise of meaning. That childlike quality. And the nature of metaphor. An aspect of humor, too. *God's creation is a bright bowling alley.* Why not?

Ma, of course, if she chose to address this at all beyond an open-mouthed gasp, would call it "cheek." She'd say Taylor had "a lot of cheek" to put God, his omnipotence and splendor, in the same squalid mouthful with a bowling alley. Not that she has anything against bowling alleys—but it's apples and oranges, oil and water. And, besides, she'd say, it was a "fresh" remark. "Fresh" as in definition number four in *Webster's Ninth Collegiate*: "disposed to take liberties: IMPUDENT."[79] A breach of decorum.

It's at line fifteen that Taylor stops his rapid-fire barrage and from the foothold of his anomalistic metaphor finally extends an image—that sun. Lines fifteen and sixteen belong to the sun itself. And seventeen through nineteen even have the good grace to stay put in the sky. It's at this point that the rhetorical charge of the poem begins to dissipate; it is the point, too, at which the reader/witness can begin to relax.

---

[78] Toi Derricotte and Madeline Tiger, *Creative Writing: A Manual for Teachers*, New Jersey State Council on the Arts.

[79] *Webster's Ninth New Collegiate Dictionary* (1988).

> Who made it always when it rises set:
> To go at once both down, and up to get?
> Who th'Curtain rods made for this Tapistry?
> Who hung the twinckling Lanthorns in the Sky?

These sorts of attributions we're used to. The sky is God's theater, his show-place. Charming, sweet. Not a laugher, though; no downgrading, no demotion. These are things he's done amidst other things and now, at least, we're beginning to look towards the celestial, the historically more fitting, expected arena for this god. No severe limitation. Meiotic deflation, yes. Funny, no. More predictable. We've accepted the artisan trope all along. So God's hanging curtains now, hanging lanterns? No surprise.

And then there's a shift in the rhetorical gears in which Taylor takes on his preacher's mantle and moves on to a little more fist banging—and then enlightenment:

> Who? who did this? or who is he? Why, know
> It's Onely Might Almighty this did doe.

Line nineteen is the line that most radically modifies the iambic pattern. If we have, up to this point, been carried along by the catalog, soothed by those few lines lingering in the sky, this line marks the point at which the Rev. Mr. Taylor demands that we sit up and pay attention. At line twenty, the poem turns around: He gives us his answer. *It's Onely Might Almighty this did doe.*

The two lines following are the summation for the catalog of works:

> His hand hath made this noble worke which Stands
> His Glorious Handywork not made by hands.

Who couldn't love that wordplay? *Handywork not made by hands.* It's glorious. And it harkens back, poetically, to those deftly played lines, one and two, at the beginning of the poem.

Taylor's on certain ground now—the balance between the effort to express the ineffable and the assertion of dogma is beginning to tip.

Then begins, in apposition to that catalog of works, what I'll call the catalog of *power*, and this is the fulcrum point at which the energies of the poem begin descending, playing out the Fall—long before his literal invocation of the Fall in the final four lines of the poem—and letting Taylor do his doctrinal job.

> Who spake all things from nothing; and with ease
> Can speake all things to nothing, if he please.

A little nudge here on Taylor's part: He's setting up the connotational scaffolding that will support his didactic thesis. These *nothing*s are again prefiguring his "nothing man"—made him from nothing via the Word, can turn him back into the *original* nothing if it suits him. As a recurring image, "nothing" is accruing depth and a frightening vacuity.

And then back to power and the world as we should fear it:

> Whose Little finger at his pleasure Can
> Out mete ten thousand worlds with halfe a Span:
> Whose Might Almighty can by half a looks
> Root up the rocks and rock the hills by th'roots.

The crook of His pinkie could create ten thousand worlds—how significant could *man* be? Nothing man. Taylor knows both his God and his poetic construction. The absence of *nothing* builds tension in this section:

> Can take this mighty World up in his hande,
> And shake it like a Squitchen or a Wand.
> Whose single Frown will make the Heavens shake
> Like as an aspen leafe the Winde makes quake.
> Oh! What a might is this! Whose single frown
> Doth shake the world as it would shake it down?

That squitchen (switch, stick, rod) introduces a notion of corporeal punishment, discipline. Parental and personal. Up close and a spur to the complicity Taylor's already set into motion in line fourteen. And whippings aside, this God's frown alone can shake the heavens, the world—in fact, shake it down! He could turn the landscape to rubble! No longer is it an issue of just the soul and salvation; the corporeal body is at risk here. If it *pleases* Him, we're human history: We're nothing. We're primordial soup.

That threat in place, Taylor drives it home with more fist-pounding to make the *Nothing* point:

> Which All from Nothing fet, from Nothing, All:
> Hath All on Nothing set, lets Nothing fall.
> Gave All to nothing Man indeed, whereby
> Through nothing man all might him Glorify.
> In Nothing is imbosst the brightest Gem
> More pretious than all pretiousness in them.

Seven *nothing*s in five lines! And he finally settles down to the focus of his rhetoric: nothing man. All those early "nothing"s come to fruition here, lend their ominous, vacuous edge to the nature of this nothing-man. God made us from nothing, has given us all; *lets nothing fall*—good puns here: lets nothing-man fall, lets nothing fall on man.

Through nothing man all might him Glorify. The climactic, doctrinal pun, the slippery, slithery bottom line of the poem. Read: Through nothing, man all might him Glorify—it's futile. Or, through nothing-man, all might him Glorify—all in the created world glorifies God via the poor, dim sight of nothing-man. . . . *Might him Glorify.* It's the reason for the poem itself. It's man's job description.

The final four lines provide the perfect doctrinal denouement: the breaking of the Covenant of Works, the Fall. The final thrust of the downward spiral, the descension to the postlapsarian state of nothing-man.

> But Nothing man did throw down all by Sin:
> And darkened that lightsom Gem in him,
> That now his Brightest Diamond is grown
> Darker by far than any Coalpit Stone.[80]

The final line, the line of *status quo*. And though that "Brightest Diamond" image is a tough one to love, I love that *stone*. Yes, I find it worth a chuckle for its allusion to the predictable hellfire and damnation we've come to expect from those generic Puritans we seldom ponder. But I respect the elegance here, the fact that it is only an *allusion*, that it comes in through the side door of hellfire. *Coalpit.* It's an admirable slight of hand.

Ontology, eschatology. Taylor's world was one metaphor. Was one arena, had one fence.

Our century is different. Ours is a century of innumerable arenas, a plethora of fences.

And more metaphors than we can shake a squitchen at.

III

Anomaly. *Dis*-ease. Recognition. Complicity. Release.

I think it's all there. *The surprise of meaning. The effect of strangeness.* The sudden bringing down: from a trolley, in a trope.

---

[80]Text of poem taken from Thomas H. Johnson, ed., *The Poetical Works of Edward Taylor* (Princeton: University Press, 1939).

Yes, of course I can hear the objections: I am predisposed towards laughter. It's true. My husband says he can find me at any gathering by following the trail of my laugh. And, yes, the unfamiliar and irregular orthography of the seventeenth century is strange and looks funny. And, sure, there's a handful of strange-sounding vocabulary that lands something like silly on the ear.

But I'm not laughing at Taylor's other work. Nor am I laughing over the works of other poets in his period. Not the *same* laughter anyway.

The appeal of "The Preface," for me, is derived from the glimpse of the man being eloquently—and hilariously—human: It is not a work intimate in its details, but a work wildly intimate because of its *urgency*. And the vulnerability that arises from that all-too-human pressure is the key to both its success and its unintentional humor. "The Preface" is alive with that humanness. Taylor wrote *from* this world *about* this world, the only world he could know. He wrote with more presence in the now than I can muster on my best of days—not the near or far future, not the near or far past, but *in the moment*. Yet he knew that singular moment as an indication of the Other. He was not writing about heaven; he was not writing abstractions. He was naming (by adamance, by inference) the author of his immediate world. In that way, "The Preface" *is* a sermon—Taylor knew what he wanted to say and, though he found language lacking, there was no room for doubt, no room for deviation. His metaphors were his art as well as his insight; what drove those images was the doctrine and belief behind the perception. And more than that. The energy, the "momentum," if you will, of "The Preface" attests to an act of desperate devotion and unrelievable frustration.

Taylor was a man. And a poet. And subject to the pitfalls thereof. In *Their Ancient Glittering Eyes*, Donald Hall recalls Marianne Moore quoting Aristotle: "It is the mark of a poet to see a connection between apparently incongruous things."[81] Divine tenor, vehicular world.

Surely a poet. And Hyatt Waggoner, in *American Poets from the Puritans to the Present*, pointed out that in Taylor's time, "The use of poetry was to help one live well—and die well."[82] Taylor seems to have done both as well as nothing-man could.

I made the trip to visit Taylor's grave. After dragging my poor husband out for the three-plus hour drive to Westfield, we then dragged our road-bleary eyes over the graveyard, stone by stone. I can honestly say I didn't feel much like laughing. But after an hour's blurry traipsing through the rain with my notebook covering my head, squinting at eroded, unreadable stones, and despairing at the great length and breadth of the cemetery itself, I heard a sound—and I witnessed my normally quiet and undemonstrative husband

---

[81] Hall, *Glittering* 173.
[82] Waggoner, *American Poets* 6.

shouting and waving like a wild man from across the graveyard. He, the good man, had found Taylor's grave.

In the rain I took pictures of the headstone, the footstone, Taylor's wives' stones, some strangers' marvelous stones. I pondered the rough angels, the strange designations. I'd been disappointed, and really, really sad for the previous interminable, soggy hour—I suspected the stone was gone, or unreadable, unrecognizable. Sad that I'd talked poor Jack into driving all the way out to Massachusetts for no reason. And I laughed like crazy in the warm rain, writing wildly while the pages of my journal buckled in the downpour and Jack held the umbrella over my head. Taylor's gravesite was well-kept, the stone legible, upright, cared for. We hadn't come all that way for nothing— and someone had been caring for Taylor.

I can't say I experienced a mystical union with the dead pastor; I'm not even sure he'd be pleased I knew his work. But I was pleased for him. His stone was a tall one, cleanly incised. And it had a lot to say:

> *Here Rests Ye Body*
> *of ye Rev.D MR. Edward*
> *Taylor Ye Aged*
> *Venerable Learned*
> *& Pious Pastor of Ye*
> *Church of Christ in*
> *this Town who after*
> *He had Served God*
> *and his Generation*
> *Faithfully for Many*
> *Years fell asleep*
> *June 24th 1729 in*
> *Ye 87th Year*
> *of his Age*

I'd call that pretty accurate. *He Served God . . .* Yes. Taylor himself said, in his *Treatise Concerning the Lord's Supper*, that "The Web of grace is wrought in the soul by the shuttle of the Word." His word, too, I think. Barbara Jordan— though certainly without alluding to Taylor at all—summed up the position of his accommodation and his grace succinctly: "All things become sacred from long gazing."[83]

It was Taylor's job. He did it well, and—even two hundred and sixty-five years later—to my delight. So I told him so. I thought he should know.

But I haven't told Ma she's in the essay. If I did, I'm sure she'd feel I'd

---

[83] Barbara Jordan, "Tutelary Poems," Section III, Line 1, *Channel* (Boston: Beacon Press, 1990) 27.

crossed some invisible line. She'd make that annoying sinus-y noise she makes before she tells me I've got a helluva load of cheek. And though she might be pleased, I'm not sure she'd laugh. But I think she would.

We do, certainly, laugh for a lot of different reasons. But my point is this: In these instances, we laugh at what doesn't fit our expectations; we laugh at what makes us uneasy. We laugh—or some of us do, anyway—at anomaly, at a sudden bringing down that carries with it an unspoken notion of culpability. There's more to it, I'm sure, but it's kind of funny, isn't it?

OF A KIND: ON ACCOMMODATION,
PTOLEMIZATION, AND AGING

When a discipline is in crisis, attempts are made to change
or supplement its theses within the terms of its basic
framework—a procedure one might call 'Ptolemization'
(since when data poured in which clashed with Ptolemy's
earth-centered astronomy, his partisans introduced additional complications to account for the anomalies). But the
true 'Copernican' revolution takes place when, instead of
just adding complications and changing minor premises,
the basic framework itself undergoes a transformation.

Slavoj Zizek

My mother is weeping again. She weeps all day most days now. She is one
hundred years old, shows no signs of clinical dementia though her memory
has holes in it, some convenient, some less so, and, when her crying crescen-
dos to an unconstrained hysteria, the less-so parts are rendered even more
less-so and her body is so profoundly racked by grieving she appears to be
the victim of an otherworldly possession. Her hearing has pretty much aban-
doned her; the few friends she might have held on to, if she had had the in-
clination, are dead or debilitated. She is filled with self-pity, and I understand
that. She is weak enough to need around-the-clock assistance and has chosen—after this last of several bouts of pneumonia—to remain in a care facility. Now she's in the system. And for the first time in her adult life she finds
herself able neither to reeducate nor to exile those around her who will not do
as she insists—and she is angry, astonished, and terribly afraid.

There is something basically opposite in the two of us: a fiery indignation, in my mother, that thrusts her forward, hackles on high, hostile to everything that might cross her; while, in me, there's a gray weariness that would have me—with resignation and a confession of culpability whether culpable or not—just lie down and melt invisibly into the earth.

So what is it in us, my mother and me, that has made us so unequivocally different when we are in so very many ways utterly alike?

The question of who we are and will be as we grow old and then older—not just Ma and me, but all of us, the we who make up the individuals of our species—intrigues me. Amidst the flux and kerfluffle of these energy bursts—high and low—we call our lives, there is a behavioral consistency in each of us that is sobering. What is it in that core of an individual self that appears to be so utterly unfailing? Why am I me, making my way through my life by doing me-things? Why is Ma who she is? Why are you *you*? Why do you do those you-things? And will you continue to do them as you grow old? What stable stuff is anybody's *me* made up of?

Of course I have a theory, but let me start with an example. Call it a baseline memory.

I am perhaps seven, perhaps six; it's the fifties. It's the middle of the afternoon on a Saturday. My father has just come downstairs from a nap. He's in his stocking feet and a little groggy still, and my mother has ambushed him at the bottom of the stairs. She is haranguing him, harping on and on, her voice growing louder and shakier until she is yelling like a fist in his face.

It is clear that while he was sleeping she has been fuming about some injustice, real or imagined, stirring herself up to a tornadic fury. And she blows—and the storm is merciless.

I've flopped sideways into my father's old green chair over by the brick fireplace with its white-enameled mantel, and I'm looking out the front window through the blinds. In the bright sunshine across the street, our neighbors, the Tullos, are fancied up for something, clean and pressed, scrubbed shiny as the bright side of tinfoil, and the four of them are heading towards their light blue sedan which is parked in their driveway. Mr. Tullo holds the passenger door open for his wife, closes it solidly when she is settled in and walks around to the driver's side. Vince and Rosemarie have let themselves into the back seat, each from a separate door, and now all four doors are shut firmly and the engine is running. My mother, just a body's length in front of me, has her feet spread, her legs braced. Her arms are flying, flinging curses and accusations as though they are cook-pots and carving knives.

And, after a bewildered, muzzy moment, and for the first time I can remember, my father engages. She has caught him unawares, half-asleep. He has been pulled out of his comfortable haze by a harridan and this time, for some reason, he fights back. His voice is raised so that she will hear him over her own. And then suddenly, as though it's fight-back-or-die, he is angry as hell, he's had enough.

Ma's stream of vituperation is transformed into a violent argument. Who knows what it's about this time. His drinking has some part in it though, that's for certain. Perhaps, in her mind, he has embarrassed her in front of a neighbor again. Perhaps he's failed to do something she asked: give her a phone message, or go to the store, go to work, soak the beans, defrost the tamales, mow the lawn. Maybe he was out too late last night. Or it might have been one of the times he'd been gone for a week or two and had returned during the night while she slept. Or maybe there just isn't enough money, there is never enough money. He might have let her down in any one of a million possible ways. He's heard them all.

But one thing I recall sharply enough to still cause me stark, unambiguous pain is that my father does not defend himself. I have never heard him defend himself. Instead, he is yelling at her to get out of his goddamn face, to stop her incessant litany of complaint, to shut the hell up and leave him alone, for chrissakes, he's just woken up, he doesn't even know what the hell she's screaming about.

But she doesn't let up. She has gotten the rise out of him she has always wanted. It's as though she says, "See? See? What did I tell you? You're a bastard. You're a drunk, you're a selfish, goddamn bum." And the shouting accelerates again and the ambient rage continues to swell.

And for the first time I'm really frightened. I feel as though my father is going to step from the landing onto the living room floor; I'm certain my mother is going to take those two steps forward that will put the two of them face-to-face. It is as though they are being drawn toward one another by the vacuum of their mutual fatigue, their shared disappointment in their rotten lives—lives so incredibly different from what each must have dreamt. It is as though there is an arc of electricity between them and both of them are going to burn.

I am the only one who can stop this before it becomes physical. I don't know if I'm crying; I don't think I am. But I'm frightened, scared enough to act. I leap from the chair and run around my out-of-control mother, who can't even see me through her deluge of invective.

Perhaps my father thinks I am running to him, I don't know. But I stop just before I get to him, at the telephone table against the bottom stair railing. I snatch the old rotary phone, pull its short, straight cord as far as it'll go and slam my behind down on the carpeted landing, the solid black bulk of the telephone in my lap, my back to my father. I hold the receiver up with my left hand for them both to see. I have my right index finger in the dial hole.

Even the air is holding still—soundlessness, sudden and as sharp as a shot mirror.

Facing my mother, I shout over the dial tone that's beaming into the air over my head and into the larger silence, "If you don't stop, I'm going to call the police." The emergency number is written on a scrap of white paper, Scotch-taped to the flat space between the upright cradles for the heavy receiver. It is there because I am often home alone. I want to be heard now. She has to hear me. They must be stopped before someone gets hurt, before everything comes apart.

Everything is coming apart.

The air in the room now has the weight of a thick San Francisco fog. A loaded cloudiness, this one fraught with shock. Then, suddenly, it is as though they have both sucked it in, taken it back, the fog, the silence, and I am poised there, the receiver in my raised hand, my finger on the dial, sitting in that vacuum, a bell jar of my own between my parents.

It seems to take a long time for them to re-enter their bodies. And when they do, my mother's is filled with fresh venom. I can see her thinking. She is growing larger in front of me. I know what's going to happen. There is nothing I can do. She hisses at my father, who has not spoken since I spoke out. She gathers her control; she has the power now. She straightens her back until she is no longer the crouched, spitting thing she has been. She says to my father in her most withering and blame-filled voice, "Now look what you have done."

Call it the wisdom of hindsight if you will, but I swear that, even at the time, I understood the dynamic. What they say is true, that the last-chance children of older parents are often the little adults they are said to be. My mother, she'll tell you this herself, had to be strong because nobody else was: She always said that. My father was quiet and gentle and sad and would leave us many times before he would leave us for good. That day, I found it shamefully impossible not to acknowledge Ma's seamless psychological slam-dunk. What was she then? forty-five? forty-six? She'd had a lot of practice. I was still a beginner, but I was learning how to survive in a household psychologically configured as ours was. I was getting good, but good for a child who also had to be strong and had found a different avenue to strength: silence. It was clearly my best defense—unless I was expected to be grateful for something and then I was as mewlingly appreciative as any make-believe child. I was capable of swooning blissfully with gratitude I did not feel. Those were the viable options as I saw them, and yet that day I spoke out. I take credit for a heavily out-of-character moment. It was the first time ever I felt some modicum of power—the clout of "cute" had disappeared when I'd become actively verbal—so, in a way, I had won, but it had cost me too dearly: I had to live with the fact that in speaking up I had given, foreseeably or not, the advantage to my mother. I had set my father up to take the full brunt of her rage. Though she had my grudging admiration for her opportunistic skill, as always my identification, my sympathies, and my broken heart went with my father. The man never had a prayer.

Of course, we can construct explanations for just about every behavior, rather in the way some of us are able to manipulate statistics to support an argument we favor, but because behavior is still the bottom line for the Ptolemaic/Copernican paradigms, herein lies the Ptolemization: The model remains the same, the factoids are manipulated to support the argument. The argument is that Ma is blame-free.

And she's tough.

My mother suffers neither humbling nor fools with any grace whatsoever; her pride is a bitch and pitiless in the extreme. In her present situation, being cared for with five other elderly people in the residential care home, she is suffering greatly from loss and outrage; it's horrible and my heart is sore for her. And when I am crying, myself, to a friend, a retired professional in the gerontological field, she says, "Your mother is throwing a tantrum," which rings true, very true, in fact, but not entirely true—because I want to believe there's something deeper going on as well. I know my mother, it seems to me, the way I know myself. And I know, too, that, despite resembling my mother in too many discomfiting ways to enumerate, in " . . . an absence of any system that might transform the / sadness of the present into a hopeful future," I would give into death without a struggle, welcome the anodyne, and bestow upon it my grateful and profane blessing on my way out (Prevallet, 43).

I am forced to marvel, again, at Ma's ability to endure.

So, after this new, less-than-independent stage of her life begins—and because I am, at sixty-one, the only living relative she has not banished from her world—I started doing some reading, thinking it might help me deal with her in some way, just give me enough understanding to lend me the patience to do what I had to. But what I discovered was far less head-on than the how-to I'd been searching for, and is, to my mind, and without a doubt, the precise explanation for my mother's ability to shed blame like the proverbial duck sheds the proverbial water.

I knew the name *Piaget*, thought he had something to do with childhood development, but never looked into his work because I am childless and, frankly, like my mother, don't care much for children. And then, in the old gerontology textbook I'd picked up and was trying hard to care about, I found an explanation of the source of Ma's Ptolemization, and it made such sense to me that I want to quote it here.

According to the Swiss psychologist, Jean Piaget (1970), the critical question in human development is how people intellectually adjust to the world. Piaget argues that all people are in continuing interaction with the environment and, as a result, they develop or construct a series of schemes (concepts or models) for coping with the world. Piaget employs this term, *schemes,* to describe cognitive structures that people develop for dealing with specific situations in their environment (Kart 165).

I read this and every pinball clang and shrill whistle in me sounded at the same time—not just regarding Ma, though certainly first for Ma, but for myself as well. And only then for everyone else. It is one of those articulations I seem to have suspected the gist of all my adult life, but was never able to any satisfactory degree articulate myself. I'm professionally trained, after all, in nothing much, certainly neither psychology nor gerontology. I'm just a daughter and a writer, who has more than once observed the repetitive dynamic, and this concept of the unfaltering self is simply one of the themata that swirl incessantly inside my head.

And whether Piaget's theories are in or out of favor now—I understand these things come and go—this is truth for me. As is this quote which is attributed to Einstein but is probably apocryphal: "Common sense is the collection of prejudices acquired by age eighteen" (Calaprice 481). Who wouldn't become prejudiced in favor of, and develop, those behaviors that get us what we need? Isn't that essential common sense? And, hence, our Piagetian schemes. Simone de Beauvoir, in her *The Coming of Age*, an encyclopedic, un-put-downable tome on aging, supports this in more general terms:

> From birth until the age of eighteen or twenty the organism's development tends to increase its chances of survival: it grows stronger and more resistant; its resources and its possibilities increase.

Of course, then she tells us in the same paragraph that senescence sets in earlier than we might have thought:

> The individual's physical abilities, taken as a whole, reach their peak at about twenty. During the first twenty years, therefore, the sum of the changes in the organism is for the good (11).

It's news none of us are probably thrilled to hear, but, news, nevertheless, that does argue for the building-up of our modes of self-preservation in those first two decades.

I think what really happens as we age, then, is akin to that your-nose-keeps-growing-until-you-die bit of misinformation we've probably all heard.

Here's de Beauvoir to explain what will really happen to your nose:

> The loss of teeth brings about a shortening of the lower part of the face, so that the nose, lengthened vertically by the atrophy of its elastic tissues, comes nearer to the chin (26).

So it doesn't grow, not literally, but does become larger, or more spatially significant, on your face. And I suppose the bad news is that your earlobes also increase in size as we suspected, but, again, they do not grow in terms of cellular growth. And if these two tidbits of information make you put one hand on your nose and one on your good ear and begin to worry, you might want to skip de Beauvoir's page twenty-six altogether. There's far more and much worse to find there. But all this is to say that perhaps our signature schemes are not literally exacerbated as we grow older. Perhaps it's that our filters atrophy or are jettisoned so that, like the nose becoming more prominent on the face, they take up more of our waking hours than they did before.

I would say that while our secondary, exterior behaviors may change as we age—alcoholics may sober up, overeaters may slim down, smokers may stop cold turkey and develop an intense, even anti-social dislike of cigarette smoke—the basic nature of our schemes, our life-maneuvers, doesn't change much. In fact, they appear *more so*: more of what they already are. It's almost as if these core dynamics become magnified or exaggerated, as if we're somehow distilled, the dilutions of secondary behaviors drained away, and the primary ones moving to and fully occupying the forefront.

M.F.K. Fisher on this:

> I have formed a strong theory that there is no such thing as 'turning into' a Nasty Old Man or an Old Witch. I believe that such people, and of course they are legion, were born nasty and witch-like, and that by the time they were about five years old they had hidden their rotten bitchiness and lived fairly decent lives until they no longer had to conform to rules of social behavior, and could revert to their original horrid natures.

> This theory is hard to prove, because by the time a person begins to show his true-born nature, most of the people who knew him when he was little have either died or gone into more immediate shadows. I still believe that it is probable, however. I have lived long enough to keep a sharp eye on a few of my peers, and they bear out almost frighteningly the same natures they first promised us to end with (234).

Hilarious! And harsh. And, really, right up my mother's funny-bone alley. She'd love it. And she'd appreciate it as long as she believed it wasn't her that Fisher was talking about.

Let me give you another example of this particular scheme from long after my father had left for good. Ma must have been in her mid-fifties at the time; I was probably a freshman in high school. She had managed to buy, on her own—a pretty spectacular accomplishment for a PBX operator—a tiny, stucco, one-story house closer to both the school and her primary job—and in a better part of town—than the apartment we'd been living in since my dad moved out and our house had been sold.

The sun was out. Ma was in a good mood. I think we were going to Hillsdale Mall to shop the sales ("I'm going to knock down any old lady who gets in my way," my mother was fond of saying, and then she'd laugh). She backed her old bronze boat of a four-door Pontiac out of the narrow driveway and then paused momentarily to dig in her purse for a hanky. She took a swipe at her nose before throwing the car into *Drive*—and that's when she saw the birds. She glanced to her right where I sat, no doubt sullenly, in the passenger's seat, and she did what she loved most to do: She tried to scare the hell out of me. She hunched down over the wheel, held on tight with both hands, her elbows sticking out and her face half-hidden. She made guttural *vroom-vroom* noises, then she gunned the engine a couple of times for real. The car shot forward towards the little clutch of what I now know were house sparrows, who were pecking away at some unseen, obviously plentiful and edible, thing in the road. At the same time that we watched those birds make their way upward into the next leg of their already too-short lives, we felt—and heard—a single, small, sickening thump. I cried out, I'm sure, in that dipthonged whine that lived so close to the surface back then, newly overripe, as it was, with its burden of resentment and disgust. Ma stopped the car right there in the middle of the road—an act very unlike her—slammed the gearshift into *Park*, then took a breath, and opened her door slowly, leaving it gaping wide into the street while she stepped out of the car with the poise of the lady she so often claimed to be and she walked to the front of the car. The engine was still running. I'd leapt out immediately and gotten there first—

but I'd imagined the sad little scene so clearly before I saw it for real that the nausea that rose at the sight was redundant. A small bird was wedged into the maw of the car, skull crushed, neck obviously broken, the smallest trickle of blood running from its open beak. Ma hesitated for quite a while as her shock receded and her crying began. She took a hugely deep, shuddering breath, and then stepped forward and she gently pulled the bird away from the grill with both hands. Little gray tufts of powder down stuck to the pitted chrome. I don't remember where she set the bird—it must have been in the narrow weedy stretch between the curb and sidewalk that marked our neighborhood as the lower echelon of the better, but not quite good, side of town—and through her sobs she kept trying to explain that the birds were supposed to have seen her coming. They were supposed to have gotten out of the way. It was a joke. She hadn't meant to kill anything. She was just playing, she said, just trying to frighten me. It wasn't about the birds at all. It was a game. She'd never hurt an animal. Never! She was just trying to shake me up a bit.

If we went to the mall instead of backing up and pulling forward into the driveway we had not so long ago backed out of, I don't recall the trip.

Ma's teariness came and went well into the evening, but by the next morning, it seemed, she was done. In the kitchen, still unshowered and in her pink robe, her coffee mug raised halfway to her lips, she said to me, as though it were a lesson I needed to learn, "Goddamn stupid bird." She said, "He should have been paying attention, he should have gotten out of the way." She moved towards me just a little, as if being closer would make her point more powerfully. "What the hell was the matter with him?" she went on. "What was he thinking? He was stupid! Something else would have gotten him sooner or later anyway, he was so stupid," she said and took a too-big gulp of her too-hot coffee and then slammed the near-full cup down on the tile drain board with a *crack!* that startled us both. A wave of black coffee leapt from the cup onto her fingers where it trickled down the back of her hand in two crooked streams. She looked at that hand as though it belonged to someone else—a look I knew well enough—and then, angrily, she wiped it on the pocket of her robe. "Goddamn bird," she said. "Stupid, goddamn bird."

I have come to understand that my mother believes she is the victim of everything and that her unconscious—I'm certain they are unconscious—deflections and displacements make her feel cleansed of any responsibility for bad choices. I know this is true and yet there must be more to it, because, as always, there is so very much I do not know.

My mother makes no secret of the fact that, since 1911, her birth, she has been nothing but the butt of one dirty trick of fate after another. Nothing at all has worked out in her favor—a piteous childhood, the Depression, the fact that no man she ever really loved had loved her back. She told me once that every single night of her childhood she'd waited for her real family to come and claim her. There she would be, living in a cold house with a huge, ragged hole in the wall where the furnace had been torn out, repossessed; or upstairs over a raucous, smoky speakeasy; or upstairs over the French restaurant, where the "rooms"—the whorehouse rooms—were on the same floor as her bedroom (she had to lock her door to keep the "gentlemen" out of her bed); or boarded out on some distant relative's farm down near San Jose for whole summers at a time with no visits from either of her divorced parents, no date set for seeing them again or for going home. She was really a princess, she said, but like everything else, that hadn't worked out.

No family of royals ever came to claim her for their own. I'm not saying her life has not been hard; it certainly has. She never graduated from high school, worked since she turned fifteen and supported the other family members until she got married, and after her marriage failed she worked two, sometimes three jobs to keep the two of us looking respectable and living decently. She was stronger and smarter, probably, than even she believes herself to have been—and smart too in those schemes that fed and still feed her most obvious protective dynamics. And—and she says this frequently—she'll be damned if she'll let the bastards finish her off. It's one of the very first things I learned about Ma: She will never let the bastards finish her off. And the bastards are everywhere.

She's tricky, though, because she can turn on a dime, as she used to say about her fabulous silver and white '57 Chevy with its white walls and the snappy Continental Kit. What I am saying is that I have observed three basic modes my mother is capable of functioning within, any one of which may be in the forefront at any given moment: When her spirits are up, when things are going her way, she is hilariously funny; it is true that her humor has teeth, that it's generally expressed at someone else's expense, but she's genuinely funny: She can slay me with her funniness; she is also profoundly depressed—as one would be, being the victim of everything; and underneath it all, she is rage-filled and bitter—this anger evidently being the charge that keeps her from giving in to her depression. She is, instead, alternately, funny, fiery, and furious, and brooks no interference whatsoever within the world she has chosen to make for herself. Anyone who dares question the logic of her scheme is quickly cast off. She is the Sheriff of the place she's created for herself and in that very small domain it's Ma's way or the highway. There are no real losses, then, because the smaller the world, the more easily it is contained and arranged to suit her. Anything other is a liability.

Yet even with all that in mind, it still took quite some time for us to get where we are now. I left California about thirty years ago; she has never forgiven me for that. I was in my early thirties at the time; she, in her early seventies, living alone in that same house in which I passed my high school years. And until about a month before her one-hundredth birthday, she was still living pretty much on her own.

She had a neighbor in his forties—the man is a saint—who lived next door. He watched over Ma, did chores for her, unbidden—not that she hadn't become dependent on him for all that he did, but she would not admit that she could never have stayed in her house without his help.

He got up on tall ladders and cleaned her gutters; he set out her trash each week, as well as the recycling; he installed her air conditioners in the summer and removed them and stored them for her in the winter; he found her a computer for email and ordering groceries; he called her from the market to see if he could pick up anything for her. Was she out of milk? bread? coffee? On Sundays she would find her favorite pastry, a Bear Claw, on a covered plate outside her front door. On Thanksgiving, a full meal, including pie and coffee, on a covered tray. On Christmas, a small decorated tree and a gift, and then later, her meal. He treated her as though she were his own mother who, by the way, was also in her nineties at the time, and lived about ten miles away, and who no doubt received at least equal devotion, despite the time taken for his attentions to his full-time job and his wife and daughter. But, as Ma points out every time we speak of him, which is every time we speak, "He came from a *good* family. His mother didn't have to work three jobs; she stayed home with her children, so the children turned out all right. I couldn't afford to stay home with you."

Ma also had a woman, I'll call her Maria, a bubbly Guatemalan woman in her thirties who, though she'd been in the States for about five years, spoke almost no English. Ma's deal with Maria was that Maria would spend nights at Ma's house, clean the house once a week and prepare some meals, along with giving Ma a helping hand with showering and dressing. But Ma was paying her an embarrassing pittance in addition to her room and board. So, Maria, at any given time, had at least two, often three, other part-time jobs, so it never went too well.

There were a large number of angry confrontations—Ma in the denunciatory lead, of course—and Maria was moving in and out pretty regularly because Ma kept firing her and then hiring her back. The last move-out was followed up by Ma's accusations that Maria had been turning tricks in the living room after Ma had gone to bed, and that she had stolen all of Ma's clothes hangers the last time she left. And then they appeared to have worked it out again. Maria returned but was still at her other jobs during the day when Ma wanted to go to the market, or Maria would have to be elsewhere when Ma had scheduled a doctor's appointment, and Ma'd already been given a "time out" from the county's Ready Wheels transportation system for the elderly because she had canceled too many rides with short notice a few too many times; taxis, she said, would no longer come to her house when she called. Anything that had to be done out-of-house had to be done with Maria. In the end, everything was chalked up to "I don't think she understands a word I say." Which was no doubt true.

All the while, though, Ma's muscles continued to atrophy; her legs were weakening even more; her circulation was diminishing; her benign tremors increasing and becoming, in a practical sense, less benign. Her hearing was pretty much gone even back then; she rarely heard the alarm clock go off, or the telephone or the doorbell ring. She'd burned up three or four tea kettles because she couldn't hear the whistle, as well as the entire Deluxe Set of Silver Seal Cookware by Guardian—which didn't have whistles—that she'd gotten when she got married. I was terrified she was going to burn herself up in the house. She couldn't hear the television if Maria was watching with her because she could only hear it at maximum volume and the noise gave Maria horrible headaches. That didn't matter much, in the end, though, because Maria only watched programs in Spanish, a language Ma doesn't understand at all. And Ma couldn't watch TV at night because the cranked-up volume kept Maria awake.

Ma'd been diagnosed years before with congestive heart failure—she used a walker and any physical exertion caused her to be short-of-breath and, if she didn't sit down quickly enough, she'd pass out. And her kidneys were just plain wearing out. She'd been making frequent—once, sometimes twice a month—ambulance trips to the hospital emergency room, the stepping up of her forays out into the enemies' world, for falls and frights and the effects of frequent and persistent bladder infections, and she was almost always sent, that same night or the following morning, the four or five miles home in a taxi. She was on a first name basis with the entire stable of paramedics and everyone in the hospital ER knew her and called her, as they should have, *Mrs. Jones*. But over time, as her visits seemed to multiply exponentially, and her demands to, age aside, "fix what was wrong" with her, became more strident, and some doctors and nurses, evidently, began to react to both Ma's tone of voice and what, they felt, was chronic misuse of the ER. It became clear, even to me, that their tones had slipped from concern to impatience, to the equivalent of *What the hell are you dying of this time, Mrs. Jones?* Ma, of course, became outraged, and though she continued to call for the ambulance she refused to let them take her to the hospital.

It was during this last, long bout of pneumonia that the bouncing back and forth between the hospital and the skilled nursing facility began. After about a month and a half full of calls telling me she was not progressing as the doctor thought she should, she called to say quite calmly: "The doctor just gave me ten days to live."

I arrived in California, breathlessly and beyond dread—I am still terrified of my mother and feel as though, quite literally, I'm drowning when we're in the same room. I had, despite my intentions not to, flown three thousand miles to comfort the woman who—though I had spoken with her, sometimes even calmly, at least once every week or two, sometimes maybe three if I got really busy or pissed off—I had not seen face-to-face in nearly twenty years.

I didn't recognize her, though she knew me immediately and called my name when I entered the six-bed room. She had lost nearly ninety pounds since I had last seen her; I had gained at least a third of that. She called to me from her wheelchair next to the *F* bed. She looked as though she'd been carved from a sweating bar of Ivory soap, but she was dressed, as she'd say, "to the teeth." She wore brown slacks with a sewn-in crease, a matching print pullover, a gold-tone necklace and earrings, and her nails were a bright, unchipped fire engine red. Her hair had been just washed and set by the resident beautician the night before.

I had planned to stay in California for two weeks, and did, and made a point of spending four to five hours a day with her. She was in reminiscent mode and told me stories of her family, some of which I had not heard before. I wrote them down. In my off hours I did what Ma asked. I began the job of clearing out the house so it could be put on the market (with the understanding that Maria would be allowed to live there until the house closed). Ma has always been a lover-of-stuff, as, alas, am I. She loves her stuff, though, the way other women love their families. And now she was frantic about her belongings—and she didn't really have a lot: a handful of objets d'art from nineteenth century San Francisco, some old lithos and prints, a busty nude in a cigar frame, some small statues from the French restaurant, and three small tables handed down from her family along with furniture she'd purchased at auctions or second-hand shops. It was made clear to me that these things had to be valued (not evaluated for sale, but valued *by me*). In my entire life, it had never occurred to me that I would someday own my mother's belongings. They were so solidly *hers* that the thought never entered my mind even during those times I contemplated her passing. I tried to calm her, assured her that they would be lovingly cared for and wildly appreciated. I told her how grateful I was that she was passing them on to me. And then between The UPS Store and United Van Lines I had them sent to my home. I had no idea where I was going to put the stuff and no idea, either, whether I could live with it—would it put a pall on my new, started-over, pretty-darn-good life? But it was on its way. Her sleigh bed and armoire were left in her bedroom. Maria would take the furniture in her own room with her when she left.

Ma's jewelry became an obsession as well. She wanted me to bring it all to the nursing home so she could sort through it, tell me what was the good stuff, what was costume jewelry, though she swore that most of the good stuff had been stolen by people who had come into her house: cleaners and ambulance people, firemen, fixers, and those men-friends of Maria's; they'd all come into her house, she kept reminding me. I found, mostly, the wide sterling silver bracelets I'd sent to her over the years—she'd always loved big, fat bracelets—and a few small gold chains she'd bought herself, her grandfather's Masonic watch fob, which, she'd told me months and months ago, had been stolen by the lady, the gardener's ex-wife, who had been caring for her during one of Maria's moved-out periods. She'd given me her own wedding set decades ago; I had it in a drawer in my bedroom at home, but never wore it. I never even wore my own. And she had four good rings she wanted me to take: my great-aunt's solitaire engagement ring, which, I had to admit, was quite a knockout—though it had a small hole in the side of the stone. How do you get a little hole like that in a *diamond*? There was, too, the oval of diamonds, fabulous and old fashioned—with a huge chunk cut out from the carved band where it had been cut off her finger on one of her hospital stays. Her own mother had had it made from *her* mother's diamonds. And there were two diamond and gemstone dinner rings—one emerald, one with three small rubies—that had belonged to either her mother or grandmother, I couldn't get that straight. The emerald, she warned me, was a phony, probably bottle-glass; her mother had hocked the real stone during the Depression.

I have all that now. They are my things. I can't sell any of them. The rings are beautiful, I've worn them, once or twice, enjoyed them, and will again. The rest of the jewelry, the bracelets I'd sent her, several chains, a cupful of earrings, I've given to friends who might wear them. I have four small tables, a very old, carved dresser, her hope-chest-sized Japanese chest with her name carved into the lid, and my great-aunt's Franciscan apple-pattern dishes and serving pieces which, despite my almost lifelong loathing of them, Ma had been saving and adding to for me. Her bulky dining room set—credenza, china cabinet, table, and chairs—I shipped to a young friend as a wedding gift; Ma was thrilled that it would be used and loved and my friend and her husband-to-be were thrilled to have it. So, most of her belongings are now settled in my home, squeezed in between my own mismatched pieces which I adore.

However, my mother has yet to be settled.

When I try to speak with her on the phone during one of her crying episodes or a convulsive eruption of, probably justified, self-pity, I would swear she could not possibly live through the night, that no breathing thing could survive such paroxysms and continue to breathe. More than a handful of times, after these calls, I've said to my husband, *If she keeps this up, she won't survive the night* and yet she does keep it up, lives through it, and inevitably has a great many particulars to report about the event, the physical repercussions, along with general injustices, and her assorted abandonments, to whoever will listen, the following day. My mother, apparently, has a heart akin to a John Deere tractor; it appears nothing can take her down. And in addition to the nights of my dire predictions, she has, in the last twenty years, pulled through at least four physician-asserted, imminent-death scenarios. I would be very surprised to find there were not at least a dozen more, because long periods of time go by during which Ma doesn't want me to know her business, and, frankly, I can live with that. I already know Ma can hold a grudge for a lifetime, and once her opinion is formed there's no changing it. Her endurances, physical, psychological, and emotional, began to take on a mythical quality when I was quite young and seem only to have gotten more convincingly mythic as I've gotten older, and I fear that when she does die, despite my familiarity with her various visceral and emotional exhaustions, I am going to be taken unawares. But her body is wearing out—no one lives forever—and if *wolf!* seems to have become her cry, it's not her fault. A passage from M.F.K. Fisher's *Sister Age* keeps coming back to mind and, even with my dreadful memory and convenient ability to forget what I don't want to know, I cannot shake it: "She was," Fisher said, speaking of a character in a piece called "Notes on a Necessary Pact," "at last, ready to die, and nothing was able to kill her" (224). Ma, I'm certain, is ready; she just can't allow herself to give the bastards the satisfaction.

And the bastards are everywhere. They run the healthcare system.

Piaget, the gerontology book tells me, broke cognitive development into four stages (sensorimotor, preoperational, concrete operational, and formal operational), but a fifth stage was added by others later: postformal thought. This kind of thought "is characterized by an increased tolerance of ambiguity, acceptance of more than one correct answer to problems, and the understanding that reality constraints are important" (166). Those first two elements sound a lot like Keats's idea of *negative capability*, and I think I've always lived with that. For Ma, though, it's always been: *Something is or it isn't; shit or get off the pot.* However, that third component of the description, that dose of reality therapy, is what Ma is currently receiving. And it's horrifying to witness; going through it can only be an order of magnitude worse.

Ma's schemes, to use the Piagetian term, preclude *accommodation* which Kart defines as "the process of changing one's knowledge or schemes to make a better match with the real world" (165). Ma is not one to *accommodate*. She has always had a slippery relationship with the real world—but now that real world has changed and her body is trapped in the alternate, undesirable universe. She spends her time now trying to figure out just how they're going to take advantage of her and getting just as upset as she would if the projected events were really taking place. But she's in the system now and the system, as we all know, doesn't give a rat's ass about Ma's schemes.

One truth is, however, that there are many caring individuals within that system who *do* care about Ma's comfort and well-being; I've met many, and most of them—in particular the hospice social workers and a half-dozen healthcare aids—have gone a long way out of their way to make Ma feel comfortable and catered-to—they have visited on their own time, sought out information she wanted, spent their own money on cushions and contraptions they felt might help Ma settle in. And she has not settled in.

It appears to be true—at least to me—that it's not that we cannot change but that in the absence of some generous insight or revelation, some re-visioning of our selves or our lives, we *do* not change. Our defenses are in place; they protect us from the assaults from beyond our pale. That is the scheme's action-imperative.

> They [the elderly] have to make a very great effort to acquire what is known as a set—an attitude, a habit of mind—for they are wholly dominated by the mental patterns adopted earlier and they lack flexibility. Once they have adopted the set they are most reluctant to let it go. Even when they are faced with problems to which the set no longer has the least reference, they still cling to it. This means that their possibilities of learning are very much reduced (de Beauvoir 34).

And Ma is not learning. And I can see her side. I can hear her voice. Why should she at this late stage? Until now she has managed; she's kept her world so small that she never had to learn the skill of accommodation. Change is more than inconvenient, it's painful, stressful—and heaven knows she already has enough stress—and it lets the enemy in. Ma's behaviors have taught her, her *experience* has taught her, it's unnecessary to accommodate anyone. She's always been stronger than everyone else. She can get along fine without the enemy, thank you very much.

> But this defense that [s]he erects against the arbitrariness of others and against the perils that fill the world by reason of this arbitrariness is itself in danger, since it depends upon the will of the outside world (de Beauvoir 469).

It's at least a triple job, then: to recognize that the scheme is no longer viable;

to unlearn it; to lose the scheme as well as the comfort of habit, of mindlessly falling back on the scheme. All of this at the same time now as having been thrown, bodily—and to her own great surprise—into the enemies' world. It does seem too much to ask. Work with what she's got? "Screw that," she told me. "I'm paying *them*; they're sure as hell not paying me." And suddenly she seems stronger. "Let *them* change."

She's caught in that crux where the forces of habit and the forces of necessity butt heads. Both forces are strong. Whether she is unwilling, or unable, to make the adjustment, I really don't know, but my money's on *unwilling*. It's the perfect set-up for a victim of everything. And if she's paying them, she is the princess after all, they should produce *what* she needs *when* she needs it.

The toilet is broken in her room now and because it's a holiday weekend the owner won't have the plumber come until Tuesday. That's four days she'll have to use the toilet that is next door to her room. It's too inconvenient for what she's paying. She's looking for another place to live. And I do understand the difficulty in changing a life's worth of tactics, but I've had to eat crow a few times myself and when I tell her so, she says, "I'm not *you*." Which is true.

She says I have no self-respect. I say nothing at all. Habits are hard to break for all of us.

My mother's deeply ingrown schemes—and oh I've got my own set I'll have to deal with, I assure you—are eating her alive. It's those bastards, the ones out there (the fate-bastards? the ones who have singled her out to work her whole life against insurmountable odds to prove . . . what?) who have made her do the things she's done. And now my mother has been released from hospice care, which means she has a life-expectancy that exceeds six months. She no longer has traces of her pneumonia, though I am told that she has "interstitial lung disease." Physically, she is growing stronger, though, paradoxically, her body is wearing out. Every time I speak with her she says, "This has been the worst day of my life." Every single day, now, is the worst day of her life. "I'm all alone," she says. "I have no one. They know that and take advantage of me," she tells me again.

"You've never been one not to speak up," I remind her.

"They're all crooks, the bastards," she says. "They won't let me go home because all my furniture is gone."

I swear that if I tried to explain to her about how I saw our schemes shaping our lives, she would, first, become incensed, and then she'd tell me. *You think you know so much. You spend more time with books than with people—what do you know? You may know books. But you don't know life.* That one I've heard before. This is her new addendum: *And you don't know what it's like here. You aren't here.* She actually did say, as clearly as anything at all, when

I was there: "I hid so much from you. I sheltered you too much. You don't know how hard it was . . . and now you have no common sense, none at all." She said, "Now you'll have to grow up."

My mother will move towards that final light—be it the ladder to heaven or the final shutting down of the optic nerve—with all her schemes and her broken pride in place and, while she's doing so, she'll complain that the light's too bright, that it's hurting her eyes. She'll be shouting, *What asshole's in charge of the lighting?* She will by no means go gently, and death, that bastard, will not have dominion until there's not a single cell left that's up to fighting. I think over and over again of how Fisher phrased the end for that character who could not die: "when her long empty life has finally wept itself to a close" (Fisher 9).

Ma is nothing if not consistent. I think she might have been about eighty when she told me someone had asked about her "golden years." She was furious. "Golden years?" she said to me on the phone. "*Golden years?* They're the goddamn shits, that's how they are, and don't let anyone tell you otherwise. The absolute, total, goddamn *shits*."

It's going to be interesting to see how it plays out with me. I don't know myself as well as I ought to. Perhaps I don't know her as well as I think I do either. I sometimes believe my own stories; I rarely believe hers. I'm selfish and, when angry, can have a tongue that's murderously sharp. I try not to speak in anger. I try to be kind, but I am not always kind. And is it too much to ask that this essay be kind? How could it be? But perhaps it could be sympathetic, if tough, or at least realistic. I hope it is. Aging itself, that moving beyond that instant of peak promise and of dropping into the downswing, senescence, is pretty unkind itself, if you think about. Romanticizing the difficulties of old age is criminal negligence. When you are a hundred, you have traded the bulk of your future for the bulk of your past. When you're sixty-one, you do the same thing, but it's a slower dawning, a recognition without the swift kick to the head that you get at one hundred. And you pray for less of a wildfire at the end. You pray for a Copernican ending, a little comfortable warmth, because in the end, the real end, it doesn't matter in the least whether one's passivity is a learned response to another's aggressions, it doesn't matter that that one was faced with something else that caused her to conjure her own aggressiveness. I'm passive. She's aggressive. That's the scheme of things.

And strangely, the sentences above were the plan for the end of this essay. But in a moment of procrastination—whether due to frustration or depression or just waiting for the impulse to give up on this essay to pass— whatever the inciting sensation was, I needed to get away from the writing of this essay for just for a while, just to catch my breath because I felt like I was drowning. I picked a book off the stack by my place on the sofa. I'd been wanting to read it; the cover was lovely, the author's name was familiar and I wanted to know her work. It had been sitting there for months, waiting for me to get to it. So, with the black dog half on my lap and already half-asleep and the brown one on the floor compulsively licking my bare left foot, I drag the cover of the book across my belly, dusting the top of it in one swipe on my tee shirt.

And then I open Kristin Prevallet's *[I, AFTERLIFE] [ESSAY IN MOURNING TIME]*. This is from "[Mythology]" in Part One:

> In time there are contraries and opposites.
> In the sky there is either a savior or a flaming ball of fire.
> The son and the sun are one and the same; they exist
>   simultaneously but in different forms.
> One and the other are one and the same. (3)

Only twice in my life have I heard voices that, surely, weren't really there. The first time was when I was trying so hard to believe in God that I was in a strain, squeezing and squeezing my eyes shut as if God could be squeezed out of me; that time I heard angels laughing at my effort. The other time, many, many years later I was coming out of a night's sleep, half-awake, trying to locate my day, and I heard a voice, genderless but strong and convincing. It said, "She did the best she could." And for a long time after that I knew it was true.

WORKS CITED

Calaprice, Alice and Freeman Dyson. *The Ultimate Quotable Einstein*. Princeton University Press: Princeton, 2010.

de Beauvoir, Simone, Patrick O'Brien, trans. *Coming of Age*. W.W. Norton & Co.: NY, 1996.

Fisher, M.F.K. *Sister Age*. Vintage Books Edition, Random House: NY, 1984.

Gorham, Sarah. "Be There No Human Here." Miller, Wayne and Phong Nguyen, eds. *Pleiades*: 31.2. pp 85-95. Pleiades Press: Warrensburg, MO, 2011.

Kart, Cary S. *The Realities of Aging: An Introduction to Gerontology*, Fifth Edition. Allyn and Bacon: Boston, 1981.

McBride, Karyl, Ph.D. *Will I Ever Be Good Enough? Healing the Daughters of Narcissistic Mothers*. Free Press: NY, 2008.

Prevallet, Kristin. *[I, AFTERLIFE] [ESSAY IN MOURNING TIME]* Essay Press: Athens, OH, 2007.

Zizek, Slavoj. *The Sublime Object of Ideology. The Essential Zizek*. Verso: NY, 2008.

SOME NOTES ON MAKING POEMS #1:
BEGINNING THE BEGINNING

Where to begin a series of short columns on making poems? In contemplating this opening installment, the possibilities seemed endless—and, even as I write this, alternatives are winging crazily through my mind.

But I have to begin somewhere, and I choose to begin at the beginning of the beginning. Yes, I really do understand that the writer's entire lifetime-before-the-poem goes into the making—but right now I'm talking about those few minutes . . . seconds? instants? recognizable as *ignition*. That beginning of the beginning.

What goes on in the mind when a nascent poem sparks? What do you experience in those moments before the pen hits the paper or the fingers the keyboard? when you recognize a poem has launched itself at the edge of your consciousness?

There are, no doubt, as many ways to recognize the poem-impulse as there are unwritten poems, but most of us are extraordinarily consistent. I have one friend who says she knows she's going to write a poem when she experiences a certain kind of emptiness, one that words might fill.

My own experience is the opposite: I tend to undergo a moment of startle and a fullness, an internal resonance that I know is a possibility beginning its move out into the world—a sudden recognition, the quickening of a found image or a particular rhythm, both preverbal impulses; or sometimes an articulated image or phrase—verbal but uncontextualized.

How do you move from that tremor of recognition towards the poem? You lean into it, write towards it. You listen; you let that initial bit of resonance lead and you follow nonjudgmentally.

It's a first draft; let your critical faculties take a break. Open yourself up to the possibilities, the ones that emanate from the spirit in you that observes and does not calculate worth. Listen to what comes to you and catch what you can on paper. You can work it hard, revise, and edit later.

But if you are not feeling that spark and still want to write? Seek surprise. And when you find it, your poem begins.

How to get to that point?

Some poets find prompts (writing assignments) given by someone else helpful (there's a being-taken-by-surprise in that, one that may take you to your own quickening). And many poets simply brainstorm a topic, explore and explode an aspect of some topical material until something catches fire.

Some find that reading favorite poems sets them on their way, some that reading work new to them or outside their comfort zone (either topic or style) may spark some new direction.

Another possibility is to write a poem in response to another poem. Some poets like to springboard their writing from a prose quote. Sometimes a poem emanates from a reaction to world or local events, news found in the dailies or on the television or radio or from your own, more intimate, life.

Most times when you write with discovery in mind, the poem's true subject will finally burst forth. If it fails to, and it may—particularly if you are not patient or receptive—you begin again.

It's my experience that the finest poems are written only peripherally to what we think of as knowledge—knowledge, if such a feat is possible, is a sorry thing, a bound thing, nailed to the floor; whereas the poems I find most effective are those that realize an urgent, momentary awareness or questioning. Those poems lift off the page. They fly or, at the very least, hover.

We write, I hope, with the spirit, the piece of us that wants to observe without prejudice, arms and eyes open—think Keats and his state of negative capability: ". . . when man is capable of being in uncertainties, Mysteries, doubts, without any irritable reaching after fact and reason."

Poems are not about telling the world something brand new; they're about taking what we know and making space for the expansion of sensibilities, about insights, however small, made within the art of the poem.

Be aware of possibility. Leave yourself open to both failure and change, to the opportunity for growth. Invite serendipity and recognition into your poem—you may find within yourself what you did not know you felt or even suspected. Just leave room for some new light to be shed for you in the process.

Do what you do. Then do more. Uncertainty is your way in.

SOME NOTES ON MAKING POEMS #2:
MATERIAL AND MATTER

"Poetry writes twice," says the poet Fanny Howe in "The Contemporary Logos." It's a vital notion for both poets and readers—and she states it beautifully.

One aspect that helps a poem *be* a good poem is the inclusion of at least two working levels, one visible and one invisible. You may hear this division articulated in any number of ways: the *literal* and the *figurative*, the *concrete* and the *abstract*, and, even sometimes, the *sensibilia* and the *sense*. I think of it in terms of *material* and *matter*.

The *material* of a poem is what's visible, the words you use, the story you tell, the thought you articulate—the *what you actually write down*.

Matter, on the other hand, is what's invisible, what the poem means, the invisible issue at hand, the abstraction at the heart of the emotional core that is evoked rather than articulated—the *what you write about*.

How do you marry the two? It works like this: For a reader, the matter of a poem is what is discovered via experiencing the material—as though the poet has created a very concrete, very visible little neighborhood (the material) through which she leads the reader on foot—right through the center of it, picking the gravel from her shoe—usually without ever giving that section of town a name. Resonance, then, often has its locus in that unspoken experience wrought from the poem. In other words, matter (invisible) takes on the form of material (visible).

As a writer, is there a rule about which the writer should wrestle with first? The matter? The material?

There is no *should*. There is only, after trial and error, what works for you.

We know by now that our writing processes vary from writer to writer, sometimes even from effort to effort for a single writer. My own tendency is to fashion my material on paper in order to discover my matter; I write to find out what I think. But Catherine Doty, an extraordinary contemporary narrative poet, says she thinks long on her material until she can "see" the matter. Only then does she begin to actually put words on paper—which is where the confluence, the poem itself, will take shape. You may have a different method that works for you, but as long as the two, the material and the matter, come together seamlessly in the end, we arrive at the same place: the functionally resonant poem, intact, and ready for a reader.

Let's look more closely. Doty's poem "Care," from her book *Momentum*, is a superb example of the matter/material dynamic.

> Unconscious, insensate, two-dimensional, punctured:
> this is the man I dream of as a child. I lean from my rocker
> to gentle the dull hair back, lift from a flowered bowl
> a dripping cloth, wring it and press it to the ribs and the wound
> between them. Someone else has plucked the bullet out, arranged
> the blankets and pillows. At the door, where they lean and yawn,
> those useless boots. My specialty is the moist hand over the heart,
> music of falling water. If he lives, a few spoonfuls of scrambled egg.
> He's any of the Three Stooges, or Circus Boy, or Mr. Greenjeans,
> that big straw hat on the bedpost. Every day at three or four or five,
> he climbs an elephant, or jigs a puppet, dresses to keep my interest,
> leaps to please me. He is a flicker of light, is all potential. Tonight,
> when I close my eyes he takes a bullet.

What is Doty's poem really about? Does it tell us its true subject via its concrete nouns? Is it about a rocking chair? Dull hair? A flowered bowl? Boots? Elephants? Puppets? Scrambled eggs? Blankets? Bullets? No, not really. Is it about the poem's cast? The Three Stooges? Circus Boy? Mr. Greenjeans? The man the speaker dreams of? No! Now look again. Are there any verbs that articulate the matter? *To be? To lean? To gentle* (note the elegant use of a common adjective as a verb!)? *To dream? To lift? To wring and press? Climb? Close?* No!

So where, then, can the true subject, the real what-the-poem-is-about, be? Or is a poem just a guessing game? A puzzle? A trick or a riddle? Well, a lesser poem than "Care" might be one or all of those things, but those are merely gimmicks-of-surprise that are not likely to hold any real value for a poem's meaning.

A good poem means more than all its words, including its title. The resonance takes place inside the reader, like a chemical reaction. So what, then, are the words of the poem supposed to do? What's their job if not to articulate the poem's real subject?

The words of a poem are the *summoners* of matter. They are words that work in concert and with other aspects of the poem to make the reader *feel* something. Together, in each poem's exact incarnation, they *mean* something they, in all likelihood, do not name. Going back to the metaphor of the town, the words, those summoners, are the neighborhood itself through which the reader passes—the dust streets or macadam roads, the houses big or small, pristine or needing a coat of paint, the landscapes litter-laden and scrappy or elegant or bare. So what, then, *is* the poem about if not its nouns and verbs?

I would say that Doty's poem "Care"—which appears, on the surface, to be about a young girl repeatedly dreaming that she saves and nurtures a wounded man—is about longing, about the desire to be needed and appreciated—and that the man that girl dreams of and her actions within that dream are merely *manifestations*, the material, of the poem's true subject which is longing.

When a writer presents a poem as *material* only, it is anecdotal—and anecdote is most often less than a poem. If the words add up to only what they *say*, the poem has somehow failed. The good poem is bigger than the poet's story.

It's not all that different from the way we live. In a poem, as in our lives, it's essential to move past the material. It's through experience that we find out what matters; our material is our way through to that deeper understanding.

A VOICE ANSWERING A VOICE: A CONVERSATION WITH RENÉE ASHLEY BY KIMBERLY NAGY

[From *Wild River Review*, April 2007]

Was not writing poetry a secret transaction, a voice answering a voice?
Virginia Woolf, *Orlando*

"Watch out for abstractions!" warned California-born poetess Renée Ashley, with a pitch of urgency only one or two tones below that exclaimed in a nearly missed automobile accident. Many years ago, I remember scribbling these words down during Fairleigh Dickinson's low-residency Creative Writing MFA program, where Ashley taught (and still teaches).

There's something about Renée Ashley that inspires vigorous note taking. Perhaps it's that Ashley exudes the appropriately intense awareness of a poet along with the steely precision of a detective. Utterly careful with the words she holds sacred, she is as resistant to vague abstractions as she is to overly "clever" wordplay and poems that in her words, "reek of competence."

Today, I sit across from Ashley at the Princeton Public Library where we meet to discuss her life and work—teaching and writing poetry. The award-winning poet's books include *Salt, The Various Reasons of Light, The Revisionist's Dream,* and *The Museum of Lost Wings.* Her novel, *Someplace Like This,* was published by Permanent Press in 2003. Ashley also received a fellowship from the National Endowment for the Arts, fellowships from the New Jersey State Council on the Arts, a Pushcart Prize, and the Charles Angoff Award from *The Literary Review.*

Ashley's call to write poetry came late and unexpectedly. "I mean you wouldn't even say the word in my household!" Ashley recounts. "I thought it was some big, scary, prissy, upper class, have-to-answer-questions-for-tests kind of thing." But one fateful writer's conference, she wandered away from the fiction writers into John Logan's poetry reading. She was amazed. "All of a sudden it dawned on me, it's somebody talking to somebody else! You know, that's what a poem is . . . And all of the fear and stigma dropped away."

Wild River Review: Let's start off with your poetry. I want to turn to a poem called "What She Wanted" from *The Revisionist's Dream*. It's an alternative reading of "Leda and the Swan" and what is interesting is how, instead of simply turning the tables, you offer a deeper complexity to the myth. I wondered if you could talk about that because your take is really not about Leda being a victim in any way. Some lines read . . .

> she wanted him
>
> like that. And she wanted him to risk
> any small thing—his life, for instance,
>
> if that were possible—to possess her.
> She wanted him to traverse oceans, cross
>
> silver bodies of perilous water: she wanted
> him reflected there, and vulnerable—blind
>
> to all but fierce need and the brave wind
> teasing her hair

Renée Ashley: Well, I think it's my bitch side. (laughs) I think you get tired of the same fiction. And you know, I'm a real opera nut. So, I've probably gone off the other end with the melodrama. But, she had a good right to be pissed. And instead of being taken advantage of, maybe she was, one could hope, in charge. I mean women get angry too, we get hungry for certain things too. And we don't often act upon them because, well if you ask my mother, because it's not "ladylike" or it's just not "good." You know, too much assertiveness, or wanting too much. I was brought up to not ask for anything. In all aspects of life, you take what you're given, keep your mouth shut, and deal. But I probably didn't remember this about myself until I wrote this poem. Anyway, this poem cracks me up. Perhaps because I think I'm being naughty!

WRR: Another poem, from your collection *Salt* is a poem, entitled "Why I

Never Came (Apology to My Mother)" —

> I was nineteen and that weekend I took
> your old Chevrolet to the coast where I goaded
> my sometimes lover, the one who put gin
> in his coffee, into beating me. His fists
> came like hammers, Mama, and when
> he had worn himself out on me, when he dragged me
> down the gravel road, I thought of you,
> and when he laid me like a carcass
> in the high grass at the side of Highway 1,
> and the sea beat a hundred yards away, inseparable
> from the throb of my body,
> I thought of you then, too
>
> but I did not come—you in the hospital
> dying and I did not come . . .

Can you talk a little bit about this poem as well?

RA: Well, that's one of the few poems I've written that came from my life. I was going out with this man because he had this wonderful dog (laughs), an Irish Wolfhound. My mom is ninety-five now, but she was in the hospital at the time having her gallbladder out. She kept saying she was dying. And the guy was a real jerk. He beat the hell out of me and left me on the side of the road. He really put gin in his coffee! Can you imagine? And his shoes were black and shiny and had pointy toes. What could I have been thinking? Oh, well. I sure loved that dog . . .

WRR: What did your parents do?

RA: Neither of them graduated from high school as far as I know. My father, when he worked, worked in a ball-bearing factory. But he was off on disability—he drank and was very ill. And they split up. My mother was a PBX operator. The old kind of telephone operator with all the cords and stuff. That's what she did. And secretarial work. Once she was the secretary at my grade school. That sucked.

WRR: Did your parents influence your writing, in your view?

RA: I don't think they did. My mother's unhappiness influenced the way I live, certainly. I guess having no books in the house was an "anti" influence, but I was an only child and my parents were a lot older. I mean my father was almost fifty when I was born; my mother was close to forty—and that wasn't as common in 1949 as it is today. Everyone thought they were my grandparents. It used to really piss my mother off. Anyway, back to the question: Let's just say once I got to the library I was in good shape.

But my mom still thinks if you're reading you're not doing anything. "Have a sandwich," she'd say, and "Talk to me." As I mentioned, she's ninety-five now, and she lives in a house by herself. She's one tough cookie.

WRR: Tell me more about the place you grew up.

RA: Oh. Redwood City, California. *Salt*, my first book, really takes place there—most of it. Some of it took place after I came to New Jersey. Redwood City is a concrete suburb of San Francisco, which has changed a lot over time. Where there used to be bay, deep-water harbors, actually, and salt ponds, there are now shopping centers and restaurants! Which, by all rights, with the earthquakes, should be at the bottom of the bay. I haven't been back in about six years.

I had to get out of there by the time I was in my thirties. I mean I didn't grow up with a sense of mobility. I thought you had to stay. Other people left, but that was other people. Once I left I thought, "Whoa! (laughs) You should have done this a long time ago." So, yeah, I'm really not happy going back there. It's not the place, really. It's the ghosts. And who I'm expected to be.

When I grew up it was just a pretty quiet, concrete suburb with a good side and a bad side. I'd lived on both. My parents were, well, not divorced, but they were split up since I was in grade school. And my father lived behind a bar for a while and then had a cabin in the Santa Cruz Mountains, in Boulder Creek, and that's very much like where I live now in New Jersey. Very forested, very mountainous. My kind of land.

WRR: Do you remember the first poem you ever read that first struck you, knocked you off your feet?

RA: I honestly don't. Not that I read. What I remember, actually, is that I never really got poetry. Although, my father had a little red leather bound copy of *Evangeline*. I've got that now. I just didn't really get it back then. I always wrote it, because I had a good ear and so I could get extra credit in grade school. But the first time I realized that poetry could be interesting—other than for extra credit or for cultivating the teacher's pet position—was really as a young adult when I went to a conference at Foothills College in California. I heard John Logan read out loud. It really was like seeing a light come on.

Logan was, well, he was evidently a very kind man, really a character physically and psychologically. I was just totally bowled over. I mean it was really amazing. He was scary he was so real. He was dangerous because he was so real!

WRR: Had you already written poetry at this point?

RA: I had written poetry, but I didn't know anything about it at that point. I didn't really know what a poem was. I wrote poetry the way kids do—mindlessly, sing-songy embarrassing stuff. I was really only writing fiction at that point.

WRR: One thing that's always interesting is who people like to read first as they begin and continue writing . . .

RA: I'm probably the world's worst role model. My life hadn't really opened up for that sort of thing. I don't think I really started reading poetry until I came to New Jersey. Oh, in California, I went to Kepler's and bought poetry, hoping someone would notice, but I don't think I read much of it. In California, there were just too many prohibitions, at least I felt there were. I was somebody else there.

But, it's funny: Though I thought I hadn't read any poetry, one day—long after I'd come to New Jersey, and that was over twenty-five years ago—a friend came up to me and said, "Your poems remind me of Edward Taylor's" and I said, "Oh that's cool. I'll go find out all about him."

So, I opened the Norton Anthology that I had in college and had carried all the way to New Jersey and my notes were all over it. You see, I had read it, but nothing had stuck. I didn't even know I had read it! But there was the word *imagery* with a long green line and an arrow running down the page to an image. And I went back to college late after having a bit of a sordid life. So we are not talking about too bright a bloom here. It was funny. Because none of it had stuck! Nothing! I was lucky I recognized my own handwriting. I still have a horrible memory. But that was really bad.

WRR: But perhaps it was digested anyway in some sort of subconscious way?

RA: Perhaps. I'd like to think so. But . . .

WRR: And you were already competent in that way, you had a good ear.

RA: Well, I did have a good ear. And there was the mixture of dictions and that sense sometimes of almost being out of control but not quite—which you know also makes a good guitar player. (Laughs)

But later, as I grew as a poet, I found out I really had to say something. You know, before, I could write all this stuff that sounded like poems, but there was nobody home. It was really late when I realized I had to say something and actually had something to say. Now, I read everything. Everything. And all the time. I'm blessed, at this stage of my life, with time. Of course there's never enough.

WRR: Do you think all good poets have to be good poetry readers?

RA: I have no doubt about it. Either that or they are far more talented than I am, which they probably are, but the thing is I think you need to see what's being done just to know what the tools are that you can play with—and especially if you hope to publish, which shouldn't be the first concern, but it is a concern.

Though, I'm pretty sure if I hadn't published I would still be writing. Because I write to find out who I am, what I think.

WRR: Does writing take you to new places?

RA: Absolutely. Writing, reading, music—they're places to me. When they're good I forget I have a body.

WRR: Do all of your poems surprise you?

RA: If they don't, they get thrown away. The idea for me is to never settle for what I meant to say. And I seldom start out meaning to say anything. I wrote one poem trying to do something specific—from an idea. I wanted to recreate the rhythms of the gospel church I grew up in. Ma used to drive me there, drop me off, and I'd walk home. But that poem was a booger. The poem is fine. I stand by the poem. But the process was hell. I hope I never have another idea. Shoot me if I have an idea.

I like it much better when I find out what *the poem's* trying to say and then start aligning the images within those terms. If I have a premise, it's time for me to write an essay. And I do love to write essays. But in a poem? I think surprise is essential. Otherwise you're just taking notes or you're just talking. Too many poems are just talking. If I want talking, I can call my mother.

WRR: Tell me three cardinal rules you have for yourself. What makes a good poem?

RA: You mean in process or after the fact?

WRR: Well, okay, both . . .

RA: In process, I would say that there must be an engine driving the poem that is not the writer. A rhythm, an image, an impulse, but not merely the writer's will.

I would also say the poem is not done until it says more than you meant to say. And everything has to be set up so that it rolls down the page seamlessly.

WRR: How about after the fact?

RA: Well, I would still say that the poem has to say more than you meant it to say . . . I think it's tough to edit for thought. The *matter* is something that has to come in the process. John Gardner talks about it as "the vivid and continuous dream." He talks about it for fiction. If something makes you realize you're reading rather than experiencing the piece, then the dream is broken—and that's a glitch. Something wrong with the piece. It's true for a poem as well . . . If I have to stop, then I've left the poem, really, and I don't want that to happen to my reader.

I like poems that have a sense of play, yet still have a serious side—the difference between matter and material—*material* being the word for the stories and images you're using and *matter*, the emotional core. I do like a sense of play. But I don't like the play to totally obfuscate the core. I have to be able to get a foothold somewhere, have to be able to get in, and have a place to stand once I get there. Then I'll be in a position to enjoy the play in the context of meaning. That's crucial for me.

I tell my students 100 things, but right now I can't think of anything else at all. They'd be astonished to hear that, I'm sure!

WRR: How about when you asked, "Can you dance to it?" I remember that rule . . .

RA: Yes, can you dance to it. Well, yeah, I like the music. The really flat prosaic poems interest me less. It's not that they don't interest me. It's just that they interest me less. Because then I have to really look at the dynamic of the traveling and the meaning. As opposed to being carried. It's very different.

I definitely don't like things that reek of competence. That's a problem. If competence is so evident that you realize it's competent before you realize what it's about or what you might experience, that seems problematic to me. Problematic, anal-retentive, and boring. Of course there are exceptions to everything. But I do hate boring. Anal is easier to live with.

WRR: Like an over-polished stone . . .

RA: Yeah, I mean let's just polish it down to dust, or kill it and pin it to a board! Beat it to death with decorum! Even if the meter is perfect and it makes perfect sense. Or when it's infused with prose logic as opposed to a poetic logic, which relies on very different things. It's easy to tell way too much in a poem.

I think people very often mistake their impulses. In the abstract, romantic notion, they want to be a poet, so they think their impulse to write is a poetic impulse. Very often they're wrong. If being a poet is the issue, a writer's in trouble. If *making poems* is the issue, you've got a better chance at doing something of interest.

I think a lot of the pseudo-autobiographical poems are prose impulses because the poem never gets bigger than the poet. It has to . . . by my definition . . . get bigger than the poet . . . to be a poem. Otherwise it's prose. And prose broken into lines is . . . a kind of sad happening.

WRR: Although maybe some prose writers feel that the writing has to be bigger than the author as well?

RA: And I think they do and I think it does. But, they've got a lot more room to play. I mean, we're [poets] really working in a bell jar . . .

For instance, we're working on some exercises in our MFA's forthcoming residency on the issue of backstory. And I think that in a lot of poems there's too much backstory. They've had something they wanted to tell. And the problem is if the thing that they wanted to tell is about themselves and they stand in front of the writing, I'm already bored. The poet stands behind the poem. The poem is the center of attention. I just want the poems to take me somewhere I haven't been before, or at least show me a familiar place in a new light.

WRR: The other thing I remember you saying is "Stay away from too much light. There's a bit too much light out there." So, is the other impulse to try and capture a universal a bit too soon?

RA: Boy! You were really listening! Maybe I should borrow your notes . . .

Well, that was a Tess Gallagher quote. She said that contemporary poetry was flat-footed and suffered from too much sunlight. And that there should be more shadow. It's probably a bad paraphrase—it's my rotten memory again—but I think that too. I think the difficulty for a lot of beginning writers is to know the difference between shadow, which is mystery, and the unanswered story questions, which are a whole different, logistical issue. But yeah, "flat-footed and suffering from too much sunlight"—that's Tess Gallagher.

WRR: I'm going to switch gears a little. Emerson wrote that poetry is a confession of faith. Do you agree or disagree and why?

RA: Well, those are two great big abstractions, *confession* and *faith*. I guess it is a confession. It doesn't necessarily need to be a public confession. I could get off on a real toot about this, but I think too often confession is equated with art. Art is not confession for me. Was it Ad Reinhardt who said, "Art is art. Everything else is everything else?" I think so. I guess my point is that we're not as interesting as we think we are. Confession is confession. Art is art.

I do have faith, though, that the act of writing will help me articulate what I don't already know about myself. I think a lot of people misconstrue the meaning of *risk* in poetry. Risk isn't telling your story. Risk is finding out something new that happened to you because of the story.

WRR: And maybe faith in the powerful ways that writing can help you connect with others and larger meanings?

RA: Yes, and that usually happens the smaller you write. You know, the more

microscopic. As soon as you go to the macroscopic and the large generaliza-
tions and the abstractions you're probably going to run into problems and
maybe sound like a pompous ass as well. And I've been known to do that. Actually I love abstractions. But they're dangerous. There's always that aspect. To
get to the large, you go through the small.

WRR: How have you experienced teaching poetry?

RA: Oh, I've learned a lot. I am forced to push my intuitions and insights
further, to articulate what needs to be tightened, arranged, deleted, and just
plain fixed in poems so that students can understand me. I love it. I've got the
best job in the world. Hate the grading thing, though.

Luckily, our MFA program is Pass/Fail.

WRR: Can writing good poetry be taught?

RA: Talent can't be taught, but craft can and should be taught. Because the
talent can and usually does let you down sooner or later. And when you run
into that pothole in your poem where something sucks or is loose or just plain
wrong, you've got to know how to locate it, identify it, and fix it and that's
where craft comes in. Like a tool box. Quite handy.

WRR: What are you working on right now?

RA: Well, in October, I spent the month at Vermont Studio Center trying to
finish my second novel. I almost made it. I'd been poking at this novel since
I completed the first one—over twenty years ago. Anyway, I almost finished
it. I write lyrical novels, poets' novels, I guess. Not just novels with musical
prose, but novels of a somewhat different shape and agenda. Let's say they're
situational rather than plot-driven.

My first novel, *Someplace Like This*, was first person, present tense. Please kill
me if I try to do that again. But this one, *Wing Theory*, is third person, present, with three point-of-view characters. Quite a change. It has the same geo-
graphical arc the first one had, a spread of experience between the East and
West Coasts. This one has to do with an artist's past, her confinement in the
assembly center at Tanforan, and later at Topaz in what can only be called a
concentration camp for Japanese Americans.

As soon as I turn my grades in, I'm going to finish it up and send it off to my agent. I'm going to do a little, not-so-demure happy dance. Then, I'm going back to the poetry book I deserted to finish the novel. If I can remember how to write a poem.

Kimberly Nagy serves as Commissioning Editor for *Wild River Review*. She is a poet, professional writer, and dedicated reader who has interviewed a number of leading thinkers, including historian James McPherson, playwright Emily Mann, and philosopher Alain de Botton.

Nagy received her Bachelor's in History at Rider University and M.A. from the Department of History at the University of Connecticut. She has worked in public relations and marketing for publishers, such as W.W. Norton, Routledge UK, and Princeton University Press.

She is currently writing a book called *The Triple Goddess Trials*, based on her *Wild River Review* column of the same name. In it, she explores every stage of women's lives through the timeless insights of myth. Find her at www.kimnagy.com

TWO INTERNS AND ONE EDITORIAL COORDINATOR
AT *THE LITERARY REVIEW*
ASK SOME QUESTIONS

[Fall 2010]

Jacklene Oakes & Anastasia Cyzewski: Thank you for your time.

Being the poetry editor for *The Literary Review* what do you look for in a sub-mission?

Renée Ashley: I'm *always* looking for something that will snap me to atten-tion and then keep me in that heightened state through to the end of the piece. I want my eyes to open wide and my jaw to drop. So many submissions are . . . boring, the same-old-same-old wearing the same old clothes; or they present me with shock for shock's sake, or peculiarity for peculiarity's sake, which only annoys me. Or the poems are just plain badly written. Or they're someone who doesn't read's idea of what a poem is. I'm looking for pieces that mean more than they say, that get larger than the poet or the poet's story. I'm looking for energy in language and language management, deep attention to line and image or concept—or prose poems that are so of-a-piece that the sentence works as strenuously as line. I'm looking for poems that wear their craft like a Speedo, craft so apparently seamless that I am propelled though the body of the poem and come to the end so eager to make a swift return to the starting point that I'm oblivious to what's happening in the room around me. I'm looking for mystery, not information. For resonance, not anecdote. I'm not looking for competence; mere competence is uninteresting. I'm look-ing for the extraordinary confluence of craft, material, and concern.

JO&AC: Are you currently working on any new projects?

RA: I am. I completed a manuscript of poems last year but haven't had the opportunity to put it in order and get it out. As I type this, it's gathering dust behind me in one of way too many wire baskets filled with documents of my various interests and obligations. I really need to do that! And I've begun a new book of poems—I conceive of books as thematic wholes—so I'm ready to begin discovering that not-yet-written book's particular surprises. I've written most of the title poem, thirteen segments. That's cooling in another wire basket, waiting for me to get back to it. For what seems like a very long time, but is really probably about a year, maybe a year and a half, I've been focusing on essay/reviews, mixing personal essays with book reviews. It's a hoot; I love it. It's incredibly satisfying. But I can't do that and any other kind of writing at the same time. I'm a one-thing-at-a-time person. And I'm glacially slow—in both writing and thinking. I'm ridiculous. Cousin to a rock. But I'm close, in theory, to pulling those essay/reviews together, with other prose pieces both personal and literary, into a book manuscript. Between teaching in the MFA and MA programs and my freelance work, this last year has been busier than ever before. My friends kid me about my *part-time* jobs that take up *all* my time. They're right. I'm anticipating a slow-down after the first of the year—I've made the arrangements—and I'm hoping to focus on the new poetry collection. Send me good thoughts, eh? I need a little time to myself.

JO&AC: Was there one event that caused you to start writing or did you start gradually?

RA: Both: gradually but forever. And also, much much later, an event.

I had a good ear as a little kid and so could win favor with my grade school teachers, with poems on any lessons we were having, as extra credit. I had extra credit up the wazoo the whole time I was in school—and, oddly, didn't need it. I was a good student. Afraid not to be. Afraid of everything, really. The good grades didn't come easily though; I worked hard. I was a very adult, very responsible kid. A piteous, ghastly little creature. And the poems I wrote back then sucked, of course, but they *sounded* good, sounded like poems might sound. (I remember, too, writing poems for a French project as an undergraduate and my teacher, the granddaughter of Frank Lloyd Wright, telling me my French was great but that my poetry was shameful and I really shouldn't try that again.)

I probably didn't write a poem that might be considered good until I was in my thirties when I really started examining craft and reading more poetry. I was always a reader—I wrote a sixth grade book report on Sinclair Lewis's novel *Dodsworth*. As I recall, it was a book about divorce and someone, or probably someone's parents, called the school to say it was inappropriate. My teacher stood up for me—Mrs. Fitzgerald said I was mature for my age and more than capable of addressing the issues without being compromised. She said, "If she can read it, she can report on it." I had no idea what the stink was about. Nor did my mom. But bless that teacher. She was good to me in many ways, tried to save me from the crap-puddles I was so often skirting.

But there was one event later, probably in my twenties. I was a prose writer back then. But at a writers' conference at Foothills College, I had an open hour and went in to listen to a poetry reading by John Logan. I came out changed. I had to hear it out loud, I think, to understand the nature of the poetry beast, a beast, I might add, with myriad backs. John Logan, bless him as well, he's gone now; he kicked something into gear in my brain. He was reading a poem about drinking at a bar and giving the cherry from his drink to a child—I'm sure I didn't dream this—and all my knee-jerk-poetry-fear-and-distaste just popped like a soap bubble. It was an "aha!" moment. I remember thinking: Oh! Poetry is just someone speaking to someone else in a sort-of-compact-electric way! The top of my head really did come off. It was an amazing experience.

JO&AC: Is there a writer or a poet that you keep rereading to inspire you?

RA: I adore, for instance, Edward Taylor's "Preface" to his "Gods Determinations." He was a Puritan preacher. The poem is a scream; it just kills me. "Who in this Bowling Alley bowld the Sun?" Wow. Isn't that fabulous? It just knocks me out. I do go back to that. Of course I have a number of favorites that I revisit frequently—some dead, some alive. I read a lot of poetry, fiction, creative nonfiction, everything. But mostly I just keep reading, period. My life has been a small one—circumscribed, not short. I want to learn things, but mostly I want to learn them from books. I'm a bit like Francophile Wallace Stevens, quite happy to absorb France from his reading chair in Connecticut. I get the larger world of experience—and I learn about writing and its possibilities—as well as being reminded that there are other people out there like me, that I'm not the only one who's just a quarter of an inch off. It's a rare day when I don't read for three or four hours. It's usually more. I'm stupid in the morning. I read at night. But I have rotten recall no matter what time it is. I go back out of both necessity and delight. But, yes, there are a few writers who are so fabulous that they make me think I should go back to work at the cheese shop instead of writing—

that I'm only managing to embarrass myself—though I don't suppose that's inspiration. And there are any number of writers who get me so excited about the possibilities of language that I want to sit down and make lines or sentences; those writers make me want to participate in the great being of whatever literature might be. Breath, probably. The great body of breath and language that is literature. That's a dream, of course, to think I might be a part of that. Aspiration, I guess, as a by-product of inspiration. Another delusion of possibility. I just add it to my already brimming wheelbarrow of delusions.

JO&AC: Do you have any friends who are writers and if so do you find it helps **your** writing?

RA: I do have friends who are writers, both prose writers and poets—and friends who are not writers and have no wish to become one! I have friends who are *fabulous* writers! Do they help my writing? Sure. We cheer each other on. Occasionally read some of each other's work, though not often. We compare funny rejection and publishing stories. But usually when I hang out with my favorite small group of writers we talk about something else; we're just a passel of people who like each other a lot, know we have this thing in common, recommend books to each other, eat and laugh, catch up, and just be generally happy to be together! I have one friend I run away with, though. We'll hop in the car when we're able, leave our usual lives behind, and spend a night or two in a hotel writing, holed up with books and computers, an anchovy pizza, a twelve-pack of Diet Coke, and a sense of urgency because for a limited number of hours we *will not be disturbed*. Under those circumstances, she and I do read each other our work. We can't get over our good luck. We are the ultimate compatibles.

Louise Dell-Bene Stahl: What has been your most memorable moment during a reading?

RA: Ha! Actually, Louise, it *wasn't* flashing that reader—who had seen it before, anyway, I can assure you. It was the time I fell off the stage stairs and in doing so screamed like a banshee all the way down, throwing myself head-first into the audience at the West Side Y. You missed that one. In fact, you were probably still in high school. Talk about a learning curve on what-may-kill-you and what won't. Evidently I lived.

THE *ITHACALIT* INTERVIEW WITH RENÉE ASHLEY
BY MICHELE LESKO

[January 2012]

Michele Lesko: As my mentor throughout the MFA program at FDU, I looked to you for balance and found it. That was an invaluable gift.

Renée Ashley: I'm so glad you found it . . . I'm betting, though, you conjured it yourself!

ML: What do you tell your students as they flounder with the spectrum of hyper-expository narrative to cryptic, insular writing?

RA: I don't have a pat answer, alas. I am a firm believer that, in poems, clarity is overrated; however, the reader must be able to find *some* place to stand, some footing in the poem, in order to want to remain there and receive the bulk of what is offered. If a poem doesn't let me in, I'm probably going to harp on image, image alignment, and the quantum leap of resultant synergies that allows the reader to make a complicit *whole* that accounts for more than just the parts of the poem. I guess that's the quick answer. As for those poems in the hyper-expository mode, I usually ask: Does this poem mean anything it doesn't say? If it doesn't mean more than the facts (or claims or stories), then it might as well be prose. A manual for your refrigerator. I've been known to ask: Why should I care? How does this poem earn the space, the poetic real estate, it takes up? If the answer is "Aren't you interested in my life?" my answer is likely to be *No*. The poem needs to get bigger than its author and its material; if it doesn't, it's just anecdote. It needs to have matter, its unarticulated subject.

I often explain the difference between the logic of prose and the logic of poetry as the difference between a wet stone wall (a mortared wall) and a dry stone wall (stones stably arranged with no mortar) and I tell those who are mired in filling in all the gaps: Let's get rid of the mortar. (Your reader is being suffocated! Poem of Amantillado!) Let the images speak. Give the poor things some air. It's perfectly possible—and highly desirable—to leave some gaps in the logic, to make leaps that the reader can participate in rather than being locked in and bludgeoned with nonessential information or needless rhetoric. Every detail of the progression needn't be accounted for. You really need to let the chipmunks dash through the cracks.

A poem, you could say, is like a bell: if you stuff a bunch of dirty laundry into the bell or make that bell too fixed, it can't resonate. It thuds. Plud-plud. But if the bell is hung with the ability to move and room to swing freely, with air circulating freely in and about the body, it's able to do its job, to vibrate after the clapper's contact. It can resonate. Resonance, in the poetic sense, includes the reader in the process of experiencing the poem's matter and consequence. Poetic logic likes air; it loves image and suggestion; it leans into negative capability; and it wants to include the reader in the work of the poem. Broad strokes, I'm afraid, but perhaps enough to answer your question?

ML: What do you learn with each new group of writers?

RA: That some things don't change. That students who do not read widely and voraciously are given to the same sorts of beginners' weaknesses and misapprehensions as the students with the same lack of hungers who came before them; that that sort of naïveté and/or laziness spawns some sort of common and erroneous idea of what a poem is. And that particular idea is usually based on ego rather than art. They need to love writing in both its noun- and verb-senses, and writing that is not their own. I learn, too, that I'm still capable of being surprised. Which is a godsend. And I learn *stuff!* My own life is small and, at this point, pretty cloistered. I learn about younger lives, which are inevitably different, either slightly or wholly, from my own and from the lives of students that came to me before them. A handful have taught me how to read poets I wasn't wild about before, showed me what to admire, what lens to look through. Their entire sets of reference are different; it's almost as though you could say their *context* is different. Their music, their social cues, their awarenesses and their obliviousnesses. It's a Sisyphean job to keep up with all there is to learn from each class. I fail, of course.

ML: Can you tell readers about learning to write in your early years?

RA: I'm not sure I did *learn* to write when I was young. I just wrote. Poems, as a child and young adult. Some essays and fiction in my twenties. And school papers, of course. I was often given a great bit of creative leeway with those, even throughout grad school. I read incessantly (no siblings, an absent father, a mother who worked, often, two or three jobs and tended not to trust babysitters, and me unable to make friends easily or often). I didn't really start looking into the craft of writing until I was, maybe, thirty. A real late bloomer. I was too shy to take creative writing classes in college—they wouldn't let me audit and just listen; if I were going to be in the class I had to be in the class and workshop my pieces like everyone else. So that was a no-go. I would have died on the spot. I wouldn't even have waited for the criticism. I'd've just keeled over and died.

ML: Perhaps tell us a little about the learning curve you experienced with your first novel and now the second novel; tell us if and how those books informed your poetry?

RA: What you might call a *learning curve* was more like a *learning crash*. I wrote my first novel, *Someplace Like This*, in my now-husband's furnace room. It took me four years. I had had interest in my stories and essays but agents and editors kept telling me I had to have a novel, so I decided to write one. What the hell, right? What I didn't understand about myself at that point was that I have no facility for plot whatsoever. Not one little soupçon of knack. After all, I've spent most of my life trying to avoid confrontation, so the idea of a protagonist and an antagonist going at it was out of the question—and if the protagonist just walks away from the antagonist, you've got no story. But I hadn't articulated that to myself when I began. I just sat down and started writing. When I was about one-third of the way through I drew up a table of contents, just naming my chapters by the plot point they covered. And so I wrote the whole book with just that. The really funny thing was that, at some point after completing the manuscript, I realized there was not one simile or metaphor in the entire novel. I had to go back and put them in. It sounds so bogus! but it's how I learned to incorporate. They came naturally to me, but, evidently, not while under the strain of Writing-My-First-Novel—I think because the "what happened" was so all-consuming for my plot-challenged mind that I had no mind left to call up trope. I'm still plot-meager. My conflicts are internal. The novels I write are lyric novels. And I like to *read* lyric novels, so, except making-a-living-wise, that works out neatly. My second novel is with my agent as we speak. It's about an artist who, during World War II, was incarcerated in one of the Japanese-American internment camps. Such a nasty business. I did a tremendous amount of research, most of which did not show up in the book at all except, perhaps, in ambient ways. And with each novel I complete, I say to my husband and friends, *Just shoot me if I decide to write another one. OK? Please, just kill me.* And, of course, there's a nascent one in my upstairs office, but I have to admit it's getting pretty dusty.

As for my novels informing my poems? If they have, I don't see it. But trying to make good poems has informed the prose tremendously. Compression, syntaxes, silences, oh yeah.

ML: In a number of your poems, from different books, different times and themes, I've noted *blue, black, bucket* and *fist* used to describe the heart. It's never hearts and candy canes with reference to your heart images (I admire that) and the heart as it speaks of more than romantic love. Can you tell me what you're finding out when you speak of the heart?

RA: Ha! Could you ever mistake me for a hearts-and-candy girl? I've certainly got my soft spots, but I'm not a girly-girl. And if I'm sentimental, I try to keep it to myself. But the heart? Good grief . . . Whose is whole? Whose isn't black and blue and rattling loose in its socket? I think I began using *heart* because somewhere along the line it was made clear to me that I shouldn't use it. It was overdone. It was weak and sentimental. Trite. And so, I tried to figure out how to do it and make it work. I'd finished the manuscript of *Basic Heart* before Stephen Dobyns's book, *Pallbearers Envying the One Who Rides,* was published. The character that is Dobyns's book is named *Heart.* The thinking and writing in that is pretty masterful. And hilarious. My first impulse, though, when I read it was to shout something really obscene, set my manuscript on fire, and drag out my mourning rags, but that lasted all of, maybe, two minutes. I'd written the book, I was sending it out. It wasn't anything like *Pallbearers.* I was sticking by it. Coincidence or zeitgeist, the concurrent *hearts*? I have no idea. *Pallbearers* is a fabulous book. I love it. But mine's a different take altogether. I once had a person at a reading—and this was decades before *Basic Heart*—say to me, *"You aren't what one could call a big fan of love, are you."* It wasn't a question. I was really taken aback at the time, but also knew he'd heard something I hadn't heard myself. It's true: I have my doubts about love.

ML: In *Salt* there are a number of poems about your hometown. It can easily be read as autobiography, yet I know you dislike poetry about merely the self and one's personal experience. What did you discover using the imagery from the salt hills of home?

RA: Well, first of all, when I was writing *Salt*, I was just really learning, via reading and practice, what a poem was—and seemingly-autobiographical narrative was filling the literary journals in those days. I've learned a lot about the natures of poems and poetic ground since, but back then that's what I knew. So that's what I wrote. I used *salt* because it's so basic—and it was so utterly *there*—and, too, because it's used to preserve and so much that I was addressing was memory. The salt mounds as image served as a unifying focus for the book as a whole, or were meant to. Life was spinning around, differently from others, and yet everyone could see the same, stable thing. Like a string of pearls: the salt being the string that held the stories/pearls together. I was trying to capture a place and a time, but I knew it had to be bigger than that, it had to mean more than *this, this, and this existed and such and such happened*. I'm not anti-personal poem at all. Much of my later work is so personal that it has to be wrung into a different language to be meaningful to anyone but me. It's not actions and reactions that are the real issue, but the interior climate and landscapes, the cold fronts and Westerly winds, the landslides and sinkholes, that will matter in the end.

ML: Another consistent image is dogs; dogs seem representative of simple being in an almost Buddhist sense. Watching your dogs, do you find a still point in their behavior and how does that propel your poems? What have your close friends, the many dogs in your life, taught you?

RA: A well-treated dog is happiness in a fur suit—who wouldn't want to be part of that every day?—but of course you must have at least two because no one should be the only one of a species in the house. I don't really think about dogs and writing . . . they're just so much a part of my life that when I'm in something-like-my-exterior-life mode of thinking, they're there. They're always there. Getting hair on my furniture, drooling on my feet, tracking mud into the house, making nests in my sheets, sitting—quite literally—on my chest. Pound dogs, lost dogs, found dogs! Steven is trying to get on my lap as I'm typing this. He's about five now, weighs seventy pounds, and has fur no longer than eyelashes. A friend gave me a DNA kit for him: Evidently he's Boxer and Irish Setter. But he's sleeker than a seal. Pooty—my girl, she's about fifteen now—usually sits near me, but she doesn't want to be held. Petted? Oh, yeah. She's got a double coat. She's Chow and Australian Cattle Dog. She never stops shedding and it's like milkweed fluff. Enough hair gathers in the corner of any room at any given time to make a whole new dog. Their photos are on my website: Hit "contact" and then "dogs"! Check them out. They're such characters. I have no family to speak of (my mother is one hundred and lives in California, she's the sole blood connection) except for my husband and a number of dear friends. I could easily just retreat from the out-side world into my rattling head, but the dogs keep me tied to the earth. All that pooping and eating and "Let's throw the stuffed armadillo out the back door again!" So, I guess I don't know what they've taught me, but I do know they have saved me.

ML: Let's talk about process. What do you need in the physical realm to write good poems?

And, to follow through with process, what prompts your poems and how do you follow through when you're on to something? I do remember being with you at Madison, when you walked toward your dorm saying, "I'm working on something, I've got to get it down."

RA: I need quiet. And, at best, no prospect of being interrupted, which is why, when I'm working, I like to work through the night. And a computer; I do compose, if I'm able, on the computer. It's so automatic; it poses the fewest obstacles between me and getting my thoughts down. I do jot things on paper when something comes and I'm on the hoof or in the car—I'm always ready for that—but I prefer the keyboard. I can close my eyes (when I'm writing prose) and just write. And, when I'm working on a poem, I can't judge a line well unless I can see it typed. I need to see how the line-ends work in concert; I need to see what I've made to happen in the left margin. And if the middles sag. Yes, I can *hear* it, but I need to see it to be comfortable before moving on.

My poems generally start with an image or a thought in combination with a rhythm. I don't write poems from *ideas*. I did that once and it was too much like painting by the numbers or filling out a tax form—and I'm unlikely to surprise myself in a poem if I'm working from an idea and, so, why both-er? Deadly things for me in poems, *ideas*. I try not to have them. Whatever I begin with usually takes the title position and the poem is discovered and aligned beneath it, one line at a time. And when it stops singing and starts just talking, then it's time to put it away until it quickens again. Which, sometimes, may be a very long time. Sometimes just after a snack.

ML: On a less technical note, how does your day-to-day shape your writing?

RA: Oh, arrrrgh. My day-to-day is stultifying, decidedly boring, and pret-ty unproductive. I don't write from my exterior life much anymore because nothing's going on. I'm trying to swear off crises. And I'm a very stop-and-go writer. I write in spurts. I'll write hot for a week or two and then not write at all for a month or for many months. And then go off on another toot of writing hot. I'm always thinking about writing—I suppose something is always percolating—but I don't *do* it much. And if you're not *doing* it, not getting it on paper, you're not writing. I'm the world's worst role model.

ML: Did you ever consider anything other than writing for your mental or spiritual expression of this journey?

RA: Oh, my! What a great notion! But my answer, I'm afraid, fails to fulfill the promise of the question. I have never been one to project into the future. The day at hand is tough enough. I didn't even consider *having* a mental or spiritual expression or journey! Not that I saw it and chose to ignore it; it just never occurred to me. I just stayed alive each day. I'm a treader-of-water. The truth—which is the same thing, but canted differently—is that there's absolutely nothing else I'm capable of doing decently. I'm wholly unfit for the world at large. Living in my head and watching fragments of that take shape on paper is all I know. I can't draw a lick, have no talent for or interest in sports, have really crappy home-ec skills, would have been a dreadful parent. Wait. I can drive just about anything. I might have made a really good long-haul truck driver—as long as there was some provision for audiobooks. But that's probably not a good life for a dog. And, besides, I'm a nester. I like having all my crap around me. Never mind. It wouldn't have worked.

ML: What detours really stand out as pivotal moments in your writing life?

RA: Hmmm. Do you mean *life* detours? If so, then the truly pivotal event would be my father's suicide when I was sixteen. I didn't write about it at all until about seventeen years after it happened; I wrote an essay and thought I was done. Then about seventeen years after that I wrote another essay and thought, *Certainly I'm done now.* But since then he's been just about everywhere. Can't shake him and am trying to keep him under control. I have a lot of guilt about my father, who was a very unhappy, very gentle man. My mother threw him out when I was really young. I used to think to myself, very self-righteously I might add, that Sharon Olds should bury her father and get over it! And now I'm in the same, if not worse, father-propelled boat. I cannot get over my father. I didn't know him that well, but enough to break my heart. And I was complicit in his suicide. That's a weight. I write a great deal about my mother, too, particularly in essays and hybrid pieces. My mother's just a funny piece of work. My father, not so funny. More emblematic, I guess. So I guess I could say there are *scenes* from my life that make their appearances and allow other baggage to come along and be explored at the same time. Perhaps they're like the thick metal pins those old fashioned audio tapes on big reels used to click onto, with the tape wound on each and strung between both: each of my parents a pin at the extreme end and I'm the tape that runs between them, pissing and moaning along. It's nuts. I'm sixty-two and still fixated on my parents. It's just plain embarrassing. Sharon Olds, I'm truly sorry.

ML: Can writing clarify our life experience or how we make meaning?

RA: I write to find out what I think, there's no doubt about that: Yes. Writing clarifies life experience if we try to be honest, in at least the parts we choose to address. The essays and hybrid pieces I've written about my mother have forced me to articulate a lot of what was simply muddy thinking before I had to write it down and make it, first, understandable and second, both meaningful and entertaining.

Remember me saying, in the beginning, that clarity is overrated in poetry? Well, it's not true in prose. I really believe articulation is the key to understanding just about everything. The trick is to push that articulation further than you'd like to—and I'm not talking about adding adjectives. Make yourself sweat. If you want to run away, you're probably on the right track.

Michele Lesko is the Founding Editor of *IthacaLit* (www.ithacalit.com). Her poems and short stories have appeared in many journals, including *The Yalobusha Review*, *The Southern California Review*, *Anon*, *Soundzine*, and *Pedestal Magazine*.

THE INNER MUSIC
INTERVIEW WITH POET RENÉE ASHLEY
BY MICHAEL T. YOUNG

[Wednesday, May 16, 2012]

Michael T. Young: Thank you, Renée, for accepting my invitation for an interview. It's a real pleasure to have the opportunity. Your last collection, *The Verbs of Desiring*, was it conceived and written as a collection from the start or was each poem written individually and then collected into a coherent book? I'm particularly curious about this because of both the linguistic daring and the cohesion of the collection. Could you comment on how you achieved this?

Renée Ashley: It's interesting that you ask. . . . That is how I write my books: by the book. I usually begin with a title and I'm obsessing about some thematic or craft issue and that becomes the engine that drives the manuscript through to completion. *The Verbs of Desiring* is really a chapbook, though, and the poems are culled from two unpublished full-length manuscripts: *The View from the Body* and *Because I Am the Shore I Want To Be the Sea*. I had a suspicion that those last two manuscripts weren't as different from one another as my previous books were from each other . . . That's so interesting! *Because I Am the Shore* is primarily prose poems now. In the larger arc of my work, then, these last two are truly transitional manuscripts. That's sort of cool! I haven't done that before—and I certainly didn't do it consciously this time. I can see such clear distinctions between the earlier books. *Salt*, the first, is very narrative and lyric, grounded, I'd say, wholly mainstream (except for one prose poem); I was learning what a poem is back then. *The Various Reasons of Light* is still mainstream, but it was my effort to learn to ground abstract thought. I had these heady-floaty goings-on in my mind and needed to anchor them to the ground. In *The Revisionist's Dream* I went back to my Comparative Literature roots and played a bit with Homer and Ovid, trying to take on some of those ideas as my own. Some, quite obviously, remained theirs. My style was still conservative I think. *Basic Heart*, however, was written after many years of . . . unrest; I think of it as my nervous breakdown book—which is a bit misleading but close enough to the truth that I won't back off from it—and that work seems to have manifested itself in a sort of embodied turmoil. That's the shorthand I use anyway. Perceptions and syntax were shattered. So, the poems in *Heart* could be called more experimental, I guess, looking at them from the outside. Though writing them felt more like *fuck it* than *experimental*. Making them felt like enactment or at least an effort to enact. I wanted the poems to be states of mind rather than to be about states of mind. So, long way around, I guess, the poems in *The Verbs of Desiring* are poems of adaptation. I'm coming back to a more balanced breath now, I think. A better outlook. That's not to say there isn't that breakdown hangover hovering in the newer poems, but I don't believe they're as deeply distressed. Let's just say they're recovering. It'll be interesting—to me at least!—to find out where these transition books are taking me. At the moment, I have no idea. I haven't been working on the new poetry collection; I've been pulling together some essays for a book.

MY: In reading *The Verbs of Desiring*, I was struck by the unpredictability of the language. Each poem seemed to shift its linguistic stance so each poem was a readjustment, a reorientation. What was the intention of this?

RA: Wow. Once again, I don't really know! I never thought of them in those terms. Are they really that different from one another? When I write, my intention is always to make the best poem possible with whatever skills I have at the time—I'm after a seamless and sharp-edged poem, a poem that has . . . balls. Also, a poem that surprises me into a truth, and, if I'm very lucky, pushes a bit beyond the limits of my previous skill set. Of course, I'm not always successful, but that's the ideal. And I bore easily—so boring myself seems wacky, right? To write a poem that's crafted well but suffering from such control that it *bores* the writer as well as the reader? I don't think so. There's enough of that stuff out there already; the world doesn't need any more. But that you, as a reader, had to readjust is possibly good news. If I gave you even footing and just went la-la-la poem to poem through the book, all on the same note or tenor, you'd get bored too. It'd be soporific, right? Something has to rise up and struggle, knock my pins out from under me—and yours from under you—or what's the point? And I don't mean that as shock for shock's sake. I have no interest in that. But more the shock of some discovery—linguistic or life-explaining—made during the act of writing.

MY: "Nothing" seems to become a presence in the collection, so that phrases containing the word "nothing" or the phrase "no thing" take on multiple meanings. At one point in my own reading I thought of the *Tao Te Ching* where the void gives birth to the one and the one to the ten thousand things. What do you see as the significance of "nothing" in the context of this collection?

RA: I'm afraid my belief system, if you can call it that—I'm a resentful atheist—gives me a lot of *nothing* to think about. I would love to be a believer. I'm just not. So I'm constantly banging into some existential door or other which swings back after the initial impact and smacks me a second time with another *nothing*. I'm not even an optimistic atheist. But, on the positive side, nothing may be the one absolute that I can comprehend. I certainly can't comprehend *infinite*. Nor can I get a grasp on *forever* which of course is party to death. When I was eight, I drowned in a motel swimming pool. I'm pretty sure I drowned and came back. I've never lost that experience of *nothingness*. It's what I believe death is. Of course, too, there's my cognitive dissonance of knowing that, once, I saw a ghost and, two other times, things that did not appear in human form but were definitely somethings belonging to the otherly. I confuse even myself, Michael. I'm sorry. But there it is. Contradictions and all. *I contain multitudes.*

MY: I especially like the poem "Oh Yes Tomorrow Expect the Ordinary." It seems to say that the ordinary is a kind of nonbeing out of which we create ourselves. It reminded me of something the philosopher Unamuno said, "To fall into a habit is to begin to cease to be." Do you find this to be true? If so, what do you think helps us to rise out of that common nonbeing into a true identity?

RA: Unamuno's theory is interesting, and I suppose that's one way to look at it, but in my experience it's backwards. In habit I know I *am*, I have time and therefore opportunity to assess the state of *me*, to see just how variant I'm being within that matrix. When I'm in a state of panic or experiencing an unusually sharpened awareness at some godawful horror or newness it's as though my molecules come unglued, fly apart, and are spun off, each separately, but all in a single burst, into the ether and I *become* panic or alertness rather than who I believe myself to be, the me I know when my reptile brain isn't blowing me up and scattering me out into the solar system. I do get what Unamuno's saying, I understand the trope, and I can see that in the abstract it can be true, and that some folks feel it *must* be true. I know people who feel that way. But to me it feels like a literary statement rather than a phenomenological one. Abstraction is a sort of generalization and my experience—as I *experience* it—isn't in the least general or abstract. I'm sorry. I'm not trying to be argumentative; I'm trying to work it out. But I just don't feel Unamuno-ish. I don't believe the *ordinary* is some vast tureen of soup in which we are denuded of our individuality. Ordinariness is just funny! It cracks me up. We're such a bunch of lunkheads! We occupy Quiddity Central. Think about it— this is an over-made argument but I still subscribe: Our parents, most anyway, tell us we're *special*, our early teachers tell us we're each *special in our own way*, and the parameters of *special* keep growing larger and larger and thinner and weaker. I think it's hooey. We work so hard to separate ourselves from the crowd—but *we are* the crowd. Good grief. Emergence theory, etc. Hell, if you listen to those voices in bulk, being special *is* ordinary. I just don't understand the hoo-ha about it. We ought to be investigating the ordinary if we want to find out about ourselves! What was the old cartoon strip that said, "We have found the enemy and he is us"? *Pogo!* It was *Pogo!* Well, same goes for the ordinary: We *are* it. But you have to understand, and in this may reside the difference between Unamuno and me: I have no adventurer in me at all. I'm a coward. I play everything safe. I keep my world small. I follow the rules as they are dictated to me by authority. I'm really, shall I say, *infinitely* timid, *infinitely* ordinary. I find comfort in habit. Habit of the body, habit of the place, habit allows me to function in an almost autonomic mode; it allows my head to do the serious wandering. However, that head's such a tightly sealed vessel that I do, periodically, get claustrophobic. But escaping to some degree— exercise (which I detest), a short trip (if I can drive), a longer trip over large bodies of water (shoot me), or a change of focus of some sort—lets my head off the hook. I have to deal with the traversing and the new place or thing, figure it out, make my way; I have to focus on something *outside* my head. I don't know . . . Is my monkey mind a "true identity"? Perhaps I'm simply not advanced enough to be able to consider something like *true identity*, I'm so busy grappling with the apparent one. It's entirely likely I have no idea what *true identity* might be. Or maybe it's like all the American poetries: There's a whole slew of true identities for each of us. I just don't know.

MY: The collection also seems to suggest that our efforts toward creating an identity are never clean, that the chaotic mess we rise from is part of us, as in the line "No one's endearment//is tidy." Or in the poem "Simple" where it says,

> . . . The whole white sky descends a grain at a time—I with it
> and the threshold disappearing. That we can find ourselves in this.

Do you find this true? If so, how do you think that untidiness influences what we make of ourselves?

RA: Absolutely true! Hail the human midden! First of all, there's nothing tidy about language because no matter how precise we are we can never know if our listener/reader understands it *exactly* as we meant it. It's that sealed vessel again. It's our own private bell jar. *The Alexandria Quartet* changed my life at a very young age. The *Rashomon* effect. Literal point of view. Futility. And there's an Einstein thing, right? about depending on the observer's position in relation to the moving train, the train's moving at different speeds? That always baffled the hell out of me until I drew the parallel between that and the language problem. So, is there really a *right* answer? Slickery, as I see it. And on top of that, supporting or perhaps sponsoring the idea of untidiness, I'm a slob. I don't think I used to be a slob—I remember telling a friend when I was in my twenties, "If you can't find it you might as well not own it!" Very smug in an unpretty, uncompromising way. That was a lifetime ago. (And I was way too old to be such a prig.) Now I can't find a thing: the filing I haven't filed for the last decade, my prescription, my watch, my keys, one of the books I need for class, my other shoe, my good black pants—and that's just last week. My walls are literally covered with paper and pictures, art and scraps, my office door is layers-deep with cartoons and quips and a great bumper sticker my best friend, the insanely good narrative poet Catherine Doty, gave me (which I keep digging out and taping to the top layer again): *I'm not myself today. Maybe I'm you.* And my desk! Oy. But it's all a mirror of what's going on in my head. Sometimes I get all the crap momentarily cleared away and my thinking clears up, my posture gets better, my priorities clearer, my strategizing becomes more orderly, etc. It's bliss—for a very short while until entropy strong-arms me again. I know there are people who are not slobs and whose thinking is precise and whose articulations are beyond exact, but even before I became a slob I wasn't one of those. My friend and colleague Harvey Hix (H.L. Hix) is one of the exact ones. He is fastidious in every way imaginable. He's always fresh-out-of-the-box brand-new-looking and articulating with the utmost clarity. But of course I can't get inside his head; there could be a trash heap in there that would unstarch me—but he has clearly found a method of orderliness. I find him miraculous. But whatever he's got, I don't have it. It seems that in this second half of my life I'm centrifugal. So with that and the way I see people interact and my observations of the physical, outside-of-my-head world and what we do to it, hell, yes we're a mess! Things flying outward every which way. *Untidy* is the least of it. *I have found the untidy and it is us.* At best, I think, we as a species are approximate, though there are exceptions, certainly, like Harvey and you, Michael—your demeanor and presentation when we met and your method and articulation in this interview were and are divinely clean, crisp, logical, and tightly ordered—who seem to have gotten some dispensation for this. But overall we're a sloppy tribe and most often our attentions are perfunctory and/or wrong-headed. Bottom line? As I said, I'm not an optimist.

MY: Dogs seem to appear in your poems frequently. Outside perhaps a love of dogs, what significance do they have for you in your poetry? What do they symbolize for you?

RA: Dogs ground me. There's nothing approximate about a dog except, maybe, his aim. They contend with what's in front of them. They're immediate. And they do not have the kind of language that strikes me as . . . slippery. And, of course, they're dependent. They need us. I have no children and have no literal family except my husband and my one-hundred-and-one-year-old mother who lives a continent away. Dogs let me love them. And they're perfect ballast; they hold a poem to the earth.

MY: You seem like a poet that is deeply stimulated by ideas, by philosophy. Do you read philosophy? Do you have a particular branch of philosophy or group of philosophers that you like and that inspire you?

RA: Oh, I wish I could read philosophy! I've never taken a philosophy class and I've tried to read some ultra-simple stuff a couple of times, but, well, let me put it this way: There seem to be no dogs in it. It appears harrowingly difficult as well as abstract. My mind wanders off. I can't hold all the increments of an argument in my head at one time. It's probably too orderly for me. My monkey mind won't let me linger. But two of my favorite poets/writers have degrees in philosophy: Kathleen Graber and the aforementioned H.L. Hix. My attraction to their work probably comes from the fact that they render their ideas concretely rather than articulating them blatantly. (And they both have dogs.) I think you have to be way smarter than I am to read philosophy with any success. I'm one of those *Oh, look! Ooooh, shiny!* people. Or like in the movie *Up!* when the dogs yell *Squirrel!!!* in the midst of their serious business (shouldn't *seriosity* be a word?) and go berserk, their reptile brains snatching up their minds and bodies like . . . well, snatchers. I'm distracted at the drop of the proverbial hat. I lose my train of thought often when I'm speaking, as well as those keys and pants I mentioned before. And my coffee cup. I'm always losing my coffee cup. With my coffee in it. And I probably have twenty pairs of reading glasses and never have a pair at hand either. Along with half a dozen open cans of Diet Coke sprinkled around the house. Here's the gist: It's the order/chaos thing. I seem to fall on the side of chaos. Too chaotic to be able to grasp philosophy per se. But writing, you see, allows me to render something that's swirling inside me and put it in some sort of order on the outside of me—and along a different avenue of speaking than philosophy takes. It's such a relief to see something you feel out there, for it to be still and sharp. It takes a load off, it really does.

MY: Do you have a favorite poem in this collection? Which one is it and what is significant about it for you?

RA: I do have a couple of favorites, though I must add that they're emotional favorites. I think the title poem is hilarious! *The Verbs of Desiring*. Nobody ever laughs, so I lamely try to explain it to people, and my friends think I'm horrible when I bust myself up because I think I'm so funny (it is *shameful*)—but I do knock myself out on that one. "The verbs of desiring" is a phrase used to describe the subjunctive—and the poem is a poem of desiring and ends on the subjunctive. But even when I explain it nobody cracks up—they laugh, but they're laughing at me, the woman standing there whose cheeks hurt from cracking up at her own joke, rather than laughing at the play in the poem. And I get it. It's OK. I love that weird sort of disjunct. It just makes the whole thing even funnier. I like "Mostly There Is Mostly I Do," too. I'm mother-phobic in many ways. And "An Art Like Any Other," which is a prose poem and, though I haven't checked the dates, may be one of the first of the prose poems that ended up being in *Because I Am the Shore I Want To Be the Sea*. I'd been wanting to write prose poems for a very long time before that one found me.

MY: You're an editor at *The Literary Review*. What do you see as the state of contemporary American poetry? Do you find it vital or sterile? Are there any young poets you find especially exciting to read and to watch out for in the coming years?

RA: Oh, I don't think I could even guess at the state of poetry from *TLR* submissions! The submissions vary, of course, from fabulous to ultra-way-too-premature-what-could-they-have-been-thinking. I don't think of "contemporary American poetry" as a single thing—it's many varied things and some of those things are vital and some sterile, and a mind-numbing percentage exists in between. We have so many different poetries! And I think my taste is pretty catholic as far as styles/schools/aesthetics go. Probably less broad regarding agendas. If the agenda is more prominent than the art I'm not going to be interested. I'm interested in poems, not propaganda. I do want a poem to let me in, and I want it to have teeth. I want it to surprise me with language and/or elegance and/or image or angle of approach. . . . I want a sort of tensile strength in it. The poem, for me, has to rise up off the page, has to be bigger than the poet, has to have some sort of torque and fire. I don't necessarily have to *like* a poem to admire it though. But to come across, in the slush pile, some vital, crisp, surprising work by a writer I'm not familiar with is so exciting! If I start naming names, I'll leave someone out and feel terrible . . . but Weston Cutter is one that comes to mind immediately. And Steve Heighton, a Canadian writer—though I *should* have known his work. He's widely published in several genres in Canada. Let's see . . . Lisa Ortiz, Scott Withiam, Mariana Toscas. Those names were all new to me. And, the folks I am familiar with . . . well, let me just say I think we publish absolutely, excruciatingly, extravagantly good poems. So the state of American poetry? There are so many fantastic poets working now! I buy their books the way the dogs in *Up!* chase and bark at squirrels. It's a good time for poetry. A good state to have real estate in even if it's only the tiniest of pied-à-terres.

MY: Are there any prose works that have noticeably influenced your work as a poet? What are they? Can you say in what way you feel this work or works influenced your poetry?

RA: Of course everything I've ever read has in one way or another influenced me and therefore my work as a poet and writer. I can only work through what I am. I'm the product of everything I've experienced including what I've read. Certainly John Briggs' *Fire in the Crucible* had a big effect on me. He articulated for me the idea of *themata*, the themes a writer will work in over and over during the trajectory that is her life's work. To acknowledge my obsessions as a part of art-process—even though I'm sometimes surprised by them—has been an enormous help. When I was in grad school, my professors were Jungians, and much of what we read and pondered and listened to (though I walked out of class the day Dr. Wiseman played Wagner's *Tristan*— it nearly pulled my heart up and out through my throat!). Oh, and *The Magic Mountain* and *Buddenbrooks*! Joyce's *Ulysses*. I still have the little bar of lemon soap that Dr. Bratset gave me! I did gain a strong sense of pattern and archetype, and though I do think *pattern*, I rarely consciously think *archetype* except in critical mode. And as I said earlier, Durrell's *Alexandria Quartet* changed the way I see language, but I was very young when I read that. The lesson stuck though. I tried to read *Justine* again recently and couldn't get through it. It seemed so . . . purple. I was devastated—I'd lost access to the source of something terribly important in my life. I'll try again someday. Certainly David Foster Wallace. And I'm reading Gaddis's *The Recognitions* right now and it's tying in so much with the poetics of information that I've been thinking about since some colleagues gave a workshop on it last year. I read a lot on creativity and creative process; I rarely remember facts of brain science—and I never remember statistics—but I do come away with a sense of having had something familiar articulated or sourced for me and that's heartening and strengthening. I read novels, memoirs, nonfiction. *Don Quixote*! *Madam Bovary*! And of course verse: Ovid and Homer. My poor mind boggles at everything I'm not acknowledging . . . How could any of it not influence me?

MY: What do you like to do that has nothing to do with poetry or writing?

RA: Watch TV, alas. I watch way too much TV. *NCIS, Bones, Rizzoli & Isles*. *The Big Bang Theory*! British mysteries. And I'm a cartoon addict: lots of noise and bright colors moving . . . I'm there. Though I'm burned out on *Spongebob Squarepants*. He just irritates me now. I still like *Phineas and Ferb* and *Aaaaaah!! Real Monsters*. *Fraggle Rock* was genius, absolute genius. I've got every episode. I loved *The A-Team*, the TV series, not the movie (which was fine but faux). Howling Mad Murdock! Wembly Fraggle, oh my. Jim Henson was a god. Is still a god. And Elmo. Oh I love Elmo! Though I never watched *Sesame Street*; it had way too many humans. I have to admit I even was fascinated by the *Teletubbies* and they were really weird. I had a friend who wouldn't eat tomatoes because she said they hadn't made up their mind whether they were a fruit or a vegetable. The teletubbies were like that—what the hell were they? Somewhat unformed and seductive and possibly menacing—underground hideouts and Big Brothery loudspeakers! I couldn't take my eyes off them. However I absolutely hated that real baby that gurgled in the sun. That was nasty. Creepy beyond just normal creepy. Really, seriously icky. My job is teaching writing, I edit the writing of others, my art is writing.

What *isn't* linked to the work? I do read a lot: poetry, criticism, creative nonfiction, novels, essays . . . But reading is so closely related to writing they're almost the same thing, another form of the same thing anyway. I do have an opera subscription with a friend, though—does that count? Sorry . . . I, too, sometimes wish I were more interesting.

MY: On the contrary, Renée. You are quite interesting and I truly thank you for a wonderful interview. Let's close with one of your favorite poems in the collection, "The Verbs of Desiring."

> How tired the self is of the self, its earth twirling in the air and
> not-air and I know a woman who ate only bread until
> > she died
> of bread. Oh the where-is-she-now. Which is not a question.

Which is a noun of circumstance.
                                        And *disquietude*: lovely
word. And *hairsbreadth. Stupor mundi. Kettle-of-fish-that-
turned-your-heart.*
                              You are returning from an alphabet ran-
sacked by thirst, by the gamut of implication neatly sung:
a tongue that speaks
                        body. A punctuated earth. You who are
resolute of hungry brutes and fooled by the beggar's bowl of
moon, tide of scat, of pellet and flop
                                        and the body's dead-
end is an assured apostrophe.
                              There are more ways to mean
than you can make note of.
                              Look! Something is pretty in the sky
—it might just be the sky—though installation's been askant.
Or what it sits upon is opposed to the level eye.
                                        A panoply of
possibilities—
                  all those bears pirouetting in your penthouse!
Oh if it or they were only.
                        Or if you. And, or if I.

Michael T. Young's newest collection of poetry is *The Infinite Doctrine of Water*, published by Terrapin Books in 2018. Find him at www.michaeltyoung.com.

OUT OF OUR MINDS WITH GUEST RENÉE ASHLEY

[J.P. Dancing Bear Interview, June 4, 2014]

J.P. Dancing Bear: Good evening, this is KKUP, Cupertino at 91.5. I'm J.P. Dancing Bear. This is "Out of Our Minds," the weekly, hour-long poetry program. I do have a guest on the line with us and I'm just going to do a quick voice check, here, to make sure she's on with you, our audience. Just say hello real quick.

Renée Ashley: Hello!

JPDB: There you go. All right. Now let me tell you about my guest. Her most recent book is *Because I Am the Shore I Want To Be the Sea*, out by Subito Press late last year. Welcome to "Out of Our Minds," Renée Ashley.

RA: Thank you very much. I'm delighted to be here.

JPDB: Happy to have you. I've been waiting for you to have a new book out so I could have you on. [laughter] An excuse, basically, to have you on.

RA: [laughter] Well, I hope, you know, you won't wait too long for the next time!

JPDB: Exactly. So let's have you read a couple of poems to get things started.

RA: Sure! I think, if I may, I'll start with "The Verbs of Desiring." [reads the poem]

JPDB: Hmm.

RA: And . . . let's see . . . This is "Oh Yes Tomorrow Expect the Ordinary." [reads the poem]

JPDB: Hmm . . . I want to start off with talking about the predominant form in this book which is the prose poem, but you've gone with a lessening of punctuation.

RA: Right.

JPDB: What is your purpose in presenting them this way, with the lessened punctuation?

RA: I'm trying to create an area where there is no way for the reader to get out. Like being inside your own head. So, if I have terminal punctuation, it's merely an exclamation point or a question mark. There're no periods. I don't want that still space for the reader to escape. I want it to feel as though it's going on in *your* head.

JPDB: So, you don't want any pause.

RA: Right. Well, I want enough pause to get to the next word, of course, but not a full stop.

JPDB: Or, a place where a reader might take a breath.

RA: Right. I don't want him to be able to stop and ask questions. I want him to get all the way through it before . . . I really . . . I think I want it to mimic that claustrophobic feeling that you get. I mean, the head is a sealed vessel, you know? And sometimes those things just go round and round. That's really what I was going after.

JPDB: And the prose form allows you to do that, too, because there is no linebreak. There isn't a . . .

RA: There's no linebreak and it creates pressure, I think, to have justified right and left margins. If the work is sufficiently compressed there should be a lot of pressure between those two uprights—which is the black hitting the white margin on either side. So, again, it's kind of . . . I think of it as a pressure cooker.

JPDB: Yeah . . .

RA: And so the meaning is pressing out against those solid margins. I hope.

JPDB: It's interesting to me because I've had a lot of prose poets on the show and I don't think I've ever heard anybody describe the form that way before, really thought out about how it's presented on the page.

RA: Well, it's a hybrid form. It isn't really codified, and it means a lot of things to a lot of different people. I simply had to have it be more than a chunk of prose.

JPDB: Um hmm.

RA: I really wanted it to have the tension and the wiriness of a poem but without the breaks and the white space.

JPDB: Right. And you've sort of somewhat answered this already, but you are fairly known for your prose poetry. What makes you continue to stay with prose poetry and gravitate to it the way you have?

RA: Probably because I haven't gotten bored yet. I mean, I have, you know, the attention span of a gnat.

JPDB: [laughter]

RA: [laughter] It takes me four or five years to write a book. I was very lucky. This book was taken the first time I sent it out. So, now I'm about half-way through another book of prose poems, but when I feel as though I'm starting to repeat, then usually I take on another subject and the form changes as well. I'm just fascinated by it because it isn't codified . . . so, how do you make it jump off the page?

JPDB: Right.

RA: You know . . . you just . . . you just . . . have to [laughter] squeeze it until it squeals. That's my aesthetic for this.

JPDB: Yeah.

RA: It's the same reason I didn't have titles as *titles*. The titles I have are lower case and in brackets. So that they're almost an aside, or a suggestion of a lens through which to read the rest of the poem.

JPDB: Right. That's interesting, too. So, and, again, everybody does it a little bit different and that's what makes it an interesting form to work with.

RA: Oh, yes! If everyone did it like this it wouldn't be interesting to *me*, so . . . [laughter].

JPDB: Exactly. Would it anger you if somebody came along and wrote almost exactly like you? Like tried to mimic your voice?

RA: [laughter] No. [laughter] I mean, I make a point of . . . my students . . . of paying attention to where their work seems to be wanting to go rather than to coerce them into whatever I'm into at the time, because that just seems cruel. They're in the space that *their* head is dictating at any given time. No, if somebody wanted to give it a shot, more power to them! The likelihood that it would sound like me, unless it was a deliberate mimic, I think would be small. I think that we're all sufficiently different that their obsessions, at least, would be something other than mine.

JPDB: Yeah. It's true. In this day and age it's a lot harder, I think, to mimic your contemporaries than it used to be.

RA: Yeah.

JPDB: Back in the day . . . like, you could write a Robert Frost parody. You know, because you knew what he was going to do, or you knew his voice was pretty solid. You could write that parody and people would get it.

RA: And I think anybody could write a parody of any one of my books because throughout the books they're pretty much the same, so that, probably, you begin to see the pattern. You'd certainly see the formatting. I do tend to think of them in terms of books rather than writing random poems and then pulling them together in a collection.

JPDB: So when you sit down to write, you're thinking about the book as a whole already.

RA: Absolutely. Well, once I'm three or four poems in, I begin to see what direction I'm taking. And I usually start with a title, so that, right there, is a leaning. Yeah, it's usually pretty clear to me, and I want it to be cohesive. I try to put it together in a sort of . . . oh, faux-Freytag's triangle, you know, for fiction, with the rising tensions of the voice getting more intense through about the first two-thirds of the book, and then lessening to release the reader at the end.

JPDB: So let me ask you this, then, what happens when you write a poem and you know it's not . . . You like the poem, in fact you may even be fascinated by it, but it doesn't fit with what you're currently doing. What do you do with that poem?

RA: It hasn't happened.

JPDB: [laughter]

RA: [laughter] But if it . . . I mean, my obsessions are obviously so strong . . .

JPDB: I have planted a seed . . .

RA: Yeah. Well, I would say "Wahoo! That's obviously going to go someplace later," and I would polish it as well as I could 'cause I only work on one poem at a time. And then I would set it aside [laughter] and go back and finish what I was doing and then see if that direction were book-worthy on its own.

JPDB: Let's have you read another couple of poems.

RA: Sure. This is "Essay on Observation." [reads the poem] I think the bears keep coming up because we have them here . . . [laughter]

JPDB: [laughter]

RA: OK. This is "Contemplation within the Framework of a Dream." [reads poem]

JPDB: Hmmm. Now, there are some poems in here that are not prose poems.

RA: Right.

JPDB: Which leads me to ask a question: Do you always start with the prose poem as your initial form and then later you look at it and you say, "Oh . . . Oh, that needs to have linebreaks after all"?

RA: No. [Laughter] Those others, the oddballs, the one with the right margin . . . I actually took a class from Brenda Hillman at Atlantic Center for the Arts and she was trying to get us to do things we haven't done before.

JPDB: Hmmm.

RA: And that's where I wrote those. But they still seemed to fit in. The nature of them, the tenor, the material, the same obsessions . . .

JPDB: Right.

RA: . . . so I just put them in.

JPDB: You know, it's interesting. You did read one earlier and I did notice it did have the similar lack of punctuation, or I should say *terminal punctuation*.

RA: Right.

JPDB: So . . .

RA: And that's one of the early ones. I mean I wrote that one long before I went deeply into the prose poem. I had a chapbook come out under that title, *The Verbs of Desiring*.

JPDB: Hmm . . .

RA: And I think they're mostly quite different in there. Yes . . . It's not all prose poems at all.

JPDB: But, and obviously that means that not all of them made it into this book, right?

RA: Oh, right . . . yeah. [laughter]

JPDB: [laughter] So do you . . . like when you do a chapbook . . . because I know a lot of people who do chapbooks and basically once they have two or three chapbooks then they make it a book. Which to me, I always view that as kind of a cheat, to a certain extent.

RA: Because they've been published twice, then?

JPDB: Well, it's not so much that, but I think, you know, as a writer you develop fans and, to me, it's a letdown to your fans because . . . you're asking them to buy something twice. [laughter]

RA: Oh . . . See . . . you must have people buy your books! [laughter]

JPDB: [laughter]

RA: [laughter] It hasn't been an issue so far for me. [laughter] I mean, I'm not a big chapbook fan for myself . . . But the two that I did, I entered contests—and they did them lovely, especially *The Verbs of Desiring* they did beautifully. But I have to admit I'm a really bad PR person for myself. I can send work out, but if I were a visual artist and had to take a portfolio and go speak to people . . . I just wouldn't. [laughter]

JPDB: [laughter]

RA: So I'm really, really bad at that kind of thing. I'm really interested in making the work [laughter] and the whole getting-it-out-there or thinking about audience or anything that is way outside is a different job to me.

JPDB: Hmm. Interesting.

RA: It's just a wholly different job, and it's one that I'm not very good at. I'm pretty good at staying in a room by myself. [laughter]

JPDB: [laughter]

RA: But going out into the world is a little rougher.

JPDB: Yeah. Nah . . . It's funny. 'Cause I used to send stuff all the time and then, I think, in the last couple of years I've really, really trailed off.

RA: It's easy to do.

JPDB: I tend to spend more time on the actual work and less time on the sending out part.

RA: I think, for me . . . I think of the work as . . . a trajectory. I wrote this thing and I have it hanging up over my wall along with all sorts of other bizarre stuff, but it says, *One of the frustrations of writing is that growth is slow,* *our work made up entirely, of trajectory.*

JPDB: Hmm.

RA: So, I'm looking kind of at the long now . . . I mean, yes, I'm trying to craft every poem to the best I'm able at that given time, and then make the book to the best I'm able to do at that time, but I want to . . . see where that takes me. It's almost as though each thing is kind of an example of the adjacent possible. Alright, I've done this; where will I end up next time? You know, where will my brain take me? And that's what I find really interesting.

JPDB: Yeah. I can honestly say that I think a good portion of what I've done in the last couple of years, as far as submitting work, has been people asking me for stuff.

RA: That's nice! That doesn't happen to a lot of people.

JPDB: Yeah. And obviously I don't want them to stop asking me, so I feel kind of obligated to respond, but . . .

RA: Yeah, of course . . . Oh, that's an honor, to be asked!

JPDB: Exactly. Yeah, and I've been lucky that way, so I don't want to dismiss it in any regard. And I really don't care. It's nice to be asked so I don't make a judgment on who's asking. [laughter]

RA: Oh, no, and the few times I've been asked nor do I, but, again, it's that not getting myself out there, and you know, if I don't meet people, who will ask me? I don't know that the books really get around that much.

JPDB: Yeah, it's hard to say, although I will say yours had more reviews than I've seen for a lot of books lately. Your most recent one . . .

RA: The new one? [laughter] You'll have to tell me where they were!

JPDB: [laughter]

RA: [laughter] 'Cause I was thinking, "Oh my goodness!" You know, there was one in *Publishers Weekly.*

JPDB: Yeah, well that's a good one.

RA: And on a blog. Those, I think, are the only two I've seen.

JPDB: Yeah, I saw another one . . . I forget where it was . . .

RA: Hmm . . . Well, yay me! [laughter]

JPDB: [laughter]

RA: The thing I did do is send out a lot of copies, and I did that myself, to reviewers.

JPDB: Right.

RA: As far as I know, three people—including the one I don't know that you know about—[laughter] . . . have taken me up on it.

JPDB: Yeah, I'm not sure there were more. That's as far as I could get, 'cause that wasn't what I was actually looking for. [laughter]

RA: I mean, that's another thing. For somebody to actually take the time to review a book . . . at least gives the book some sort of . . . I won't say *honor,* but worthy-of-attention, be it good, bad, or mixed. At least somebody thought it was worth talking about.

JPDB: I agree. I'm one of those people who doesn't believe that there are bad reviews . . . just in that, if somebody's calling you out, or calling your work out, they're not calling you out. They're calling the work out.

RA: It's true, but it would be hard to take. [laughter]

JPDB: Exactly.

RA: [laughter]

JPDB: But there's something about it that is obviously worth mentioning or talking about, so . . .

RA: Well, I certainly hope so.

JPDB: I guess it's the same thing as "There's no bad publicity."

RA: I guess it's true, but some of us are awfully mooshy, you know, and everything seems personal. Even when your brain says it's not.

JPDB: [laughter] Yeah.

RA: I go whimpering away if something . . .

JPDB: [laughter]

RA: I remember when somebody wrote about my first book that it was terribly prosaic, and I thought, "The man has no ears!"

JPDB: [laughter]

RA: And then I thought, "No, that's not the right . . . [laughter] . . . not the right response. You should be ashamed of yourself." So I try to put myself in my student's place, because I'm a killer. [laughter] They call me "The Slasher," which I think is really funny. However at a different school, they called me "The Dragon Lady"!

JPDB: [laughter]

RA: I'm getting a reputation for something. Anyway, I'm very, very big on compression, and I'll mark out whole sections of where they're just talking, you know? Blah-blah blah-blah blah-blah-blah-bla-blahbah. And they're usually stunned.

JPDB: Yeah.

RA: But they also usually get it by the time they get their Master's Degree, but, still, at first, they just can't believe that I don't appreciate that their grandmother died. You know? [laughter]

JPDB: [laughter] Well, the other thing you see is the conversational thing that gets people started into a poem . . .

RA: Oh, yeah. Yeah.

JPDB: A lot of times you can just get rid of that, you don't need that.

RA: Yes. Yes. The pre-writing that forgot to be pre-.

JPDB: [laughter]

RA: Yes. Well, that's also part of that . . . I guess the trajectory runs through everything, because that is the beginning of the bridge.

JPDB: Um hm . . .

RA: Right? That's that stuff in the beginning that gets you to where you are going. You just have to learn to recognize it.

JPDB: Right. It pulls you out of the dark and gives you focus.

RA: Stephen Dunn said a fabulous thing—though he says he didn't say it but he did, I was there—

JPDB: [laughter]

RA: He said, "The poem doesn't start until you surprise yourself."

JPDB: Interesting.

RA: Which I think is fabulous, because I can see, when I'm reading something, if my posture changes, suddenly they've got my attention. If I'm slopped back in the chair, with my usual dreadful posture, I'm just going duh-da-duh-da-duh-da . . . , you know? But I can tell, I sit up, I lean into the book or the piece of paper when a poem actually ignites—and it always seems very clear to me. So I think that's that moment of surprising . . . where, probably, the writer surprised herself.

JPDB: Hmm. Yeah. We're coming up on the break, so I want to have you read a couple of more poems.

RA: OK. This is "An Art Like Any Other." [reads poem]

JPDB: Hmm.

RA: This is a short one. It's called "My Father Is Ashes." [reads poem]

JPDB: Hmm. And we are going to take a break. My guest, in case anybody tuned in late, is Renée Ashley and she has been reading from *Because I Am the Shore I Want To Be the Sea*, which is out by Subito Press. And I hope I'm saying that right. Did I say that right?

RA: I think so!

JPDB: We'll be back with her on the other side to have her continue reading and sharing her thoughts. All right. You are listening to a public radio station.

[Station break.]

My guest on line with us is Renée Ashley and we should have her read a couple more poems.

RA: I'm listening to you name all these towns, and I'm from out there. I spent my summers in Boulder Creek, and more than half of it in Santa Cruz and Soquel, so—ah! I'm getting a little homesick.

JPDB: [laughter]

RA: All right. This is "All My Suicides Have Been Men." [reads poem]

RA: This is a short one called "What Is Visible Is What Mostly Is."

JPDB: You had mentioned you were born in Palo Alto . . .

RA: Yeah!

JPDB: So, I always wondered, do you ever get back this way, or . . . does that just not happen?

RA: Umm. My mom was alive until two years ago. She died at one hundred-and-one-and-a-half.

JPDB: Wow.

RA: Wow, is right 'cause she told me all the people in my family died at fifty . . .

JPDB: [laughter]

RA: . . . so, for ten years I held my breath waiting to drop dead in the street.

JPDB: [laughter]

RA: [laughter] So, I went back to clear up her things, and now I have a couple of friends there, but really not a lot of time. And I love where I live now, too, and I couldn't afford to move back there, certainly. [laughter] Yeah, though I did go to Santa Cruz . . . maybe eight years ago? And I used to know that town like the back of my hand. I could crawl on my knees to find the corndogs . . . I couldn't find my way out of town. [laughter]

JPDB: Wow. [laughter]

RA: [laughter] It had changed so much. I drove around for over an hour before I actually made it out of town. It was so crowded! Since the university, it has just powered up to the tenth power!

JPDB: Yeah. I always think, because I know people who grew up there and remember it when it was somewhat more of a fishing kind of community.

RA: Oh, absolutely. Yeah . . .

JPDB: You know . . . with some oddball surfers . . .

RA: We used to stay in these little cabins that were all smooshed together about a block from the ocean, which, of course, are all gone now. But it was an entirely different place.

JPDB: Yeah. Well, the same thing is true . . . I knew people who grew up in San Jose, and they remember it before the big Silicon Valley bust . . . I mean boom.

RA: Oh, yeah! Well, that has changed even Redwood City, which was where I lived. Boy, has that changed!

JPDB: [laughter]

RA: Again, *crowded!* [laughter] *Really* crowded! In fact, there are now roads where there didn't used to be any land! It was the bay! They've filled in a bunch of the bay. I think that's kind of amazing. I remember I was going to the Salvation Army and my mother said, "You won't be able to find it," and I said "Pfffft! Of course I can find it!" I couldn't find it.

JPDB: [laughter] Wow. Well, it is weird. Now I have friends who have been gone from the Bay Area for thirty-five years, and they'll say the same thing. It's so weird to see pictures of it or to walk through and nothing looks the same. It's like a whole different place entirely.

RA: Yeah. Well, I think it is a whole different place. It's got a different kind of energy; it's got a different demographic, certainly. It's kind of amazing.

JPDB: Yeah. It's funny because recently I watched *Cosmos* where he was talking about, you know, the planet of the past . . .

RA: Yes . . . yes.

JPDB: . . . you know, being a whole different planet [laughter] than the one you're on now.

RA: Uh huh . . . Yep.

JPDB: And I just . . . That guy blows my mind so many times it's unbelievable!

RA: Yeah! My husband . . . We sit there and go, *"Really?"* [laughter]

JPDB: [laughter] Uh, but, yeah, I think about that when people talk about things being so different.

RA: Incredible. I've been gone about thirty years, I guess.

JPDB: Yeah. [laughter]

RA: It's weird that the world just goes on without us! that it doesn't stay the way we remember it. And I probably don't even remember mostly correctly, so . . .

JPDB: Well that's true, that's what they say about memory is that it's an inaccurate form of . . .

RA: Oh, my heavens!

JPDB: [laughter]

RA: [laughter] I've been reading about it for creative nonfiction classes, and I make them read Schacter's *The Seven Sins of Memory.*

JPDB: Ummhmm . . .

RA: . . . and they're just . . . they're traumatized. [laughter]

JPDB: [laughter]

RA: . . . and these are adults, you know? who already have jobs. They're absolutely . . . "Really? Really, I could be wrong?" and I say, "Yeah." [laughter]

JPDB: [laughter] OK. Let's have you read a couple of more poems.

RA: OK. This is "How to See It." [reads poem]

JPDB: Hmm.

RA: And this one is called "Look." [reads poem]

JPDB: I want to ask you . . . The book title *[Because I Am the Shore I Want To Be the Sea]* suggests some sort of—to me it does—The grass is always greener on the other side sort of situation. . .

RA: Exactly . . . [laughter]

JPDB: [laughter]

RA: Yes. What more can I say? I can't even quibble with that.

JPDB: [laughter]

RA: I'm *astonished* at the ability to change our wants, right? When we get what we want, it's no longer what we want, so we want something else. It's that state of wanting . . . that . . . I don't know. . . must pump up the dopamine and then you get a dose when you get it and pffft! you're out, you know? and . . .

JPDB: [laughter]

RA: . . . you're off to something else that's going to send those things flying. I'm constantly astonished . . .

JPDB: Yeah. . . It's a great title, and I was wondering, do you see the individual voices in this collection in this sort of way? you know, kind of all speaking to those wants? or . . .

RA: I think it's a theme that I don't seem to be able to get away from . . .

JPDB: [laughter]

RA: [laughter] There's this wonderful book called *Fire in the Crucible* by John Briggs on creativity, and he talks about how we always hear, "Oh, you know, a poet writes the same poem over and over again until he drops dead and that's when he stops writing the poem." Brigg's talks about these *themata*—our obsessions, our abstract obsessions, the things we goofed up and would like to change, regret. [laughter] That sort of thing. And they just . . . I think they tend to eat us. I feel like there's a giant PacMan of regret [laughter] just about to close his mouth around me most of the time.

JPDB: Hmm . . .

RA: [laughter] . . . in many ways and for many things.

JPDB: That's interesting. That's a deeper answer . . . [laughter]

RA: Oh, you're just too psychologically balanced to [laughter] understand. [laughter] I'm just, you know . . . I'm . . . I don't know . . . I have felt, since 1967, I have felt responsible for my father's suicide.

JPDB: Hmmm . . .

RA: And I was sixteen at the time, and I wrote about it when I was thirty-one, and I wrote about it when I was forty-seven, and I thought, OK, I'm done. I've written this out, and I'm done. Oh, my goodness . . . In rereading this book . . . [laughter] he's everywhere. He's everywhere. Clearly I can't shake it, you know . . .

JPDB: Yeah . . .

RA: I didn't pull the trigger, but . . . We had a big fight . . . and then he shot himself at my mom's house. He lived in Boulder [Creek]; we lived in Red-wood City, and he had come for Easter, I think.

JPDB: Right.

RA: It's the first fight I ever had with my father. And I'm carrying that . . . I feel really bad that I did that.

JPDB: Hmm . . .

RA: I think he would have done the act at some point anyway. He was a ter-rifically unhappy man. But I was the catalyst for that particular time. I can't get rid of that.

JPDB: Wow . . . I wanted to ask you . . . 'cause I don't normally ask authors to read because normally they pick up on the thing that I . . . but there is one I did want to get you to read at some point . . .

RA: Sure.

JPDB: Which is "Utterance and Origin."

RA: Oh, sure . . .

JPDB: It's the last poem in the book.

RA: OK. Thank you. There is one thing about writing these poems in blocks: [laughter] You don't find them as quickly when you're trying to!

JPDB: [laughter]

RA: It's crazy, they all look the same! OK. OK, here we go . . . OK. Funny, it's the one I had set to read last . . . I marked that one "last." "Utterance and Origin." . . . [laughter] [reads poem]

JPDB: Hmm. I've read that one several times . . . [laughter] I just wanted to make sure that . . . I wanted to hear you read it, basically. [laughter]

RA: [laughter] Is it what you expected?

JPDB: Yeah, yeah, I . . .

RA: I mean sometimes it isn't. We read things that aren't really on the page.

JPDB: Well, that's true, and everybody has a different way of presenting. Which is . . . I'm cool with that, in fact I encourage it. On this show we've done several times, where we've had, either people read other people's poems or I've gone out and found people who have read and recorded . . .

RA: Oh, that's nice! Yeah. That's really nice.

JPDB: Yeah. And then wherever I can find an example of the author reading it, then I . . . then you can juxtapose, you can see, side by side, where the emphasis is placed.

RA: Right . . . Well, because the author knows what she intended.

JPDB: Right.

RA: The reader can only know what she achieved.

JPDB: Exactly.

RA: She has no way . . . I mean it's that whole intentional fallacy thing . . . She, the reader, has no way of knowing what you meant to say—only what you said. And I think there's all sorts of interference for us . . . for the writer . . . I think we don't always know what it is we've said.

JPDB: Right. Right.

RA: It's funny. After this, I started writing a whole . . . It struck me so funny . . . I think I'm *so* funny, it's just awful . . .

JPDB: [laughter]

RA: [laughter] It's just embarrassing, but I started a whole series of poems called "from Her Book of Difficulties." [laughter]

JPDB: [laughter] I would be remiss if I let you get out of here [laughter] . . .

RA: [laughter]

JPDB: . . . without talking about *The Literary Review.*

RA: Oh! OK.

JPDB: Because you're the poetry editor there and . . .

RA: Well, I was until a few months ago, but I can . . .

JPDB: Oh, really!

RA: . . . certainly talk about it. Yes.

JPDB: Oh, no! I didn't realize that.

RA: I did it for seven years, and I was reading all my students' work, I was reading every single poem in the slush . . . and there were many . . . [laughter]

JPDB: Wow . . .

RA: And it got to be . . . It got to be somebody else's turn, I decided. [laughter] I loved it, but I need two lives.

JPDB: Right . . .

RA: . . . to get it all done.

JPDB: Wow . . .

RA: But I'd be *happy* to talk to you about what I was doing when I was doing it.

JPDB: Well, I was going to say that, just from what you said about reading your students' work and critiquing that, it seems to me you probably applied the same . . . measurement to the work you were reading for the magazine.

RA: Um . . . much more stringent! [laughter]

JPDB: Right, but I mean you were looking for things that were going to make you shift, basically.

RA: Yeah. Yes. To make me lean forward . . . and I have offered, you know . . . arrogance, but, anyway, I have offered people editing, and saying, "Look . . .

this isn't working for me," or, "What can we do . . ." and I actually never had anybody admit to being mad at me, and everybody took my editing choices.

JPDB: Wow . . .

RA: Yes, which is unusual, I think.

JPDB: Yes, I can speak to the other thing happening.

RA: Yeah! [laughter]

JPDB: [laughter]

RA: But you know sometimes there would just be this *f-a-b-u-l-o-u-s* poem and a stinker of a closure. [laughter] I mean, they wrote this incredible, energetic thing . . . and then didn't know how to get out of it.

JPDB: Yeah . . .

RA: And sometimes . . . if you just point that out to somebody or say, "Perhaps . . . You started this and didn't explore this any further . . . You stopped too soon." My experience is that people have been glad of it.

JPDB: Yeah. No, I remember there was a . . . and he's a pretty well known author now, but I remember getting a set of . . . It was probably the third time he'd submitted work to me and I had noticed through almost every single one of them that he had the very same thing, which was just kind of a petering end . . .

RA: Hmm.

JPDB: And I was, like, "You know, you're frustrating me." I finally wrote to him and I said, "You're frustrating me, because I love these poems but they just peter out at the end and I'm not happy with that. I want more." And he wrote back to me and said, "Oh, thank you very much for the critique," and then sent me work that actually did what I was looking for.

RA: Yeah! I mean, they honestly, they can't read it cold. I can't read my stuff cold. Because, first of all, we're too close to it, second of all, we have that scrim of intention . . .

JPDB: Uh huh . . .

RA: It takes a cold eye.

JPDB: Yeah.

RA: I always approach it gingerly, but I don't mince words once somebody lets me in.

JPDB: Yeah.

RA: I mean . . . I get about half my income, now, from editing and . . . —not the magazine, but people's manuscripts and that kind of thing—and [laugh] I get a negative reaction and then two weeks later a note saying, "Perhaps I was hasty. . . ."

JPDB: [laugh]

RA: [laugh]

JPDB: I've always been appreciative of anybody who is willing to make a comment because I feel, you know, it means I did *something* right for them to do that.

RA: Well, it takes time to do that! They've thought about it. They didn't just dismiss it.

JPDB: And I think I've only argued once with an editor and it had more to do with aesthetics than anything else. Because I think they were locked into a particular aesthetic and not open-minded enough to took at, you know, work that . . . I always have a problem with people who adhere to just one school of whatever, or . . . Just because I think that it's too limiting, and it's . . .

RA: Right. Right. There's a whole big pie out there.

JPDB: Exactly.

RA: . . . and it's got all sorts . . . I mean poetry just comes from every angle and there's room for all of it, even if I think it's bad . . . there's room for it.

JPDB: Yeah.

RA: But I do think I have a pretty broad aesthetic and it's all doing something different—as long as it does it well.

JPDB: Right. We've come to the end of the hour, so I want to make sure we get at least one poem in, hopefully two.

RA: Aah! OK. Is there something I haven't read that you'd like to hear?

JPDB: You have done a pretty good job.

RA: [laughter] Oh. Here. I'll do my mother poem. This is "I Have a Theory about Reflection." [reads poem]

JPDB: Hmm. And if you have another short one you'd like to share . . .

RA: Yeah. I'll read the first part of the title poem. This is "Because I Am the Shore I Want To Be the Sea, Part 1." [reads poem]

JPDB: Hmm. Renée, thanks so much for . . . I know it's late where you are, so I appreciate your staying up to be with us.

RA: Oh, I loved it. Thank you very much.

JPDB: And have a nice night, and I'll contact you in a little bit.

RA: Fabulous. Good night.

JPDB: Bye. OK, and that was Renée Ashley and her book is *Because I Am the Shore I Want To Be the Sea*, Subito Press [pronounces again, differently, then laughs]. So, you may want to look for that.

J.P. Dancing Bear is the editor of *The American Poetry Journal* as well as the author of six full-length collections of poetry, the most recent of which is *Cephalopodic*. He is also the author of six chapbooks. Find him at www.jp-dancingbear.squarespace.com.

WHAT ARE YOU READING?

BECAUSE I AM THE SHORE I WANT TO BE THE SEA

INTERVIEW BY MATTHEW THORBURN

[June 5, 2014]

Matthew Thorburn: Why prose poems? Do you find that prose poems offer unique opportunities that poems in lines don't—and vice versa? How do you decide a poem will be a prose poem, rather than in lines? Were the poems in *Because I Am the Shore I Want To Be the Sea* always prose poems?

Renée Ashley: Prose poems seem such a challenge to me, partially because the form isn't codified, so if a writer says it's a *prose poem* then it's a prose poem—but if that poem doesn't jump up and do something striking and do it well, then it's just a dollop of, at best, competent prose. I knew there had to be a dynamic that could make it into something I couldn't construct in another way. And I love the rigor and effect of extreme compression, which I think is one of the keys to making something leap off the page. I wanted the sense of pressure that only justified right and left margins could give—the feeling of being trapped inside a sealed vessel, always at the moment of about-to-explode, no way out—the way we are, so often, in our heads. Or the way I am, anyway. I think of the prose poem as a sort of pressure cooker. That's what I wanted: no energy leaks and the content volatile, forcing itself against the physical limits of its containment walls. The pressure, to my mind, should be bi-directional: verbal pressure inside pushing out against the rigid, vertical dividing line between text and white space and the visual, structural pressure, the rigid margin of external, white space, pressing back.

I seem to know from the onset—or at least believe I do—what impulse is propelling an act of writing. I can hear it in the pacing or see it in the embrace of focus. In *Because . . .* I went very consciously after the prose poem form. It took me years to find what I felt was the right mix. Every poem I wrote, for so long, was so obviously lineated that I began to think I was never going to be able to write a decent prose poem. Only when I utterly gave up and felt resigned to just prose and poetry, did I somehow find a way in. My aesthetic was formed as I tried things out—I kept what worked for me and discarded what didn't. I wrote a lot of essays during that period-of-can't-make-the-prose-poem-happen, a form that seems to me the polar opposite of the prose poem—it's so elastic. I'm pretty horrified to admit that a few of the poems that appear in block form in the book were not conceived as prose poems—and this is something I've never done before, change a piece into something it wasn't intended to be. I reworked and pruned them, I think, into better poems in the prose poem shape. (With one exception which is kind of a personal joke.) There were only two or three of these, thank heavens. The after-the-fact shaping is not nearly as satisfying as having the work ignite in the shape it will take in the end. I did it for more cohesiveness on a book-scale rather than on the poem-scale. But I wouldn't do it again; it's unnatural and much too convenient a compromise. I'm not certain verbal art from such an impulse is really that plastic. I'm such a hidebound old thing.

MT: I find your use of capitalization combined with limited punctuation (that is, no periods) really interesting. For me, this gives your prose poems a very lyrical feel: meaning is sometimes blurred or doubled as thoughts overlap or bump up against each other, and everything moves very quickly. The poems convey the feeling of a mind in motion, moving swiftly from thought to thought. How did you come to this approach—and what is the appeal of it for you?

RA: Thank you, Matthew! I'm so happy it reads that way. Yes. No terminal punctuation but question marks and exclamation points. It was about the pressure again. Each phrase or clause needed to run into the next without a full stop; I didn't want the reader to have a pressureless gap through which to escape; I had to keep up the momentum and the horizontal tensile strength. I used capitalization for the orchestration of sentences or fragments and also to take advantage of some ambiguities that I felt added in a positive way to the pressure-pot. I wanted speed and profluence to compound the pressure that was forcing movement, building momentum, and the sense of being trapped in a thread of thought with no exit. The appeal? The possibility of transferring the sensation of head-as-inescapably-sealed-vessel to paper. That was the ideal I worked towards; I didn't achieve it exactly, of course, but it's what I was aiming for. And also, in the book, there's more white space between the lines than there was in the manuscript: the poems manifested there as much denser and impenetrable. I can understand, though, why the publisher and designer wanted more space between the lines of text. It was difficult to read them in their more compact form; I admit it.

MT: How does a poem start for you? In particular, how did "[contemplation within the framework of the dream]" or "[oh yes tomorrow expect the ordinary]" start? And what was your writing and revising process like with these poems?

RA: I inevitably begin with a title or first line, an image with a rhythm. I let that beginning generate (sound and association) what follows so that, if I succeed, the dynamic of the poem evolves almost naturally, however strange the poem itself may turn out. All art is artifice, I know, but I'm after a seamless quality that exists in nature. A hybrid, if you will. I rarely, if ever, know where a poem is going to end up, in fact I almost never do, but the poem creates itself from top to bottom, the first line or sentence feeding the second, the second the third, etc. Every once in a while, near the end of a poem, I'll have to change the order of some lines—or sentences in the case of the prose poem— but more often not. I can't move forward until what I have feels right—approximate doesn't do it for me—otherwise I'll generate something that won't align well in the end. It's not an efficient way to work, I know. But it's the only way I have.

Both poems you mention were prose poems from inception, but "[oh yes. . .]" is a kinder, gentler poem than ["Contemplation . . ."]. That's the penultimate poem in the book. At that point, I'm trying to ease up on the reader and begin to release him back into the world, not raise his blood pressure.

MT: These poems feel like a sequence to me, almost like the chapters of a very succinct novel. It's a subtle feeling, but it seems like certain themes or ideas or images (or animals) surface and resurface throughout the book. Did you envision writing a sequence or a collection of prose poems from the beginning, or did they gradually build up momentum, or . . . ?

RA: It's funny. Others have said this to me—about a buried narrative—but I never saw it when I was putting the book together, and I haven't had a chance to just sit down and read it through to see if I can find it. But as for returning themes and images, those I'm aware of. In John Brigg's book, *The Fire in the Crucible*, he talks about a writer's *themata*, the themes that a writer returns to in her work again and again, and heaven knows I've got mine in spades.

And that, in fact, may be one of the sources of the sealed-vessel feeling that I so often experience, the I-can't-get-away-from-me feeling. Those recurring themes are so obvious, in fact, that, years ago, someone I didn't know at all, came up to me after a reading and said in this really withering tone, something like, "You don't think much of love, do you?" and instead of thinking, *Oh, wow! He's actually read my work*, I laughed. I had to admit it: Nope. No, I really don't. I hadn't articulated that to myself before that night. It was like this nova of recognition that burst out of my mouth in the form of a laugh. He was horrified, of course, and probably never read another thing I wrote— but it was such a surprise! But coming back to sequence, I do order poems in a book according to a vague tension-model of Freytag's triangle, easing in, building intensity, then backing off, and that may be a contributory factor in the sensation of sequence.

With the exception of my first book, *Salt*, in which I was learning what a poem was, I've written my books as books rather than eclectic compilations. I'll have, maybe, five poems toward a new manuscript when I'll recognize what hobby horse I'm riding into the ground this particular time and I'll construct the book on that arc. In my second book, *The Various Reasons of Light*, I was learning how to ground the abstract; that was definitely my conscious project. In my third, *The Revisionist's Dream*, I went back to my Comparative Literature roots. The fourth one, *Basic Heart*, that's my "nervous breakdown book" though, luckily, I didn't have one—but it was written during a patch that was about as rough as it's gotten. And *Because I Am the Shore . . .* was definitely meant to be a book of prose poems. I'm far too much a seeker-of-similarities-and-patterns to work randomly; I see a pattern, I begin to recognize some obsession-of-the-next-four-or-five-years, and work *with* it rather than letting it work against me.

MT: What's next for you, writing-wise? Are you writing more prose poems?

RA: I am! It takes me, on the average, four or five years to write a book. And I'm about half-way through another book of prose poems. I'm also pulling my essays and reviews together into a single book-length manuscript—wish me luck on that one! That's sure to be a best seller! They're almost all hybrids: essay/reviews, personal essays/craft essays, interviews. It'll be ready to send that out by the end of June, I think. I don't know yet, though, what I'll do after this next collection of prose poems is completed. I don't usually recognize the new impetus/obsession until the current project is at least past the half-way mark. Evidently, that's how I get things finished, one thing nudging the nearly-completed other thing off the road. I may jot down some notes, etc, but I don't allow myself to focus on anything new until the previous project is bagged up and ready to leave home. It can get frustrating. I work on only one poem at a time. I can, though, work on a poem and an essay at the same time—they're such vastly different animals that there's no danger of my cross-breeding them and creating two identical monsters.

MT: And lastly, what are you reading these days?

RA: I read a lot of essays. I recently finished *The Empathy Exams*, which was really interesting and beautifully written though I did feel the heavy hand of theme on the book-scale. The individual essays on their own were fabulous. And that same author's, Leslie Jamison's, novel, *The Gin Closet*, which was superb as well. David Grand's *Mount Terminus* is an odd, beautiful, and brilliant novel; I finished that not too long ago. Oh! The first volume of *My Struggle* by Karl Ove Knausgaard kept me mesmerized but I haven't put my finger on why yet; I've got the second huge volume in my pile. Maybe I'll find out there. Fascinating. Oh! And Lloyd Jones. He's the most wonderful writer! He's a New Zealander, but born in Wales, I believe. He's famous for his novel *Mr. Pip* which a friend in New Zealand gave me a long time ago and which was surprising and just marvelous. I just finished his *biografi* and couldn't put it down! It's part travel, part creative nonfiction, in which he talks about a trip to and the history of Albania—not something I'd consciously seek out! But I read it in two days and I'm a slow, slow reader. Could. Not. Put. It. Down. I've just started his memoir, *A History of Silence*. I've only read about five pages and I'm smitten. Clean, musical, divine prose. I've got two more of his novels in my pile. And I've just read Ellen Akins' new novel-in-manuscript; she writes the most intricate, amazing characters and her sentences are gorgeous, to die for. She's a remarkable writer and this new book is going to really get a lot of attention, I think. It's brilliantly strange and familiar. I believed every word. I also listen to *a lot* of nonfiction in the car (I'm often in the car for long stretches of time). And, of course, I read a ton of poetry. I've got poetry books in piles everywhere as well as scattered around the house (just like I do pairs of reading glasses). I like to dip into them. Who's on my tables now? Let's see: Alex Lemon, Mary Ruefle, Kathleen Jesme, Rusty Morrison, Cole Swensen, Dennis Nurkse, Martha Collins, Frank Bidart, Saskia Hamilton . . . I know there are at least half a dozen more lying open around here . . . I also want to reread Helen Vendler's books of criticism. She's astounding: such a lover of poetry and so smart. And Stephen Burt, who slays me. I want to reread Ellen Bryant Voigt's book on syntax. There's *so much* I want to read! I admit it. I'm a book addict. And life's too darn short!

Matthew Thorburn is a poet and essayist. He's the author of six collections of poetry. The most recent is *Dear Almost: A Poem*. Find him at www.matthewthorburn.net. His interviews with writers, first published on that site as the "What Are You Reading?" series, now appear on the *Ploughshares* blog as a monthly feature.

PERORATION RATHER THAN POSTSCRIPT:
EVERY DOG'S A LOST DOG, THE BLUEBIRD
OF NESS, AND NEXT TIME

My mother, Carmen Jones, the focus of so many of the pages in this book, died at one hundred and one-and-a-half years of age at six a.m. on August 5, 2012, though I remember thinking, when I finally saw the death certificate, that it had been one day later. I had completed the essay, "Of a Kind," just months before. The ringtone on my cell startled me out of my first-cup-of-coffee haze, blasting out Janis Joplin's "Maybe" at about nine a.m. Eastern Daylight Time. I was in my dorm room—the faculty floor, no different than any other floor—getting dressed for a long day of residency workshops and lectures. After I stifled Janis, the voice that came through the phone was unfamiliar, soft, apologetic, young-sounding, and male. I knew what he was going to say well before he told me his name, which I failed to write down; that voice had already given it away. I'd been expecting this call for thirty years.

While he was speaking, I had a vision—literally—of a flat, brushed aluminum bar, rectangular, long, narrow, and, less than a quarter-inch thick—I swear it was this oddly clear and specific—unbending and burnished, and turned so that I could see the shape of its small, blunt end. It simply existed in the blue-tinged air; then, along its length, the knife-sharp corners started softening downward, dropping, as if in slow, heatless motion, into a molten roundedness, its unsafe contours disarmed. And I knew far more quickly than I could have put it into words: I was no longer capable of writing about Ma with the sharpness I had experienced while she was living. I, too, had lost my edge. No one in the world could hurt me like my mother and, for the first time in my sixty-three years, she could not.

My original plan—Plan A—for the two weeks at the artists' colony, was to finish up this collection with a preface that touched on the ideas of hybridity, the concept of minglement and writing and thinking, themata, and discovery as process, just a handful of preparatory pages to make clear the importance of divergent thinking, and the way I make sense of the small parts of the world that I do find a way to make sense of. After that call I was in a place where a preface seemed both impossible and impractical. My mental state dictated not a beginning, but an ending, the conclusion of the ambient context of my entire life before that moment. The axis of the planet Renée had shifted, the tectonic plates had broken free, and more things in heaven and earth, Reader, were coming to an end, than were dreamt of for my Preface.

If you've read the essays that precede this one, you know my mother was funny—*wicked funny*, as my friend Eric would say. And she was more than just a little wicked as well. She had the usual I-married-a-drunk issues—shame, secrecy, grievous and, often, displaced rage. She had, as well, a bitter resentment of any exchange that smacked of someone with balls enough to disagree with her, and then, of course, another compounding wallop of shame if she imagined the treachery had been witnessed by some third party. She was a difficult woman, like I can be. We were too much alike and far too different for any easy rapport. We disappointed each other in too many ways to count. Ma had always relished pointing out that I was exactly like her. Nearly every time we spoke, she repeated the godawful clause, *You didn't lick it off the wall*, in the way some other parent might have said, *Nice job! I'm so proud of you.* To Ma, I could be only an extension of herself, an extra, fully functional and inoperable limb.

The doctor offered his condolences that morning and my silence, which I could not control, was the type that follows sudden comprehension rather than an angry or emotional holding back. But, to break the clearly uncomfortable lull, he offered me answers to the questions it never occurred to me to ask: comfortably, she had passed comfortably; she was just no longer strong enough to fight the recurring pneumonias combined with her interstitial lung disease that had left her breathless and on oxygen for years. And all through that nearly one-sided conversation my heart and brain were in a state of stasis, of a single, protracted "Oh." I was wondering whether this were the first call of this nature this young resident had had to make. "I'm glad she was calm. I'm glad she was in the hospital," I told him, then added: "She felt safer there," which had always been true.

The staff, she had made very clear, at both the convalescent home and the assisted living house, were cruel, lazy, and incompetent—except for one woman whom Ma trusted, a part-timer—and she called the residents of both places "nuts" and "vegetables" within earshot. I was hoping, too, that knowing she would have preferred dying in the hospital would make that poor young man feel better. In the end, he, very kindly, asked if he could do anything for me and was there anyone he might call for me. There wasn't a soul I could think of.

Nor was there any reason for me to go to California. Ma's friend Peter, who owned the house next to the one that had been her own, very generously offered to clear out her room at the assisted living home. Directions for the disposal of Ma's body were already in her hospital file along with her *Do Not Resuscitate* order. Ma had taken care of it. "So you don't have to bother yourself."

After years of saying she was going to sign the Neptune Society papers (a funeral organization whose contractual duty would be to collect her body, cremate it, and sprinkle the ashes in the ocean) she'd read about a scandal. A huge pile of ashes and bone fragments, she reported, had been found on a corner lot somewhere in California and traced back to the Neptune Society. Evidently truckloads of ashes had been dumped there over the years. And though we both knew the subtext, we both said that we thought it screamingly funny, though horrible, certainly for the duped customers alive and dead, not to mention the families. Then, many years later, she'd signed the papers and sent them a check and reminded me she'd always loved the ocean. Out of curiosity, I looked up the Neptune ash-scandal villainy. In the spring of 1984, someone in Sutter Creek, California, hiking, I imagine, had found what appeared to be human bone fragments "in heaps" strewn across a remote hillside. The owner of the land was a pilot hired by the Neptune Society, and several mortuaries, to scatter cremated remains "at sea or over the Sierra Nevada." That was close enough in Ma-speak.

Ma had always insisted: no viewing, no wake, no service, no obituary, no garage sale. She didn't want people gawking at her body or talking about her when she couldn't be around to tell them to go to hell. All I had to do was send a check for the two hundred dollars she had warned me about for a cardboard box they would cremate her in. A law had been passed after she had paid her fees: no unboxed bodies in the crematory's retort.

There was nothing for me to do the day of her death but explain to my students what had happened that morning—though I didn't tell them about the vision—and ask them to bear with me if I seemed a little spacey. They were more than understanding. I think I kept saying it aloud, "My mom died this morning," to put it out into the world, to see it outside of myself—a statement of fact, like *A semicolon is normally used to separate independent clauses.* Or, *No, James, it's not a good idea to have sex with your sister.* I said: *My mom is dead. She died.* A redundancy no one called me on.

As far back as I can remember, Ma insisted that all the women on her side of the family had died in their fifties, which was the reason that, for a decade, I made no long-range plans—pretty much held my breath waiting to drop. And, if what she said were true—it turned out not to be, by the way—my mother had used up two lifetimes. The reason I had no children? I told her she'd usurped my only child's allotment of life. I said it as often as the subject came up—admittedly it was rare—and she responded with vigor that it was "because of those damn dogs" of mine, not her. And I don't remember a single instance in which she did not, with a wistful voice, add the coda, "You're better off anyway. They only break your heart." And the conversation would dwindle from there down to some other laughable or lamentable topic.

The truth was, of course, I had no children because I'd been lucky. I'm far too involved with dragging my own sorry self through each day to be capable of humanely towing along someone else—even a small someone else. I do believe there is some truth to the notion that some people shouldn't have children; there are genetics and predispositions to consider: Both my parents were deeply depressed, my father's manifesting in silence and alcoholism, a product, Ma told me, late in my own life and offhandedly, of the loss of the great love of his life, his first wife—he had a *first* wife?—who died very shortly after they were married; my mother showed her own in an addiction to a resentment so soul-searing that I honestly believe she was capable of deeply enjoying almost nothing.

Born Carmen Regina Schweyer, she'd said she'd long ago dropped *Regina* and changed her middle name to *Delores*—from *queen* to *sorrows*. After her death, while going through her papers, I found that she hadn't changed her name legally, but had simply, as was her wont, decreed that it was so. I often wear a bracelet of hers, a narrow cuff, made by my father, of twisted and flattened stainless steel rods, handed over to me decades before she died. Her initials are engraved into the top: CDJ. The J was for Jones, her married name.

It's impossible to sort out her true threads from her untrue ones. My mother lied with frequency, and, I think, for a lot of reasons. For her one-hundredth birthday, because she'd told me the doctors said she had ten days to live, I flew to California—though when I arrived, she was out of bed and looking pretty robust for a dying centenarian. I had packed a blank journal and asked her to tell me some stories about her life. I thought that, in her *extremis*, she might tell me something other than the five heartbreakings-slash-character-builders I'd heard repeatedly all my life. And she did give me a few small anecdotes along with some variations of the ones I'd heard in my youth.

She could not stop obsessing about her birth date; I would find that the date on her birth certificate was incorrect because her mother, after she had divorced—a huge scandal at the time that made the front page of the newspaper, *The San Francisco Call*—had knocked a few years off her own age and lowered the ages of Ma and her younger brother, as well, to make herself appear a more appealing catch. Ma was convinced that her life insurance policy—a small one purchased shortly after my birth in 1949—wouldn't pay up if I couldn't give them the correct date: April 19, 19*11*. They would ask me, she said, and I was to tell them she was born in nineteen-*eleven*, not twelve. Got it? I assured her I had it. I repeated it for her. I wrote the year and her directions on the flyleaf of my journal. Then I asked why her mother would think a single year would mean so much to the new husband. I was stunned to hear Ma say, "I don't know. I don't know. I've lied about everything all my life. I just don't know anymore." I wrote that down too. It was as though she had opened her mouth and a truth had simply fallen out and, apparently, flopped there, wide-open, on the tray-table between us. Then, as though she'd said nothing remarkable, she scuffed her fingers in the air over the table as if to brush the words, like crumbs, away.

Never, never, not even when called face-to-face on an obvious untruth, had she ever admitted she lied. I do understand that memory is unreliable; I've read Daniel Schacter's *The Seven Sins of Memory* and I've committed every one of them myself. But I'd known that, all my life, my mother had lied— to me and everyone else—yet the relief I felt at her words was exhilarating: I wasn't as crazy as I thought (though I hadn't even realized the lying had contributed to what I thought of as *my* craziness). I had gotten very good at tone of voice, and could spot one of Ma's fabrications most of the time. I just think I grew up figuring that talking to Ma was like testing the ice on an imaginary, but nevertheless deadly, pond; I had to be really, really vigilant and even then, if my attention lapsed for a fraction of a moment or the lie was something I really needed or wanted to hear, I could fall through and drown. And all of a sudden, the ice had become terra firma and my footing more confident. It turned out her birth certificate had the correct date and her distress and promptings had been for naught—assuming 1911 really was the year she was born. The Neptune Society did give me a call, though, because when she had filed the paperwork with them, some of the information she'd supplied conflicted with public record. I couldn't help them. I wasn't even sure of her mother's first name. The story had changed too many times.

It still seems to me that I've never understood what *forgiveness* might actually entail, the parameters of the feeling or the act. Is it possible that her death had operated with a sort of automatic activation switch? Like the glass doors at the supermarket that slide open when you weight-trip the switch or break their beam of light as you cross them? Might the vision of the softened aluminum bar have been a manifestation of forgiveness operating with the same sort of trigger? Because that's what it felt like.

I'd always understood, I think, that she did the best she could. Our world was miniscule and she was the woman behind and in front of the curtain, essentially a single and older-than-average mother with few skills. And yet I never went hungry, never was homeless, never was cold or dirty, and though I was swatted a few times—remind me to tell you about the hairbrush and the vacuum cleaner hose sometime—I never was beaten, never locked in a closet, never locked out of the house. The crime I'd been convicted of, I'm certain, was that I simply was incapable of loving her *enough*. I also loved my father. I loved books and school. I loved our cats. I loved our parade of dogs. I had spread my love too thin to satisfy her. Ma had begun motherhood, I'm certain, with a faulty premise: She made a child so someone would always love her, love only her, and love her unconditionally. Her life was already a disappointment at thirty-eight; people were treacherous. And then she'd been cheated all over again.

When Ma was still in assisted living, she told me someone brought a little rescue dog to the house to visit. I think it was a poodle. It did tricks. Ma would say, "There's a little dog coming from the pound and he dances on a balloon." I assumed she meant *ball* but I have no evidence of that other than the *éclat* of imagining a little dog's nails and weight atop a balloon. She might have meant *with* a balloon. It doesn't matter. Her mind was still pretty sharp but her word recall was beginning to falter. Nevertheless, those visits were, I think, literally, the only bright spots in her last year-and-a-half. She anticipated the dog's arrival and, on the several occasions she expected him but for some reason he didn't make it, she was crestfallen. Those nights she'd have the aids help her to bed right after dinner. The dog didn't have to dance on a balloon for her to love him. All he had to do was show up. If Ma got to see and hold him, to sink her hands in his fur, if he got onto her lap and licked her face, she was happy. She said he was always freshly bathed; he was soft and friendly, loved people and dancing on his balloon. She, and, I admit, myself as well, had *always* liked dogs better than people, but she'd been known to state the fact to any or all. They're so easy to make happy, dogs. They're so grateful. And they can't talk back.

Our very first dog was a fawn-colored, short-haired stray: no tags, no collar. We lived on Warrington Avenue, my parents' first house outside of San Francisco proper. Probably the first house they owned at all. I must have been . . . three? Maybe four? My father still lived with us. In fact, it's likely he hadn't yet been fired for breaking his contract by moving out of San Francisco County, so he was probably at work when, at my mother's instigation, we coaxed the dog, with a loaf of Wonder Bread from the tiny corner market back to our house a half-block away.

I named him *Snooky,* after Snooky Lanson, a singer on the TV show *Your Hit Parade.* And when we moved, around the time I began school, to a tract of stucco homes built in 1946 called *Redwood Village,* maybe a mile north of (unincorporated) Warrington, Snooky came too. I have no idea how long he stayed; it was likely a few years, but *stayed*, in Snooky's case, was a relative term. Ma explained, after the first few of his many disappearances, that he was a hobo dog. He'd be our dog for weeks or months and then he'd go away. Then he'd return. And at some point off he'd go again. He'd disappear for days or weeks, sometimes a month, perhaps more. Then he'd come back home. And his job, as he evidently saw it, was to trot alongside me as I rode my blue bike up and down the sidewalk between our house on Flynn Avenue and the Spring Street intersection. I wasn't allowed to ride on the street. Snooky would run alongside just beyond the concrete curb at the edge of the macadam road as though he were there to catch me if I fell. There were days he ran beside me for so long the pads of his feet grew raw. When I was sick, he sat on the couch with me and watched TV. He'd nuzzle me when I was sad. He was a sweet dog and took care of me. But he had his own business to take care of as well; he did what he had to do, I guess. I like to imagine that when he left me he went to the home of some other little girl that loved him just as much; that he stayed with her until he felt, for whatever reason drove him to it, he had to leave again. And that then he'd go on to some other child. Or he'd come home to me. I don't know what I imagined back then. It was just a fact: Snooky came and went and, when he returned, I was the one filled with a sense of belonging. One day he left and didn't come back. I don't remember grieving, only waiting. And when we moved across town to an apartment many years later, just before I entered high school—I must have been thirteen or fourteen—I was stricken by the idea that Snooky might return and we wouldn't be there. It still makes me feel hollow and sick when I imagine him coming back to find that we had left him behind.

For Ma, every dog was a lost dog. "Lost dog!" she'd shout whenever she saw any dog at all: loose dog, leashed dog, tethered-in-a-yard dog, dog in a driveway, dog in a park, dog in a car going past, head behind the glass or poking out of the window in the breeze, small dog in someone's arms, large guide dog for a blind man, any dog. "Lost dog!" she'd cry and she'd laugh. That shout was the one time I knew for certain I'd see her huge and rare, genuine smile. It was a game and it wasn't a game.

There were nights, after I left home, when she had "lost-dog" sleepovers. She'd seduce some dog into the house with a palm full of roast beef or shreds of chicken. "He's lost," she'd tell me on the phone. Sometimes she might add, "But he's pretty clean. And he seems to have a collar." And sometimes, "I can't quite make out his tags." And in the morning, after he'd slept on her bed, she'd share her breakfast with the animal or go to the neighborhood market and buy him his own. And, always, after he ate, the dog would stand by the door asking to be let out. She'd open the door, and he'd trot back to wherever he came from—to someone who, no doubt, was frantic about his whereabouts—and she'd call me to say, "That ungrateful little son-of-a-bitch went home." Then she'd sigh deeply and say, without a trace of irony, "He wasn't lost at all."

If, however, a disoriented, dirty, and footsore dog appeared, if he were collarless, unkempt or smelly or had runny eyes or a wound, she'd feed him, clean him up as best she could, and feed him again. She'd take him to the vet if she thought it was necessary, and then put the word out to the neighbors she was still speaking to: "Some selfish, shit-ass bastard let this nice little dog get lost. Can you imagine?" Only then would she call the *Tribune* and pay for a Lost and Found ad. The owner inevitably came and she inevitably responded with both relief and a broken heart. And after the dog and its master had gone, she'd call to say, "What's the matter with that goddamned asshole?" Her tone would have singed the eyebrows off a person standing near her. "What the hell kind of goddamned asshole loses a dog like that? Can you imagine losing a little (or big) dog like that?" Her closing coup was always, "He could have gotten hit by a car! Someone could have stolen him!" Her outrage was profound and real. Then she'd gather herself up, a bit calmer for having had the outburst. "Well," she'd say every time, "if the goddamned dog shows up again, I'm keeping the little (or big) shit."

Once Ma died, I began to see some of my early poems, those I considered dog poems, in a different light. In the middle of a public reading, I stopped stunned. How could I not have seen that poem for what it was? I continued the reading, of course, but, frankly, was flabbergasted at the blatant connections. One, "Lost Dogs," is a sestina—a poem with repeated words, teleutons, at the ends of lines—about love and about staying home. Now it seems goofy not to have seen the connection, and the poem seems prescient at the same time, though I'm not and it isn't. I wondered if I'd licked those themata, lost dogs and home, off my mother's wall. Not being able to return to her own house to live was really the worst thing that had ever happened to Ma.

Another poem, called "What We Don't Understand," calls up Ma and my relationship with her, though that wasn't at all my intention when I wrote it.

What We Don't Understand

> . . . Myth gives man, very importantly, the illusion
> that he can understand the universe and that he
> does understand the universe. It is, of course, only
> an illusion.
>
> Levi Strauss, *Myth and Meaning*

looks up at us and begs. It sits up. Bends
its outstretched paws at what would be the wrists—

we think it looks like us, or something like us,
but . . . different somehow. It has a tail. And there's

something in the eyes, something deep. But it wears
strange clothes: a collar, thick fur. And it knows

we're lost, we haven't got a clue. Wouldn't know one
if we saw one. And it's true, we don't, we wouldn't.

But its tail thumps like our poor heart beating
and what we don't understand welcomes us home,

gives out its message in sharp, nearly comprehensible
bursts. We love that. And we bark back, our blunt

tongues wagging. We think what we don't know
loves us, but we can't even call it by name.

So we give it a name. It's mysterious. And for all
we know we might be saying *footstool, pig's eye,*

Or *rich, black dirt.* We'll never be sure. But we
go on. And we brag; we write long and painful essays

On our progress. Others read them. But what we really
   understand
is this: We want. And what we can't comprehend

is unfathomable. What we hear is the wind
and our own fears rumbling. But we could

be mistaken. We are often mistaken and
so little is visible—for instance,

the wind and what we do not know. What
we don't understand. What sounds

like it might be our home—unknowable
wind and the black, thumping heart of the world.

So now—my Plan B—in which I've come to this artists' colony to pull together both my thoughts and this book of essays. I came to this same artists' colony this same time last year to do the same thing and failed: I'd wanted to turn a book review in before I left home, but it had spun woefully out of control and I had to complete it at the colony. Then, just before I completed the review, the galleys came in for my book of prose poems, *Because I Am the Shore I Want To Be the Sea*, and I had only two days to turn it around. The two projects ate up more than a week. By the end of my second and final week, though, I had in my bag a maybe ten-page section of the final essay, and I was not displeased—though I hadn't, yet, broached the subject I had originally intended to treat. During that stay, I broke three pairs of over-the-counter reading glasses—not out of pique, but out of carelessness—which might have been a new two-week record for me; my bedroom and studio had a freak infestation of both stink bugs and wolf spiders, and on the day before I was scheduled to make the drive home, my husband called at seven A.M. to tell me my beautiful, old, superhero role model for a you-can't-get-me-down attitude dog, Pootie, had died during the night in her favorite spot on the sofa. I packed up and left within the hour.

This year, I got off to a rocky start before I even arrived. I had satisfied all my student obligations, had nothing due to anyone, and, in a fit of eagerness, left at seven A.M., Monday. I figured I'd miss the commuter traffic, arrive in Virginia sometime after five, get settled in, and sleep the sleep of one in for the long haul. I got past the construction on Ringwood Avenue, one of the two southbound egresses from my borough, before the workers and policemen had even arrived at work, but once up the ramp and onto Interstate 287, traffic just stopped. There had to have been a nasty accident somewhere up ahead. It took me more than an hour and a half to get to Exit 35, a trip that normally takes forty minutes tops. And after I crawled past Exits 41 A and B, the off-ramps for Interstate 80, the traffic picked up. Then I was flying. The weather was fair, and what was scheduled to be an eight-and-a-half-hour drive would now be closer to nine-and-a-half, but no sweat. It was plenty doable. I had the audio file of Daniel Dennett's new book, *Intuition Pumps and Other Tools for Thinking*, on my iPod and by the time I got to Virginia I figured I'd be forty-five minutes more intuitive than I would have had I not been caught in traffic.

The first chapter of *Intuition Pumps*, by the way, is on the topic of failure and is fabulous.

What was it Thomas Edison said when he was working his way towards the successful incandescent light bulb? "I've not failed," he said, "I've just found ten thousand ways that won't work." Successes? We like to just stack those up as deeply as possible and watch them glow. Our failures we're not so quick to shine a light on. I knew how I had failed last year—letting job obligations overwhelm my own writing. That wasn't going to happen again.

When I finally crossed over the Virginia state line I felt a change in myself, as though the whole book, including this essay, were coming together. Like the brooms in Disney's "Sorcerer's Apprentice," the pages were swirling around me organizing themselves into a cohesive, readable whole. I maintained that sense of power and promise right up to the moment I saw that the black-and-orange board hanging over the highway, signs I think of as *amber alert signs*, spelled out *Accident ahead. All lanes closed.* After a couple more signs, with declining mileage indicators, I poked the GPS and requested a detour. It sent me to Route 11 and through Harrisonburg where I—and close to everyone else on the planet—sat in traffic. I was boxed in by huge tractor-trailers and saw nothing of the "Historic Downtown" I'd glimpsed a sign of. I felt like a pea being pressed between two cinderblocks. My GPS told me to get back on 81, and, when I tried the on-ramp was closed and, from the overpass, it was obvious it was closed much farther down as well. Every lane was deserted for as far as I could see. You could have landed a jumbo jet on that highway. A herd of jumbo jets. So, I just kept going, set the GPS to avoid Interstate 81 and traveled more than a few back roads. I pulled into the long, winding, uphill gravel road that leads to the colony at seven P.M., the night around me at least as dark as tar. Though my headlights were on, the rural Virginia evening just gobbled that light up. I drove slowly and tentatively because I remembered—one of the best features of the colony—that cars and cows share the road. I was nearing the last, sharpish turn that would bring me to the parking lot for the Fellows when, out of the corner of my eye, I noticed that the atmosphere outside the passenger side of the car seemed perilously close to an even darker shade of black than the driver's side was offering me. It was a black that appeared not air-like, but convincingly solid, a wall. Startled, I slowed down to a stop and the wall shifted. The solidity I'd sensed was the broad side of a black bull, just about the size of one of those eighteen-wheelers I'd wrestled with for breathing room in Harrisonburg. It was the biggest damn thing I'd ever seen that saw me back. The head swung around towards me on its massive neck to let the perimeter of my headlights reach two very watchful eyes. Last year the fields on both sides had been dotted with assorted, beautiful, moony cows and the occasional smallish-to-moderate-sized black bull. But nobody expects an extraordinary, edge-of-the-road battlement of an all-black bull to appear, as if suddenly, out of a deep black night.

I drove *very* slowly into the parking lot and just sat there until my heart moved down from my throat back into my chest, and I walked into the residence hall in time for two readings by prose writers in the common room. The readings, too, took my breath away.

As did dragging up the stairs to my bedroom my far-too-stuffed duffle, a backpack full of computer and printer and cords, another backpack full of books, and various last-minute totebags (a ream of paper, two pairs of boots, a tin lunchbox filled with office supplies, some Honeycrisp apples, and two four-packs of Red Bull Sugarfree). It is a fact that I always travel with too much stuff—Ma and I both loved our stuff—the difference being that mine inevitably includes far too many books, a crazy number of books. This trip, amidst the whimsy and good intentions of a dozen others, were three particularly apt books: Rebecca Solnit's *A Field Guide to Getting Lost* (who could resist such a title?), Alain deBotton's *The Art of Travel* (who can resist such writing?), and a book I found at a garage sale which struck me as particularly funny, *Finding Your Way in the Outdoors: An Outdoor Life Book* by Robert L. Mooers, Jr. (a wholly literal book on how to stay alive in the out-of-doors and get back to civilization should you become lost). The likelihood of my getting lost in the out-of-doors is smaller, of course, than one of those angels who might be dancing on the head of any given pin. I rarely leave the house if I can help it, and, when I do, seldom get far from my car. I had already set out the Solnit and deBotton to bring, and it seemed serendipitous to have found *Finding Your Way*. I didn't dare leave it at home.

Besides, I knew that, in the front of the residence, the rolling hills would be covered with cows—though I would never have even guessed I'd be shocked-near-to-death by the black solidity of a bull the size of Rhode Island—and this little paperback I'd found was written by *Mr. Mooers*.

Come on. You'd have brought it, too.

This morning there was a bluebird out my studio window—a bluebird! We don't see them at home, or at least not at my home, in northern New Jersey. It's my first real bluebird. There's actually a passel of them out there in the grass behind the studio complex.

My studio is a huge room, maybe fifteen feet by fifteen feet. It has windows on three walls, and a door that opens to the out-of-doors and faces a silo and water tower. It also has a door that opens into a small foyer that has another door that opens into a long hallway and, then, into a warren of hallways along which, at irregular intervals and irregular angles, there are doors that lead to other studios. My huge, wartime-margarine-colored room is greatly taken up by an intimidating white Yamaha grand piano and an electronic keyboard on a table over on the back wall. It's a studio that accommodates both composers and writers. There's a desk on the silo-side wall. A lamp, a bookcase, a sweet little three-level divider tray for my work. To my left is a bed—fully made up though I have a bedroom in the residence building—in case I want to nap or spend the night with my work. There's a more-shabby-than-chic—and really comfortable—wheat-colored rocker-recliner for reading, thinking, or just closing my eyes for a moment or two. There's a heater on the stable-side wall, a bathroom down the hall and to the right, and a kitchen where, if I go a bit farther past the bathroom and turn left, lunch will be delivered at 11:30 A.M. and will remain, for our delectation, until 1:30 P.M. What writer—or any artist at all—could ask for more?

And now I have a bluebird. The bluebird of happiness, I'm hoping. The thought makes me curious and allows me to indulge in a bit of procrastination-type-exploration. www.bluebirdofhappiness.net brings me up to something like snuff by telling me the first sighting they know of for this rare bird is in a play for young folks by Maurice Maeterlinck in the early 20th Century. "Happiness," the site says, "as the moral of the story imparts, comes from seeking rather than finding" and that children in the play learn that "[t]rue happiness . . . is usually found close to home. It comes from making the journey, not from reaching the destination." I think that's true. I think that's what writing is. We go forth and change and also stay the same. We need to know that to be happy. I need to know that in order to be happy. Ma, alas, never figured it out.

One of my favorite poems is William Dickey's "Happiness," from his collection, *The Rainbow Grocery*, a marvelous, under-celebrated book, as Dickey was a wonderful—and full of wonder—and under-celebrated poet. "Happiness" begins, "I have sent you this bluebird of the name of Joe /with 'Happiness' tattooed onto his left bicep." But of course he doesn't arrive. The fourth line reads, "And all you can say is you think your cat got him?" which seems a pretty tidy summing up of human reasoning to me.

Next time I come to the colony, if I come back and I hope to come back—this essay will have been completed—I'm bringing a bird guide. Or perhaps I'll write my own philosophical bird guide and take into consideration some birds-of-a-different-color. Perhaps the ecru bird of seemliness—Ma would have encouraged that one—or the golden bird of holiness, the purple bird of wordiness. Perhaps just one black bird, then, one of fussiness. Or prissiness. Or arbitrariness. It would be hard to choose.

I've got, after today, two more days at the colony. I'll go home again, not with a wholly completed manuscript, but with a plan for the order of the essays and a solid draft of this final piece. At home I'll do the fine tuning, assemble its twenty-seven electronic files and then print the entire manuscript out and begin my first assessment of the book as a whole. No doubt some essays and/or interviews will be dropped; perhaps even one or two will be added over the next year. What stays will get a final buffing, then the whole thing will go off to a writer friend or two for a cold, editorial read.

I know I've said this before, but at home, I have a piece of typing paper taped to the wall over my computer with big, thick, black letters that spell out: *One of the frustrations of writing is that growth is slow, our work made up entirely of trajectory.* It's me talking to me. We move along increment by increment. *Bird by Bird*, as Anne Lamott says. It's true for writing, certainly. And for life too.

And even though I'm very close to completing this essay, and even though this is the only obituary my mother will have, and it's already late, I can't disallow the possibility that I might have to apply to this colony again next year, and for the same reason. After all, both years I've come, I've been certain I'd succeed.

But life intervenes, as does death, and with each of experience of intervention, however small, I am changed. As is my perception of everything around me.

RENÉE ASHLEY is the author of six volumes of poetry: most recently, *The View from the Body* (Black Lawrence Press) and *Because I Am the Shore I Want To Be the Sea* (Subito Book Prize, University of Colorado—Boulder). She has received fellowships in both poetry and prose from the New Jersey State Council on the Arts and a fellowship in poetry from the National Endowment of the Arts. A portion of her poem, "First Book of the Moon," is included in a permanent installation by the artist Larry Kirkland in Penn Station, NYC. Ashley teaches in the low-residency MFA in Creative Writing and the MA in Creative Writing and Literature for Educators at Fairleigh Dickinson University.

CPSIA information can be obtained
at www.ICGtesting.com
Printed in the USA
FFHW022013061218
49778498-54277FF